The
NIGHT PARADE
of ONE HUNDRED
DEMONS

a Field Guide to Japanese Yōkai

written and illustrated
by
MATTHEW MEYER

Edited by Zack Davisson

First Edition published in 2012
Revised Edition published in 2015

ISBN-10: 0-9852184-2-8
ISBN-13: 978-0-9852184-2-3

www.matthewmeyer.net
www.yokai.com

This book is dedicated to my wife, who first introduced me to yōkai,
and to all of the patrons who supported this book through Kickstarter.

Aaron W. Thorne, Abigail Joslin, Adam Baily, Adrienne Choma, Adrienne E. Jimenez, Alex "Gus" Wendling, Alex Schröder, Alex Webb, Alexander Burel, Alexander Lucard, Amanda Merritt, Amir Lohi, Amy Archambault, Amy C. Franks, Andres, Andrew Caplan, Andrew Harkness, Andrew Lohmann, Andrew Stafford, Andy Lacroce, Angelia Pitman, Angelique Blansett, Angie Shinmore, ann sprayregen, Ann Wagner Hall, Anna Petrik, Antti Luukkonen, April Gutierrez, Ash Brown, Axel, Baas Beens, Baptiste Augrain, Beatriz Rinaldi, Ben W Bell, Ben Whittenbury, Benedikt Betz, Benjamin (Florn) Daws, Benjamin Workman, Bob Bercaw, Bonnie Lee Elizabeth Evans Barnes, Bonnie Watson, Brad Broge, Bradley Gabriel, Bredon Clay, Brent P. Newhall, Bret E Hall Jr, Brett Camper, Brian Dysart, Brian Fitzpatrick (Game Knight Reviews), Bronwen Everill, Buddah, Campbell Ruddock, CarbonIII, Carl Shapiro, Carol Duckworth, Carolina Velis, Carter P. Allen, casbot, Cassandra Marketos, Cassy Adamson, Catherine Docherty, Cedric Howe, Chad Fahs, Champ Wu, Chantal Fournier, Charles Richard James Potts, Cheryl L Costella, Chip & Katie, Chiye Azuma, Chizuru Adachi, Chris Tokuhama, Christal 'Mari' Blair, Christina Hughes, Christopher Nickell, Clark & Carrol, Clayton March, Corey "Tickles" Callahan, Craig and Anne Jorgensen, curt sherman, Damian and Cath Lauria, Damon-Eugene Rich, Daniel Rider, David Aston, David Bennett, David Fooden, David Hunter, David Inacio, David Kafrissen, David Spence, David Stanley, Dawn Oshima, Deborah Grant, Deborah Silver Goodman, Deborah Spiesz, Deborah Teramis Christian, Debra A. Sartori, Derena Ryan McCray, Devon E Rampe, Diana E. Williams, Doug Conant, Doug Roos, Doug Sarver, Doyle Joanne, Dr Paul Dale, Drew (Andrew) South, Duke Lelo, Dylan Holland, Dylan Kurtz, Dylan W, Dziek Dyes-Bolt, Ed Hanson, Edward Garcia, Eleanor Bracey, Elisa Ristuccia, Elise Beck, Eliza Frye, Elizabeth Neronski, Emil Petrinic, Emily Short, Emily Simpson and Mason Breed, Eric Sipple, Erica Jablon, Erik & Anna Meyer, Erin Palette, Ernesson Chua-Chiaco, Espen Steinsnes, Evan Huntoon, Faye, FBP, Florian Schmitt, FlukeNukem, Frances McGregor, Francesca Verdier, Frank A Laycock, g, Gabriel Novo, GC Lim, Gene Shekhtman, George J. Fronimopoulos, George Martinez Jr., Gio, Gloria Fan, Gordon Garb, Grankvist, Greg Zuro, Guillermo Martinez, H Lynnea Johnson, Heather E. Pristash, Heidi Ellis, Helen Febrie, Henning Colsman-Freyberger, Hitomi Meyer, Holden Mcgroin, Horizon Factory, Hunter H., Ian Gregory, InnocentSystems, Ivo A A Araújo, J Doe, J. Muzacz, J. Myllyluoma, J. Schultz, J.S. Jobski, Jack Smyth, Jackie Lin, Jacqueline Skelton, James Pond, Janna Solis, Jason and Sylvia Wodicka, Jay "circuitree" Kim, Jean Chen, Jeff Matsuya, Jeff Melin, Jeffrey Campbell, Jemolian, Jen Blaikie, Jenna Lovelady, Jeremy Depaul, Jeri Smith, Jess Scott, Joe Watkins, john guthrie, John Herzfeld, John Hodge, John McCord, John R Sacco, Jonathan Jacobs, Jonathan W. Smith, Josh Catone, Joshua Beale, Jude Griffin, Julie and Jim Vick, Julie Felix, Julie Renae Campbell, Justin and Brittany, your fans from Yokosuka, Kalaya Wichacz, Karla Steffen, Kate Mastroianni, Kate Trgovac, Kate Walton, Kathryn Halapoff, Kathryn Sikorski, Katy Richard, Kazuko Matsuda, Keara Giannotti & Neil King, Keigo Kiyohara, keiichiro ota, Kelly Hoolihan, Ken Liu, Keoma Shaw, Kestril Trueseeker, Kevin Ivan Smith, Kevin Walker, Kris Haamer, Kristian Jaech, Kyle O'Brien, Lars, Lars Ericson, Laura Hertel, Laurali L. Carroll, Laurel Swayze, Laurence W. Brown, laurent b, Lee S. Tratnyek, Leo Hourvitz, Leora Effinger-Weintraub, Leslie Barrett Beck, Liz Dowell, Liz R, Logan Gittelson, Lorena Morgan Wolfe, Lowen Warrington, Lucy Payne, Luke Chin, Lynne Whitehorn-Umphres, M. Draheim, Maarten Broekman, Madeline Carol Matz, Maggie Young, Margaret, Marie Minako von Kampen, Mark, Mark & Melissa Riccobono, Mark R. Scappini, Jr., Martha Heuser, Mary Prince and Kelly Lowrey, Matt Erik Katch, Matteo Rossi, Matthew "Senjak" Goldman, Matthew Gatsby, Matthew Paul Waldschmitt, Matthew Urgo, Mauro Ghibaudo, Max Henderson, Max Kaehn, Maximilian Hötzl, Maxmillian Kuliev, Micha Savelsbergh, Michael Brewer, Michael D. Blanchard, Michael O'Dowd, Michael Quandt, Michel Claussmann, Mike DeMille, Mike Frysinger, Mike Urano, Moose, Natalie S. Wainwright, Nathan Bradley, Nathan Smyth, Neil Graham, Nick Coombe, Nick Tantra, Nicola Evans, Nikki Tran, Norbert Barrion, Noriko & Hiroto Ichihashi, Norman Shing, Olli Toivanen, P.E. Reiman Family, Patty Kirsch, Patty Mitchell, Paul Robinson, Peter Riordan, Peter, Emma & Gabriella Rossi, Philippe Barreaud, Poocan, Pramod, R. Scott Daniels, Rachael Bloom, Reverance Pavane, Richard and Cheryl Everill, Richard DiTullio, Richard J. Anderson, Robert "Ski" Cudinski, Robert & Linda Hewitt, Robert E. Stutts, Robert I. Lee, Robert Lee Mayers, Robin Svensson, Robin Whittle, Roger Jacobs, Ron Carroll, Ross Jenkins, Roy Zemlicka, Ryan Cook, Samantha de Graffenried, Sarah J. Christensen, Sarah Tribedi, Saravanan Thirumuruganathan, Satchel Clay Fenenga Parker, Scaut, Scott King, Sean Holland, SEM, Serge Vincent, Seth M Johnson, Shane Williamson, Sharon Teavae, Shawn Finley, Shayna Harris, Sheila Mazur, ShimmerGeek, Sian Harrop, silence, Simon Davis, Simon Lieu, Simone D Bennett, Soochon Radee, Sorrow Pennefather, Steph Turner, Stephen A. Caldwell, Stephen Hill, Steven Moy, Sue Lawton, Susan Bailey, Susan Patrick, T.S. Luikart, Tagno25, Tara Gibbs, Tara Zuber, TD Gammon, Ted Aaron, Tenkai Yamauchi, Tereza Kulovaná, Teymour Sursock, thomas bourke, Thor Deacon, Tif T, Tim R. Schreck, Timothy Blank, Timothy J. Lashley, Tina Chiu, Tomaste, Tony Grob, Toshimitsu & Mikiko Umeda, Tree Khartam, Trevor Thompson, Tury Koopa, Vadim Troshchinskiy, Vanessa Krause, Veronika Knurenko, Victor Gargiulo, W. Ellery Samuels, Ph.D., Waipo, Yingju Lan, Youkai Lonely Hearts Society, Zach, Zachary Norris, Zack Jones, Zane Smith

Contents

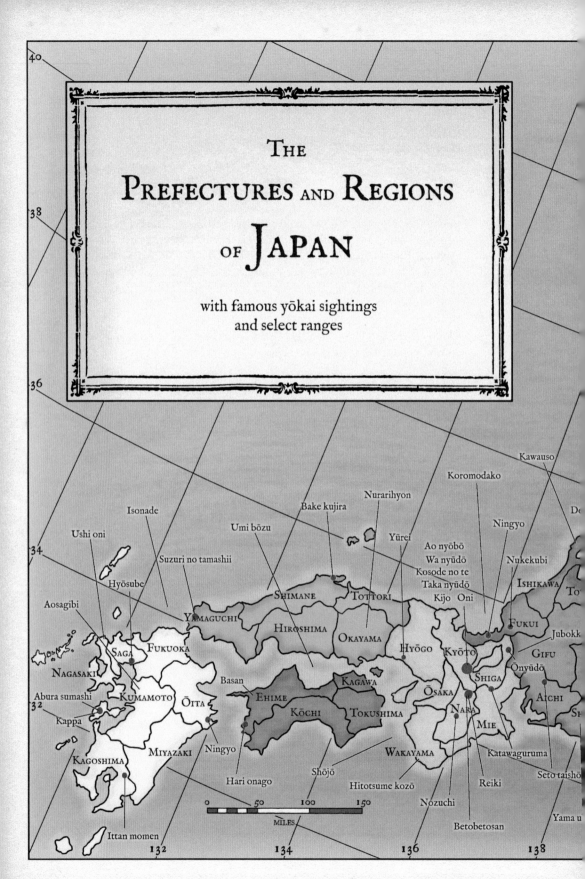

THE PREFECTURES AND REGIONS OF JAPAN

with famous yōkai sightings
and select ranges

Kawauso

Koromodako

Nurarihyon

Bake kujira

Isonade

Ningyo

Umi bōzu

Yūrei

Ao nyōbō
Wa nyūdō
Kosode no te
Taka nyūdō

Ushi oni

Nukekubi

ISHIKAWA

Suzuri no tamashii

Kijo Oni

Hyōsube

SHIMANE   TOTTORI

FUKUI

Aosagibi

YAMAGUCHI

HIROSHIMA

OKAYAMA

FUKUOKA

SAGA

HYŌGO KYŌTO

GIFU

Ōnyūdō

SHIGA

NAGASAKI

Basan

KAGAWA

ŌSAKA

AICHI

Abura sumashi

KUMAMOTO   ŌITA

EHIME

NARA

KŌCHI   TOKUSHIMA

Kappa

MIE

MIYAZAKI   Ningyo

WAKAYAMA

Katawaguruma

KAGOSHIMA

Shōjō

Reiki

Seto taishō

Hari onago

Hitotsume kozō

Nozuchi

Yama u

Ittan momen

Betobetosan

132   134   136   138

Jubokk

To

De

0   50   100   150
MILES

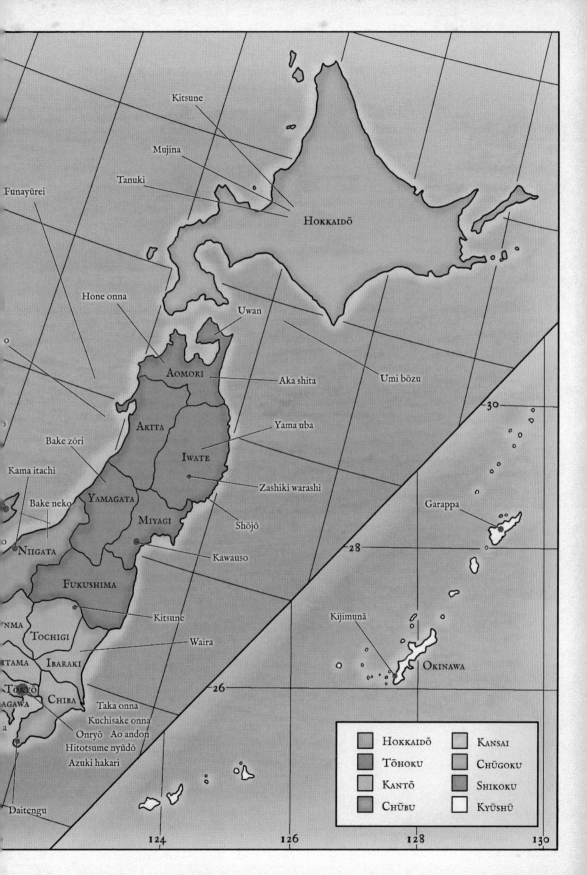

Kitsune

Mujina

Tanuki

HOKKAIDŌ

Funayūrei

Hone onna

Uwan

AOMORI

Aka shita

Umi bōzu

AKITA

Yama uba

Bake zōri

IWATE

Kama itachi

Zashiki warashi

Garappa

Bake neko

YAMAGATA

MIYAGI

Shōjō

NIIGATA

Kawauso

FUKUSHIMA

Kijimunā

NMA

Kitsune

TOCHIGI

Waira

ITAMA

IBARAKI

OKINAWA

TŌKYŌ

26

AGAWA

CHIBA

Taka onna

Kuchisake onna

Onryō   Ao andon

Hitotsume nyūdō

Azuki hakari

Daitengu

30

28

■	HOKKAIDŌ	■	KANSAI
■	TŌHOKU	■	CHŪGOKU
■	KANTŌ	■	SHIKOKU
■	CHŪBU	□	KYŪSHŪ

124   126   128   130

LANGUAGE NOTES

Japanese is one of the most difficult languages for native English speakers to learn. This is due to its difficult conjugations, three writing systems, and various levels of "polite" speech. Fortunately, the one area where Japanese is not difficult is pronunciation—with only five vowel sounds and no diphthongs, Japanese is an easy language for English speakers to pronounce.

However, in written form even transliterated Japanese can be difficult. Words are often pronounced differently than they would be in English. To further complicate things, there are numerous Romanization systems, each following different standards. The result can be various spellings of the same word.

To ease this confusion, here is a brief guide on how to read and pronounce the transliterated Japanese words in this book.

VOWELS

The five Japanese vowels are a, i, u, e, o, pronounced like bot, beet, boot, bet, and boat, respectively. In cases of two vowels or double vowels—because there are no diphthongs—each vowel receives a full syllable without being blended. For example, in English the name koma inu would be read as ko/mai/nu. However, in Japanese it reads with four separate syllables: ko/ma/i/nu.

MACRONS

It is common to find combinations like aa, uu, ee, oo, ou. These pairs are often indicated by macrons: ā, ū, ē, ō. This is partially because combinations like aa look awkward when transliterated into English, and partially because combinations like ee, ou, oo might be confused with their English pronunciations. For example, ōnyūdō is more legible than oonyuudou. These long vowels are treated like the double vowels above and read as two syllables. For example, ōnyūdō is read not with three beats as o/nyu/do, but with six beats as o/o/nyu/u/do/u.

COMPOUND WORDS

Japanese is written primarily with ideograms called kanji, and most words are only one or two characters long. Because Japanese compound words are shorter than in English, they are not delineated in any specific way. This is generally not a problem when reading names in Japanese. However, reading the same words in English can lead to a long string of letters that are difficult to digest.

Names like hitotsumenyūdō, suzurinotamashii, and usutsukiwarashi are more difficult to read in Latin characters than in their native script. In this book breaks have been inserted into phrasal names and before common suffixes to make them more legible. Broken apart this way, names like hitotsume nyūdō, suzuri no tamashii, and usutsuki warashi are comparatively easy to read.

INTRODUCTION

WHAT ARE YŌKAI?

Put simply, yōkai are supernatural creatures of Japanese folklore. The word in Japanese is a combination of *yō*, meaning "bewitching," and *kai*, meaning "strange." Yōkai encompasses more than just monsters and demons. It also includes certain kinds of gods (*kami*), ghosts (*bakemono*), magical animals, transformed humans, urban legends, and other strange phenomena. Over the years, many different words have been used as translations—such as demon, monster, goblin, and spirit—but each of these words carries cultural baggage. None of them quite does the trick of capturing the essence of yōkai. It is a broad and vague term. Nothing exists in the English language that matches up exactly. Like samurai, geisha, ninja, and sushi, yōkai just works better left in Japanese.

WHERE DO YŌKAI COME FROM?

Japanese mythology is an amalgamation of a several traditions. The foundation comes from the folk religions of isolated tribes living across the Japanese islands. Later, these tribes merged and forged their beliefs into the Shinto religion. Contact with China and India brought Buddhism and Hindu cosmologies, which were incorporated seamlessly into the existing folklore.

Japan's oldest recorded histories go back to the 8th century CE. These books contain the creation myths and legendary prehistory of Japan, including stories of emperors descended from the gods. Over the following centuries, other books and scrolls were written which catalogued the legends and folklore of Japan. These works contain the earliest records of Japan's gods, demons, and other supernatural creatures.

From the 17th through the 19th centuries, Japan experienced an unprecedented flourishing of culture and art. Ghost stories exploded in popularity, along with tales of monsters and strange happenings from the various regions of the country. During this period, the first mythical bestiaries were assembled by folklorists and artists like Toriyama Sekien and Sawaki Sūshi. These entrepreneurs collected the oral traditions of rural Japan—adding a few monsters of their own and creating mass-market entertainment for commercial consumption by the growing urban population. Yōkai bestiaries begun as collections of painted scrolls, and later expanded into multi-volume illustrated encyclopedias of strange tales and supernatural stories. Toriyama's *Illustrated Night Parade of One Hundred Demons* set the stage for other famous artists. The yōkai tradition was born, and would eventually expand into every aspect of Japanese culture.

After fading away during the WWII war years, yōkai reemerged during the 20th century and were popularized by manga artist Mizuki Shigeru. His comic series *GeGeGe no Kitarō* re-introduced yōkai to post-war Japan, and caused a second explosion of interest in supernatural monsters and ghosts. Mizuki's comics and illustrated encyclopedias brought yōkai out of the distant past and into modern Japan, where they have continued to be an important aspect of popular culture. The influence of yōkai can be felt in Japanese books, movies, animation, product design, video games, and more. Today, as Japanese culture becomes more and more global, yōkai are becoming known all over the globe.

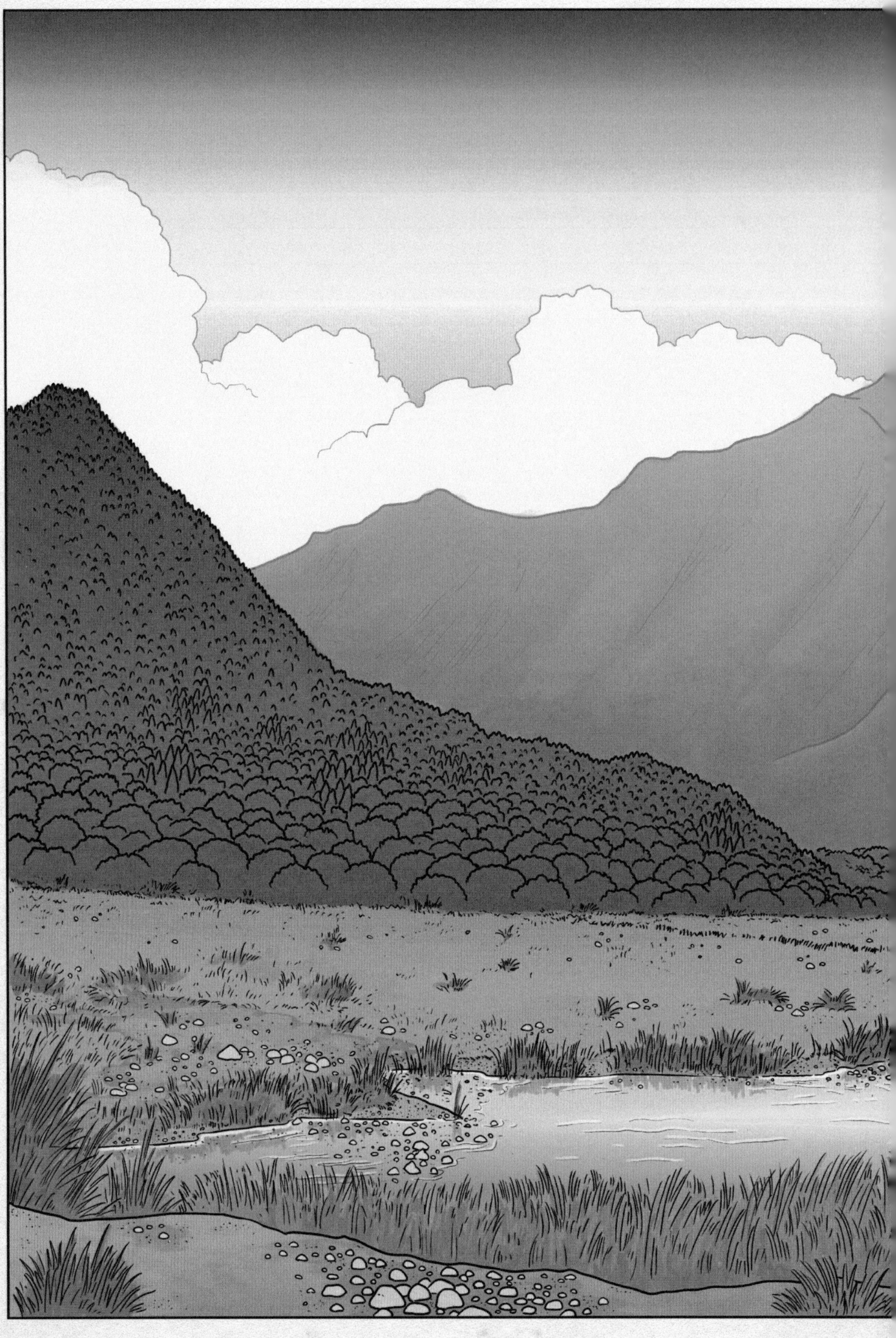

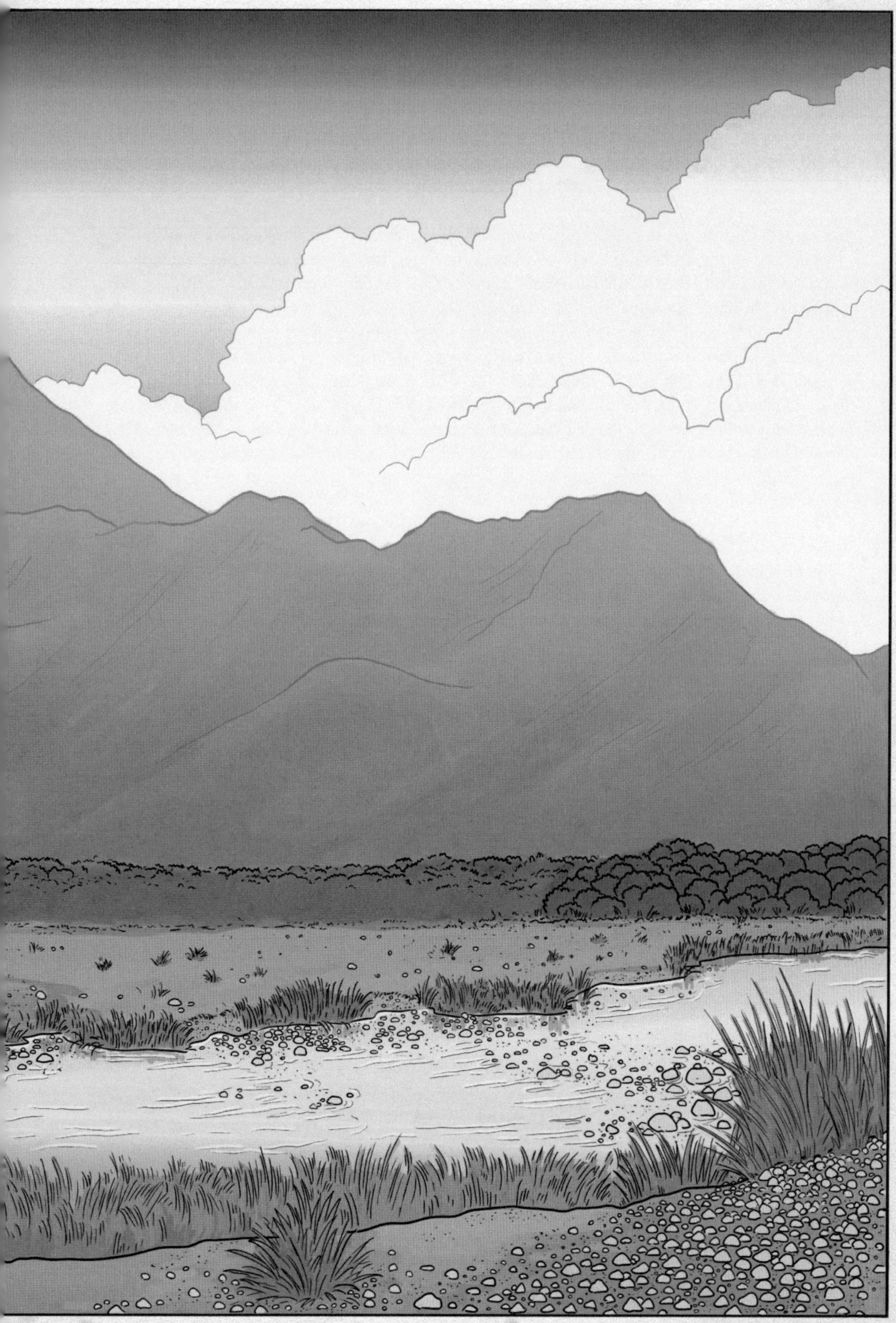

KAPPA 河童

TRANSLATION: river child
ALTERNATE NAMES: kawatarō, kawako
HABITAT: rivers, lakes, ponds, waterways, cisterns, and wells; found throughout Japan
DIET: omnivorous; prefers cucumbers and human entrails

APPEARANCE: Kappa are aquatic, reptilian humanoids who inhabit the rivers and streams flowing over Japan. Clumsy on land, they are at home in the water, and thrive during the warm months. Kappa are generally the size and shape of a human child, yet despite their small stature they are physically stronger than a grown man. Their scaly skin ranges from a deep, earthy green to bright reds and even blue. Kappa bodies are built for swimming; they have webbed, thumbless hands and feet, a turtle-like beak and shell, and an elastic, waterproof skin that reeks of fish and is said to be removable. Other inhuman traits include three anuses that allow them to pass three times as much gas as humans, and forearms attached to one another inside of their shells—pulling on one arm lengthens it while the other arm contracts. But their most distinguishing characteristic is a dish-like depression that lies on top of their skulls. This dish is the source of a kappa's power and must be kept filled with water at all times. Should the water be spilled and the dish dry up, the kappa will be unable to move. It may even die.

BEHAVIOR: While younger kappa are frequently found in family groups, adult kappa live solitary lives. However, it is common for kappa to befriend other yōkai and sometimes even people. Possessed of a keen intelligence, kappa are one of the few yōkai able to learn human languages. They are highly knowledgeable about medicine and the art of setting bones. According to legend, friendly kappa taught these skills to humans. For fun, they love causing mischief, practicing martial arts like sumo wrestling, and playing games of skill like shogi. Kappa are proud and stubborn, but also fiercely honorable; they never break a promise. Kappa will eat almost anything, but they are particularly fond of two foods: cucumbers and raw innards—particularly human anuses.

INTERACTIONS: Kappa are revered in Shinto as a kind of water god. It is not uncommon to see offerings of cucumbers made at riverbanks by devout humans. In return, kappa help people by irrigating fields, befriending lonely children, or competing with adults in sports and games.

Kappa can also be crass and dangerous. Lakes and rivers where they live are often marked with warning signs. Kappa particularly despise cows and horses, and will attack the animals for no reason at all. Mischievous by nature, they loudly pass gas in public and love to peek up women's kimonos. Sometimes their mischief turns violent. Kappa have been known to kidnap or rape swimming women, and kill people. A kappa's preferred method of attack is to drown its victims, or bite them to death under water. Kappa also devour humans alive. Usually they go for the rear end to get at the *shirikodama*, a mythical ball of flesh located just inside the anus.

In the water, there is no escape for anyone who crosses a kappa. On land, however, it is possible to outwit one; the honorable kappa will feel obliged to return a bow. If it can be tricked into bowing so low that the water in its dish spills out, it can be overcome. Once bested, kappa have been made to swear loyalty and friendship to their victor for the rest of their lives.

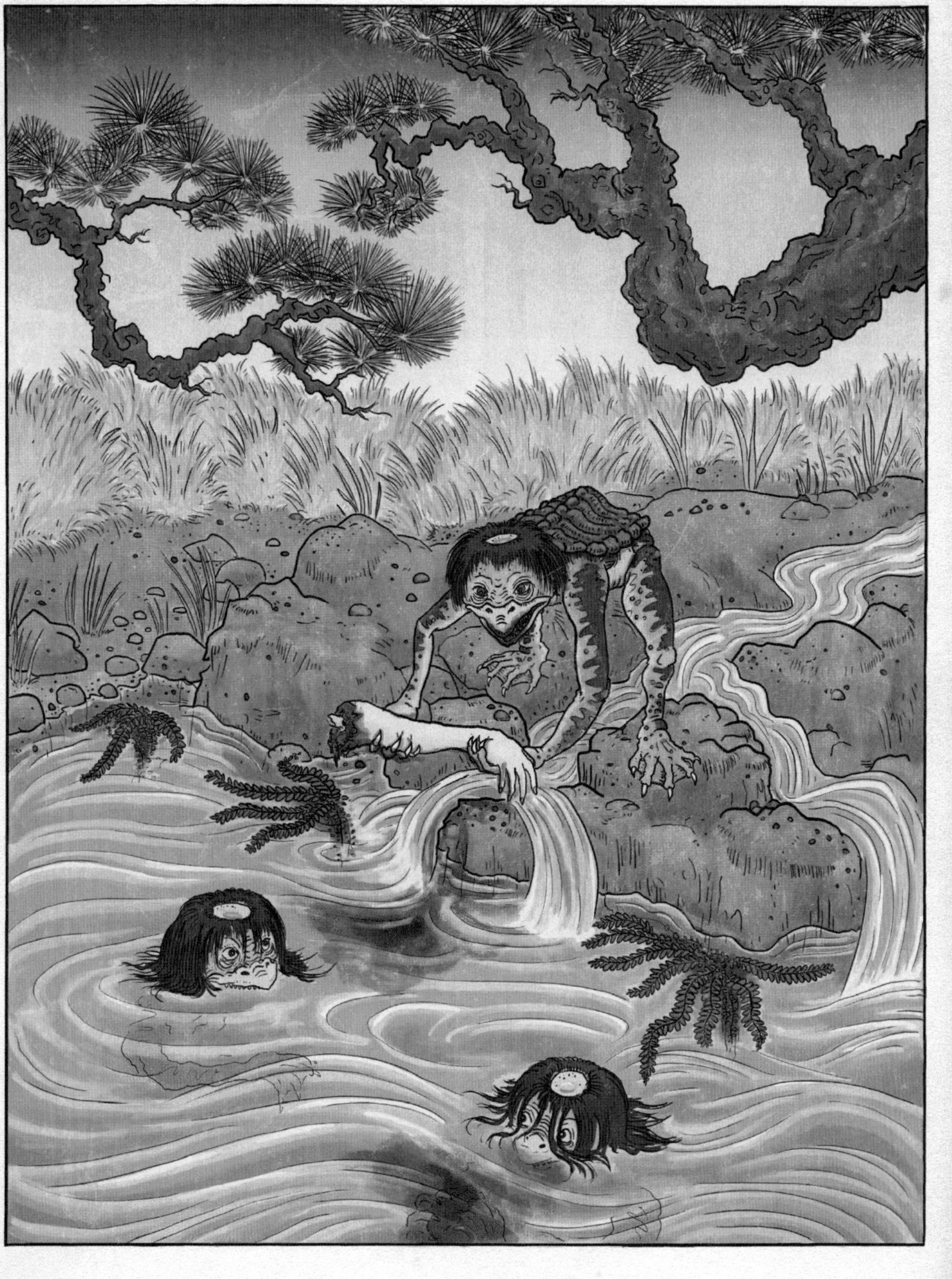

Garappa ガラッパ

Translation: a regional corruption of kappa
Alternate names: gawappa
Habitat: rivers, lakes, ponds, streams; found only on Kyūshū
Diet: omnivorous; same as the kappa

Appearance: Garappa are river spirits found on the islands of Kyūshū in southern Japan. Close relatives of kappa, they resemble them in many ways. The two are often confused with each other, although there are a number of important differences. A garappa's limbs are much longer than those of a kappa. When garappa sit down their knees rise high above their heads, unlike the stubby kappa's knees. Because of these longer limbs, garappa are taller than kappa when standing upright. Garappa also have slightly longer and more streamlined faces.

Behavior: Garappa are shyer and more elusive than kappa. They tend to avoid populated areas and instead, wander back and forth between the rivers and mountains. Garappa live in smaller groups, or by themselves. Because of their shyness, garappa are more often heard than seen. They have two distinctive calls: "*hyō hyō*" and, "*foon foon foon.*"

Interactions: While garappa encounters are much rarer than kappa, they share a similar relationship with humankind. Extremely fond of pranks and mischief, garappa love to surprise people on mountain paths, or trick travelers into losing their way. Like kappa, garappa are physically stronger than humans and are easily capable of overpowering grown men larger than themselves. They are extremely fond of sumo wrestling, at which they are highly skilled. Garappa are also sexually aggressive and are known to assault and rape women.

Despite their reputation as tricksters, garappa are absolutely dedicated to keeping their word. When captured or bested in contest by humans, they can be forced by their victors to promise to stop drowning people, playing pranks, making noises in the woods, or similar concessions. Over the centuries, Shinto sects who revere garappa have worked to earn promises from them to cease doing evil. As a result garappa attacks have become less and less common over time. Garappa occasionally even serve humans by catching fish or planting rice fields, and they are credited with teaching the ancient people of Kyūshū the art of making poultices.

Yōkai-Human Hybrids

While humans and yōkai rarely intermingle in "that way," there are a number of stories of rape by yōkai, and even voluntary pairing between humans and supernatural creatures. It is possible for humans and yōkai to have children together, and the children of these couplings sometimes have inhuman strength reflecting their supernatural nature. Sadly, many cases are also fatal. In one case of rape by garappa in Kagoshima, the impregnated woman was eaten from the inside out by the hungry offspring. Eventually the creature emerged from its mother's stomach in a gory mess. The horrified villagers tried to kill it with fire, but it vanished into thin air.

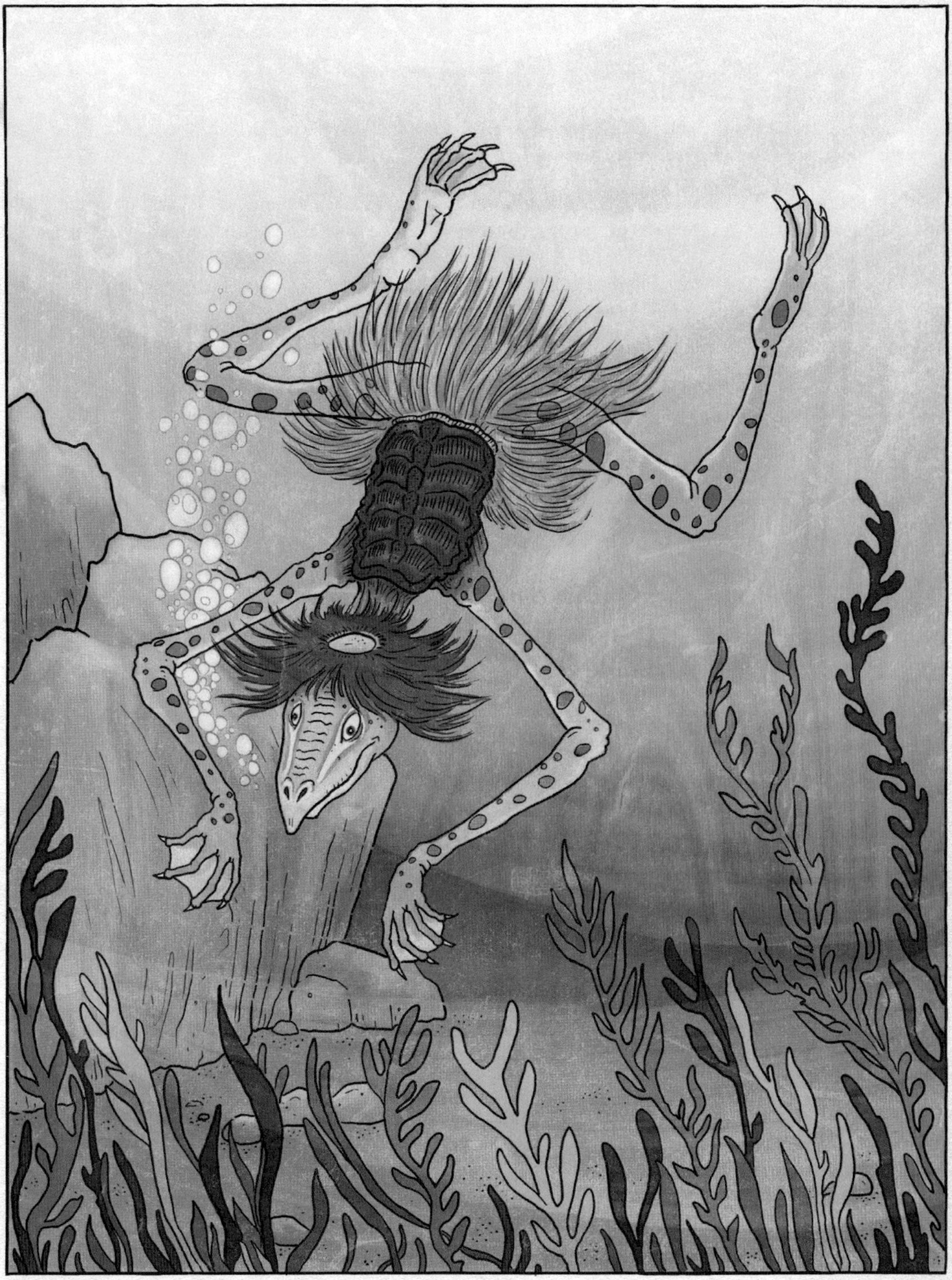

Hyōsube 兵主部

TRANSLATION: onomatopoeic; written with characters connoting warfare
ALTERNATE NAMES: hyōsue, hyōsubo, hyōsunbo, hyōsunbe
HABITAT: rivers and streams; found primarily on Kyūshū and in West Japan
DIET: omnivorous; prefers eggplants

APPEARANCE: Hyōsube are squat, hairy humanoids found mostly in the southern and western parts of Japan. Cousins of kappa and garappa, they are more savage and belligerent. Physically they are short, with bald scalps, sharp claws, and a mouth full of sharp teeth which are prominently visible due to the malicious smile they wear. Their skins are covered with a pelt of thick, greasy hair that gathers dust, oil, and dirt. This repulsive pelt constantly sheds wherever they go. Their name is said to come from the "*hyo hyo*" call that they make. However, written in kanji, the characters have a martial connotation.

BEHAVIOR: Hyōsube live near rivers, where they catch wild fish and generally keep away from humans. Their favorite food is eggplant—they are capable of devouring whole patches in the blink of an eye. Like kappa, hyōsube love mischief and hate horses. They are generally more violent and malicious than their cousins, but they retain a strong sense of honor.

INTERACTIONS: Hyōsube are capricious, insolent, and extremely dangerous. Simply looking at a hyōsube can cause a terrible and contagious fever, which can spread and turn into an epidemic. Hyōsube cackle with an evil laughter which is also contagious; an unlucky person who hears a hyōsube laugh, and who laughs himself, will be struck with fever and die within hours.

A hyōsube's thick hair builds up with dirt and grime; they love nothing more than to sneak into houses at night and slip into the bathtub. When a hyōsube finds a bathtub it likes it often returns every night, leaving behind a thick scum of greasy body hair and a horrible stench. Once, the unlucky owner of such a house emptied the bathwater and threw out the hair and grease. This angered the hyōsube so much that it slaughtered the owner's horse the next night. When another unfortunate dumped his bathtub and some hyōsube hairs accidentally landed on a nearby horse, the animal promptly dropped dead. In yet another tale, a woman spied on a hyōsube ravaging her eggplant garden; the next morning her entire body had turned purple. She died soon after.

Hyōsube are occasionally honored at local Shinto shrines, usually worshiped as gods of war for some military service performed for villagers in the past. Farmers living in areas inhabited by hyōsube often leave offerings of the first eggplants of the harvest in hopes that the hyōsube will spare their fields for the remainder of the year. Those who do not leave offerings can find their fields trampled.

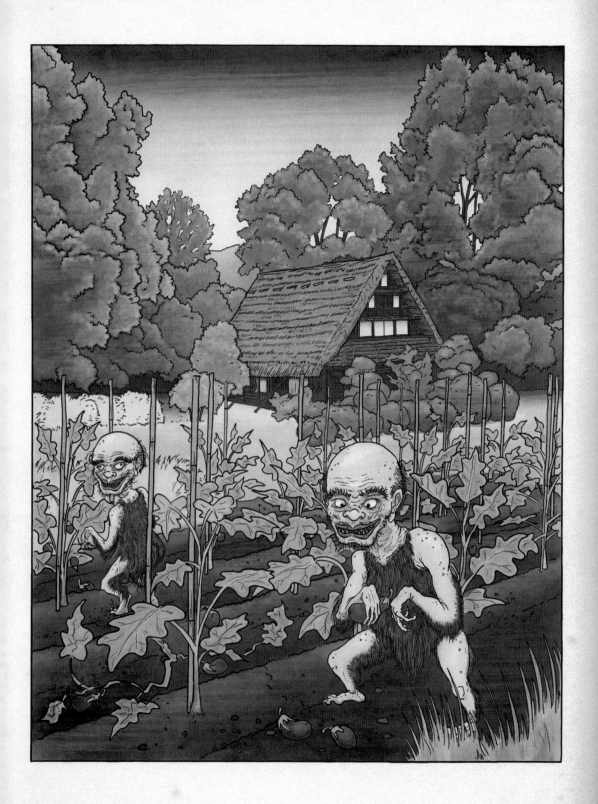

KIRIN 麒麟

TRANSLATION: none; based on the Chinese name for the same creature
HABITAT: areas ruled by a wise and benevolent leader
DIET: purely vegetarian; never harms another creature

APPEARANCE: The kirin is one of the rarest, most awesome and powerful creatures ever known in East Asia. It is a regal animal, holy and highly revered. The kirin is often considered a god in its own right. Resembling a deer with scales like a dragon's covering its body, the kirin is a chimerical beast. It has a tail like an ox and a flowing mane. Its body and mane are covered in brilliant, holy fire and its face is the picture of utter serenity.

BEHAVIOR: A gentle animal, the kirin never eats the flesh of other beings, and takes great care never to tread on any living thing, even insects. When it walks, it does so without trampling a single blade of grass. Its beauty is only surpassed by its rarity; the unicorn-like kirin only appears during periods of world peace. They are seen only in lands owned by wise and benevolent people and during the reigns of noble and enlightened rulers, where they herald a golden age. Although kirin never harm good and pure souls, they are swift and fierce to attack if threatened, breathing holy fire from their mouths.

INTERACTIONS: Because kirin are beasts of purity and goodness, they have been used in carvings and paintings as symbols of these virtues since early times. They are also seen as symbols of justice and wisdom. Because of their holiness, images of kirin frequently adorn temples and shrines. Omens of great luck and fortune, the appearance of a kirin is believed to be a sign of the arrival of a great leader or a wise man.

ORIGIN: Kirin were introduced to Japan via Chinese myths and legends where they are known as *qilin*. Over time, the Chinese and Japanese version diverged into slightly different creatures. In Japan, the kirin is considered to be the most powerful and sacred beast of all, surpassing the hōō and tatsu.

Giraffes are also called kirin in Japanese, named for the traits they share with the holy kirin. Their long legs, scale-like pattern, gentle nature, and the knobs on their heads must have reminded the first Japanese to see a giraffe of this most sacred of beasts.

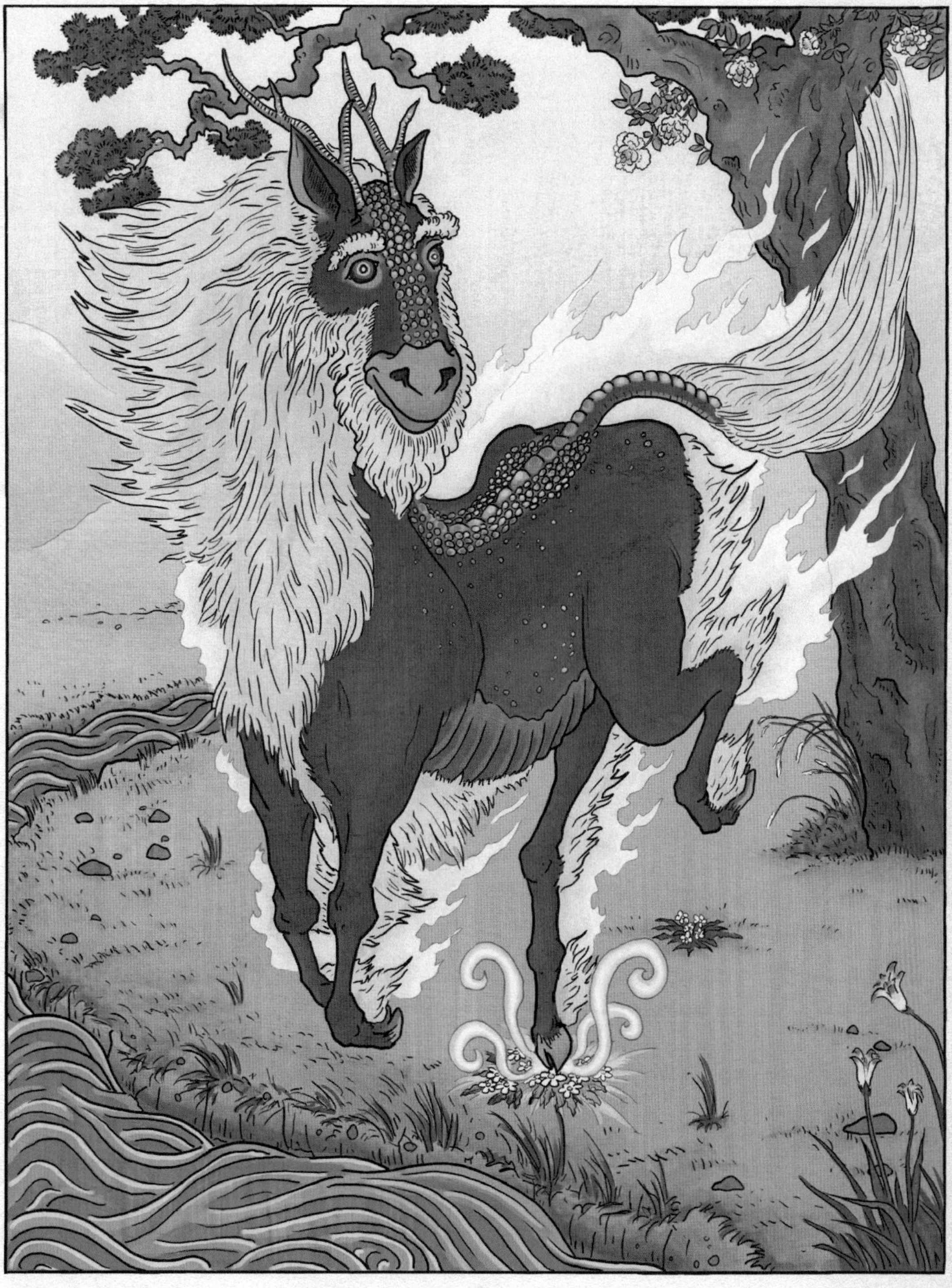

Hōō 鳳凰

TRANSLATION: none; based on the Chinese name for the same creature
HABITAT: paulownia trees; only appear in lands blessed by peace and prosperity
DIET: only bamboo seeds

APPEARANCE: Hōō are beautiful, peaceful, phoenix-like creatures honored across East Asia and worshiped as divine spirits. They are described as having the beak of a rooster, the jaw of a swallow, the head of a pheasant, the neck of a snake, the back of a tortoise, the legs of a crane, and the tail of a peacock. Brilliantly colored with the five colors of the Chinese elements—white, black, red, yellow, and blue—they have five distinctive tail feathers.

BEHAVIOR: Hōō are creatures of utter peace and never cause harm to other living things. They eat only bamboo seeds, and nest only in paulownia trees. When a hōō flies, it is said that the wind stops, dust settles, and birds and insects grow quiet. Because of their purity, they appear only in lands blessed with peace, prosperity, and happiness. They flee to the heavens during times of trouble. The appearance of a hōō is an extremely good omen, said to signify the beginning of a new era.

INTERACTIONS: The hōō is a popular motif in Japanese paintings, crafts, kimonos, and as designs on temples and shrines. As a symbol, it represents fire, the sun, and the imperial family. It also stands for the virtues of duty, propriety, faith, and mercy. Its five colors represent the five elements of wood, fire, earth, metal, and water.

ORIGIN: Hōō come from Chinese mythology, where they are known as *fenghuang*. Originally they were considered to be two distinct birds: the male hō (*feng*) and the female ō (*huang*), symbolizing yin and yang and the duality of the universe. Eventually the two creatures merged into one and their combined name was used. The combined creature is still considered to be female, and is often partnered with the tatsu, which is considered to be male.

The hōō is one of the most revered and holiest animals in Japan. Second only to the kirin in terms of power, it is the most sacred bird in the Japanese pantheon.

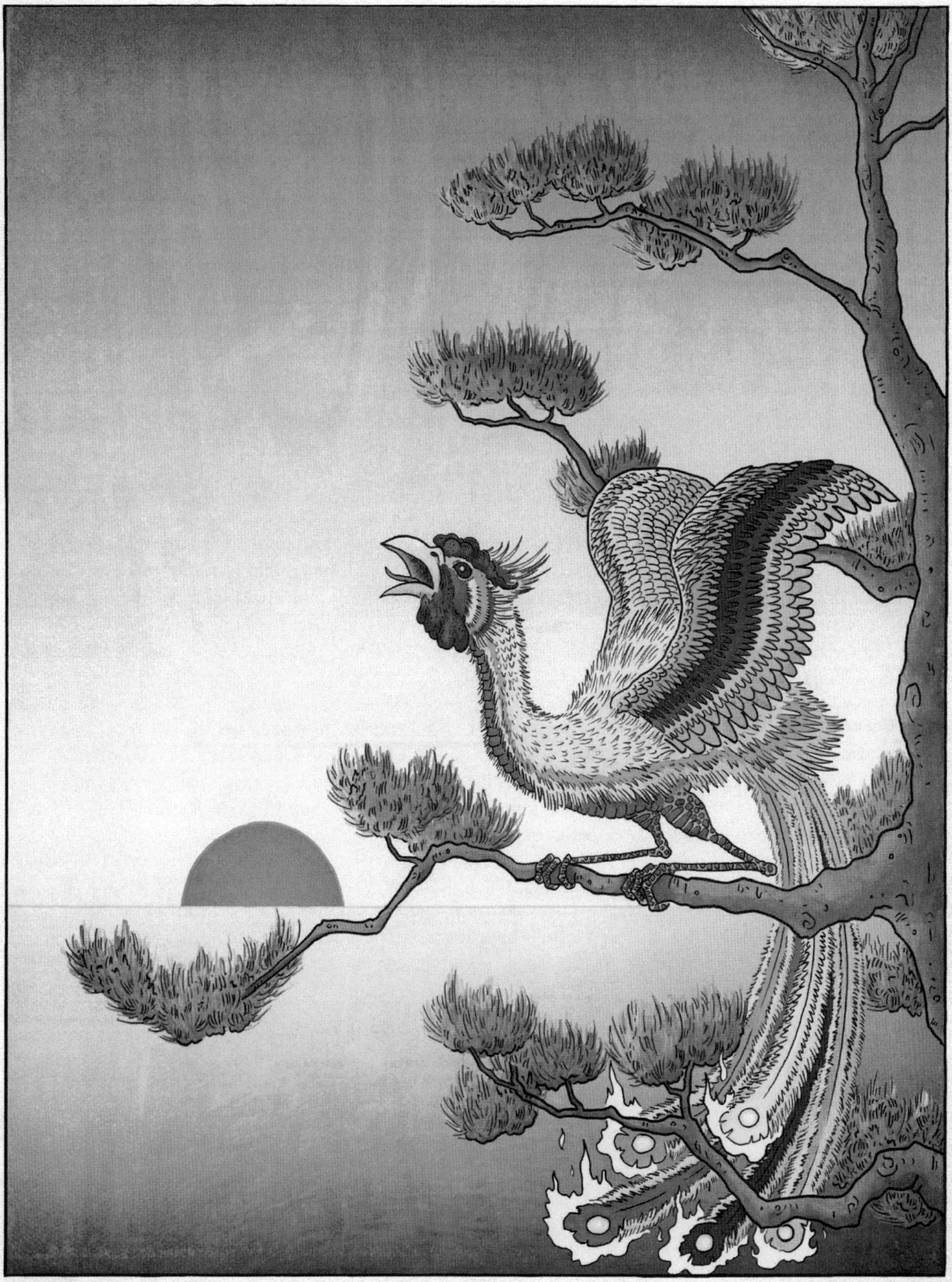

Tatsu 龍

TRANSLATION: dragon
ALTERNATE NAMES: ryū, ryō, wani; known by many specific individual names
HABITAT: rivers, waterfalls, mountains, lakes, seas, and palaces deep in the ocean
DIET: capable of eating anything

APPEARANCE: Tatsu, Japanese dragons, are similar in appearance to the dragons of China and the rest of the world. They have long, scaled bodies, serpentine tails, sharp teeth and claws, and often have horns, antlers, spines, and beards. Some tatsu have multiple limbs or heads. Many disguise themselves as humans and are never seen in their natural forms.

BEHAVIOR: Tatsu are strongly connected to water—be it rain, rivers, seas, or oceans—and are considered to be water gods. They live in splendid palaces at the bottom of deep seas, or in other secluded places. They usually live far from human-inhabited areas, but occasionally make their homes near Buddhist temples. Like Western dragons, they hoard vast amounts of treasure and keep powerful magical artifacts in their homes. Many are great villains, tormenting mankind out of spite, while others are pure and kind, offering their wisdom and power to those seeking it. Some tatsu even allow worthy heroes to visit them, and lend their magical items to noble warriors.

INTERACTIONS: Tatsu rarely concern themselves with human affairs unless it affects them directly. They accept worship and sacrifices from humans; many temples maintain the holy grounds of local dragons, and countless Japanese make pilgrimages to holy mountains inhabited by tatsu. Tatsu receive prayers for rain or for protection from floods, and other water-related requests. Fireworks festivals, ritual dragon dances, and other local celebrations honor these dragon gods all over the Japanese islands.

ORIGIN: Tatsu are one of the oldest supernatural creatures known in Japan. The first recorded stories go back to the earliest written accounts of Japanese history and mythology, the *Kojiki* and the *Nihongi*. Over the centuries, tales of the Chinese *long* and Indian *naga* were incorporated into Japanese mythology. Today's Japanese dragons are an amalgamation of these imported myths merged with the indigenous water deities of prehistoric Japan.

LEGENDS: The Japanese imperial family, the oldest hereditary monarchy in the world, is supposedly descended from dragons (as well as other gods). The monarchy is said to have been founded in 660 BCE by Emperor Jimmu, the legendary first ruler of Japan. His father was the son of Toyotama hime, who in turn was the daughter of Ryūjin, the dragon god of the sea. So by tradition the emperor of Japan is the direct descendant of a dragon.

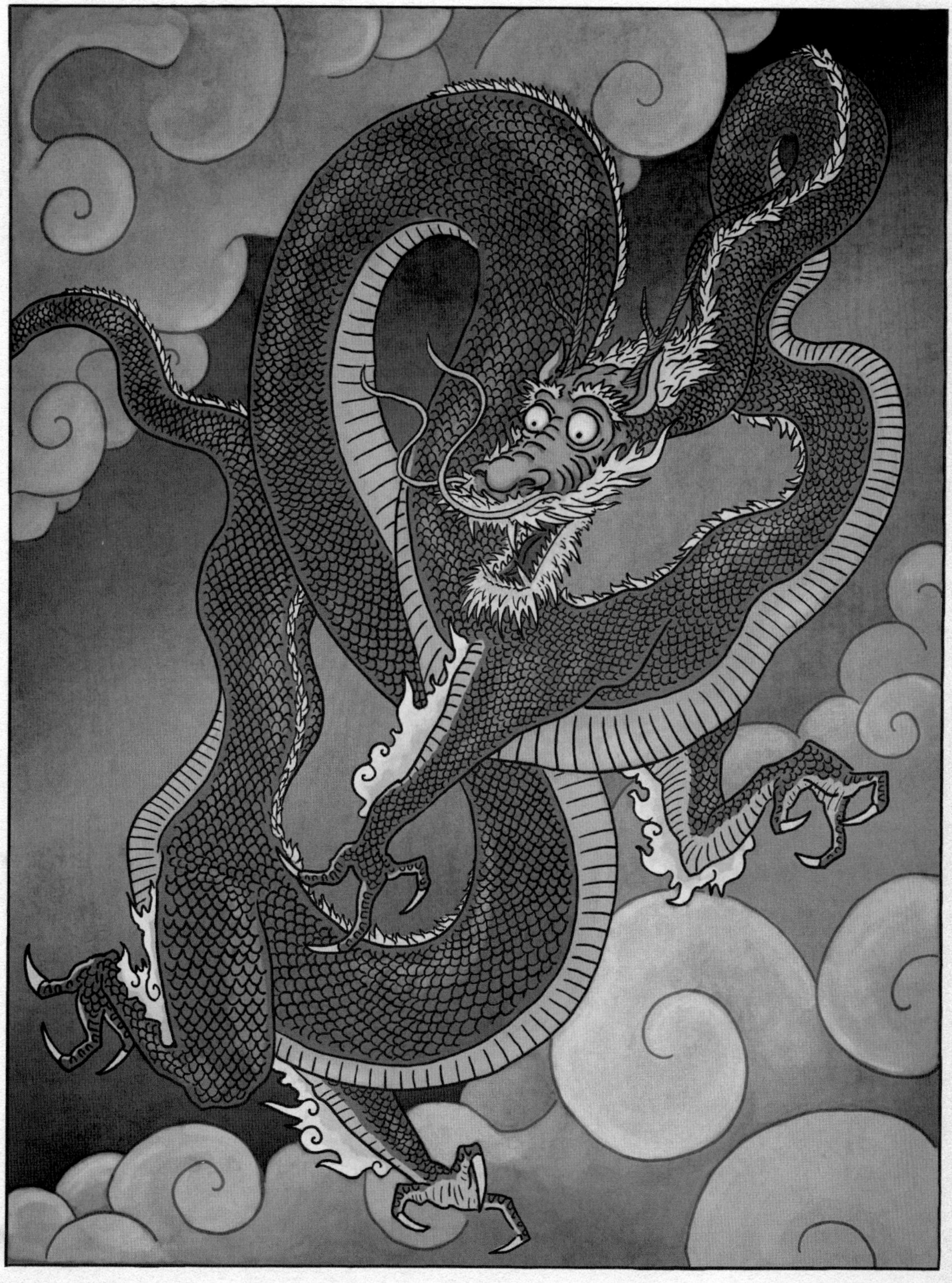

Baku 獏

TRANSLATION: none; based on the Chinese name for the same creature
HABITAT: deep in thick forests
DIET: bad dreams

APPEARANCE: The baku is a strange, holy beast that has the body of a bear, the head of an elephant, the eyes of a rhinoceros, the tail of an ox, and the legs of a tiger. Despite their monstrous appearance, baku are revered as powerful forces of good and as one of the holy protectors of mankind.

BEHAVIOR: Baku watch over humans and act as guardian spirits. They feed on the dreams of humans—specifically bad dreams. Evil spirits and yōkai fear baku and flee from baku-inhabited areas. Because of this, health and good luck follow baku wherever they go.

INTERACTIONS: The baku's written name and image have been used as symbols of good luck in talismans and charms throughout Japanese history. In the old days, it was common to embroider the kanji for baku onto pillows in order to keep away bad dreams, sickness, and evil spirits. Fearsome baku images are commonly carved into the pillars above temple doors and on the columns supporting temple roofs. Baku are one of only a handful of holy creatures honored in this manner.

ORIGIN: Legend has it that when the world was new and the gods were making the animals, the baku was put together from the leftover bits and pieces at the end of creation. That explains its bizarre appearance, and why it is considered a favorite of the gods.

Today, the Japanese word baku also refers to the tapir. The animal was named for its uncanny resemblance to this holy chimerical beast.

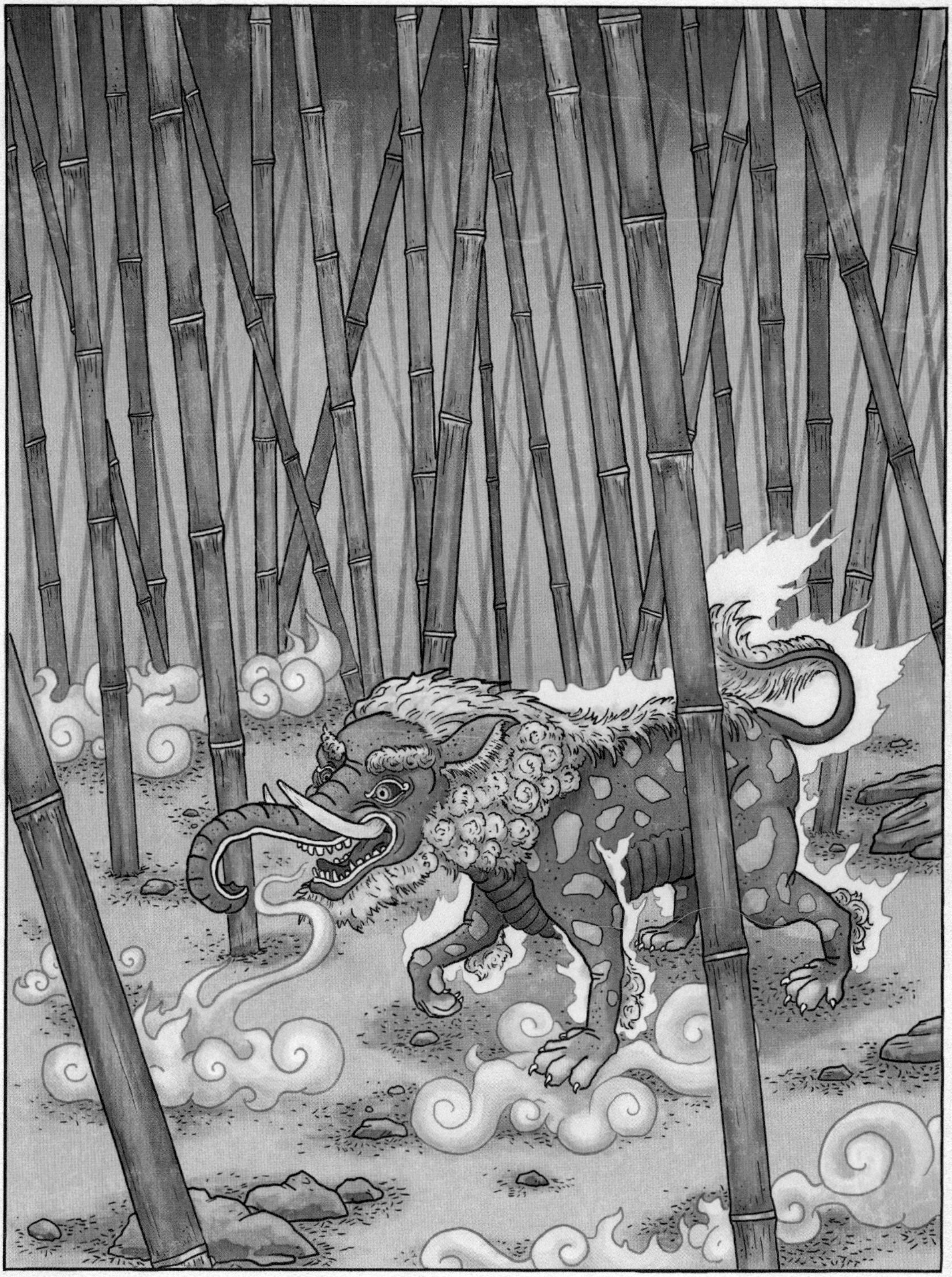

Koma inu 狛犬

TRANSLATION: Goryeo (an ancient Korean dynasty) dog
ALTERNATE NAMES: shishi ("stone lion"); refers only to the open-mouthed koma inu
HABITAT: shrines, temples, and holy areas
DIET: carnivorous

APPEARANCE: Koma inu are noble, holy animals, usually employed as guardians of sacred sites. They can range in size from a small dog to the size of a lion and—due to their resemblance to both creatures—are often called lion dogs in English. They have thick, curly manes and tails, powerful, muscular bodies, and sharp teeth and claws. Some koma inu have large horns like a unicorn on their heads. However, many are hornless.

BEHAVIOR: Koma inu are fierce and noble beasts. They act like watchdogs, guarding gates and doorways and preventing the wicked from entering. They live together in male-female pairs and are always found together. In their pairs, the female usually guards those living inside, while the male guards the structure itself.

INTERACTIONS: Koma inu are a ubiquitous symbol at holy sites in Japan. Stone koma inu statues are almost always found at the entrance to Shinto shrines, often with more inside the shrine guarding the important buildings. The pairs are usually carved in two poses: one with mouth open in a roaring position, and one with mouth closed. Symbolically, these creatures represent yin and yang, or death and life. The open-mouthed koma inu represents the sound "*a*," while the closed-mouthed koma inu represents the sound "*un*." These sounds are the Japanese transliteration of the Sanskrit "*om*," a mystical syllable which symbolizes the beginning, middle, and end of all things. A Western analogy would be alpha and omega.

ORIGIN: Koma inu were brought to Japan via Korea, which in turn received them from China, which in turn received them from India. China is where they first began to symbolize the Dharmic philosophies of Indian religions. In China these dogs are called *shishi*, which means "stone lion." This name is often used in Japan as well, though it only refers to the one with its mouth open. The other one, and the two of them collectively, are always referred to as koma inu.

PEARLS OF WISDOM

Koma inu, tatsu, and other holy beasts are often depicted carrying round pearls or decorative balls, either cradled in their mouths or in being grasped their claws. These balls are representations of the jewel or pearl of wisdom, a common theme in Buddhist art. It is a symbol of vitality, life, and the jewel-like perfection and purity of Buddhist wisdom.

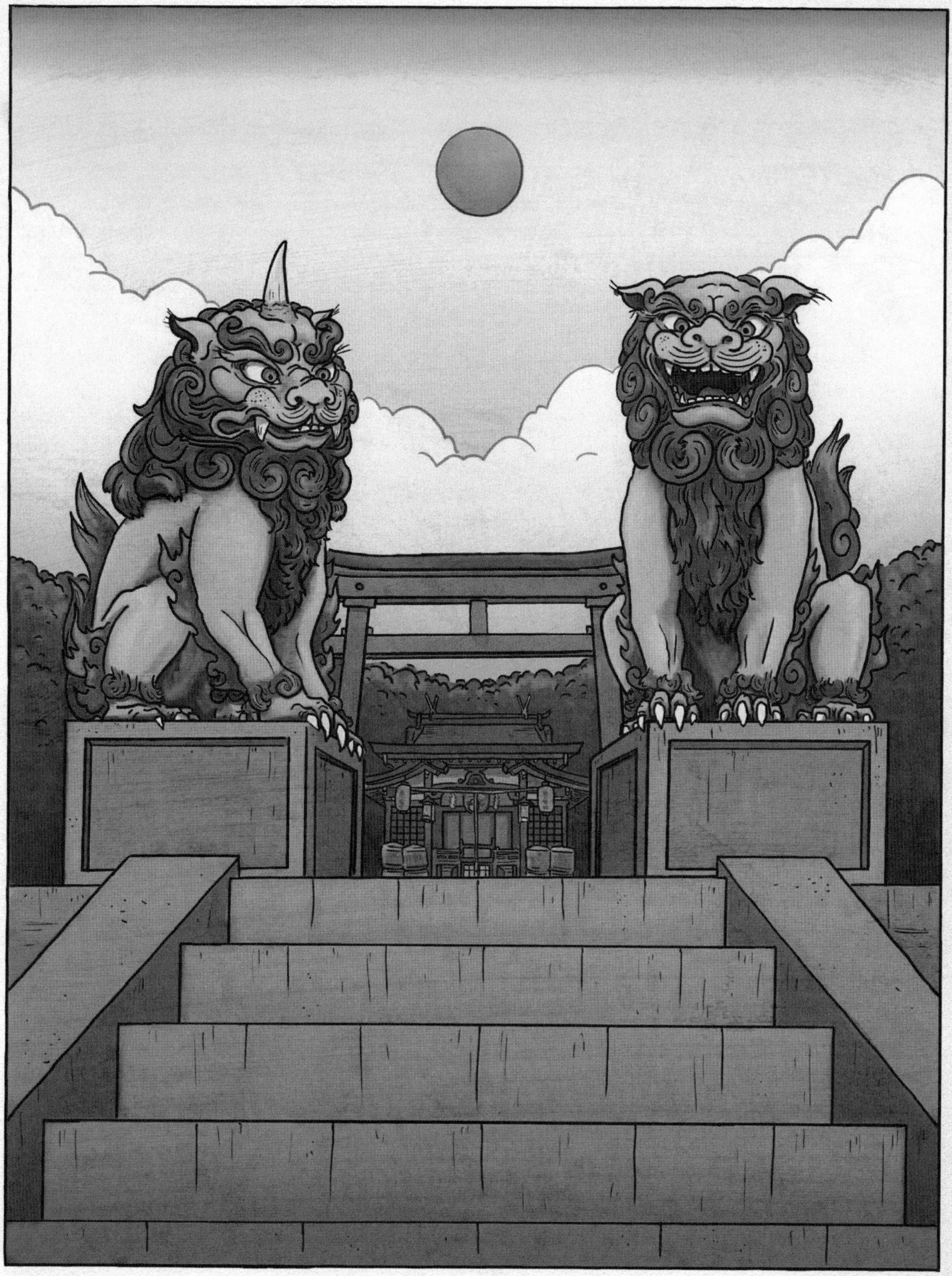

Nozuchi 野槌

TRANSLATION: wild mallet (named for its mallet-like shape)
HABITAT: fields and grasslands; found all across Japan
DIET: carnivorous; usually feeds on small animals like rats, mice, rabbits, and birds

APPEARANCE: Nozuchi are one of the earliest recorded yōkai in Japan. They are powerful and ancient snake-like spirits of the fields, known for their bizarre shape and habits. Short, fat creatures shaped like mallets, Nozuchi are about fifteen centimeters in diameter and just over one meter long. They have no eyes, nose, or any other facial features save for a large mouth located on the tops of their heads, pointing towards the sky. Their bodies are covered in a bristly fur, much like a hairy caterpillar.

BEHAVIOR: Nozuchi make their homes inside of large trees, particularly on the tops of hills. They are slow movers, and get about by rolling and tumbling down slopes, then slowly inching their way back up. Their usual diet is wildlife—mice, rabbits, squirrels, and other small animals—however, they are able to eat things much larger than themselves. In Nara, they are known to feed on deer. They can devour a deer in a single bite, pulling the whole animal into their small, stumpy frame.

INTERACTIONS: Nozuchi have been known to attack humans who come near their nests, rolling downhill and snapping at their feet. Their bites are dangerous, resulting in terrible, mangled wounds which quickly lead to a high fever and death. A person who is touched or even merely seen by a tumbling nozuchi can contract this fever and die. Fortunately, nozuchi attacks are easily avoided. Stick to higher ground where they cannot tumble, or climb a tree if no other high ground is available.

OTHER FORMS: Nozuchi can transform into a humanoid shape, though they rarely are seen in this form. They take the shape of a human priest, but with no eyes, nose, hair, or ears. The only feature on the head is a large, gaping mouth pointing upwards towards the sky. Wicked monks who are banished from their temples to live in the wilds sometimes gradually turn into nozuchi. These nozuchi are more likely to maintain a humanoid form than a serpentine one. Care should be taken not to confuse a shape-changed nozuchi with a nopperabō, which has a similar appearance but poses a different threat.

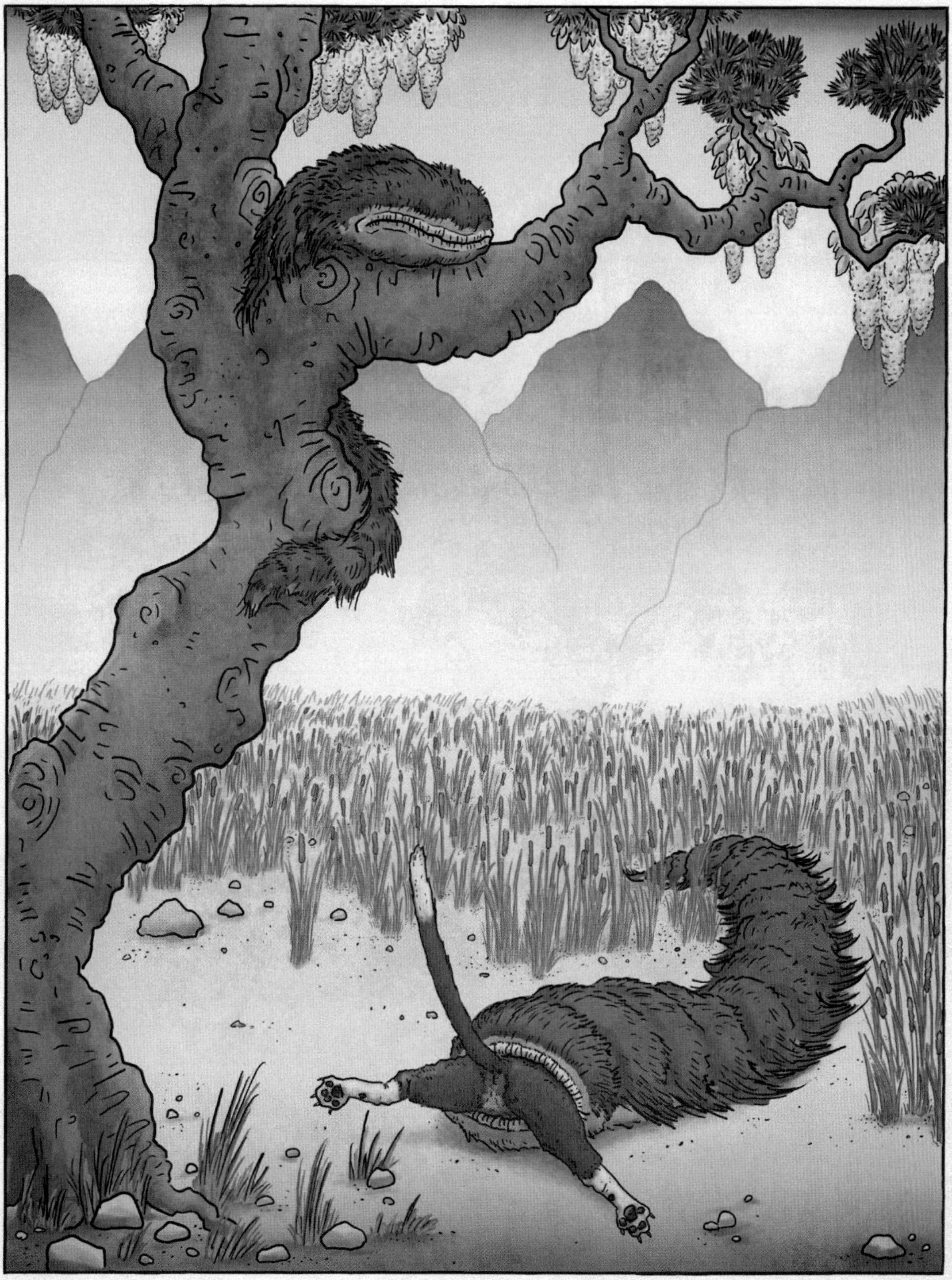

ONIBI 鬼火

TRANSLATION: demon fire
HABITAT: grasslands, forests, watersides, graveyards
DIET: life energy

APPEARANCE: One of the more dangerous types of fireball yōkai, onibi are a beautiful, but deadly phenomenon. Their name means "demon fire," and they certainly earn that moniker. They look like small balls of flame, usually blue or blue-white (red and yellow onibi are less common), and appear in groups of twenty to thirty orbs. The orbs can range in size from three to thirty centimeters, and usually float around at eye-level. They appear in places surrounded by nature—most often during the spring and summer months, and particularly on rainy days.

Onibi are found all over Japan. In some areas, they manifest the faces and even voices of the victims whose life force they have drained. In Okinawa, onibi are said to take the shape of a small bird.

INTERACTIONS: Onibi do not create much heat, but the orbs possess a different danger. Living creatures that draw too close are swarmed by dozens of orbs, which drain away the life force from their victims. Soon nothing is left but a dead husk on the ground. During the night, onibi are often mistaken for distant lanterns, and people have vanished into the forests chasing after these phantom lights. Travelers should take care not to be lead off their paths to their deaths by demon fire.

ORIGIN: Onibi are born out of the dead bodies of humans and animals. It is not known what causes onibi to develop; sometimes they appear and sometimes they do not. Intense grudges and malice are also able to create onibi. They are considered to be identical to the will-o'-the-wisps of English folklore.

HI NO TAMA 火の玉

There are many different yōkai which appear as glowing orbs of light. It is difficult to tell the difference between onibi, kodama, hitodama, kitsunebi, and the many other kinds. Though similar in appearance, they have different origins and attributes. Some are mindless while others are intelligent; some are harmless while others are deadly. Despite their differences, all of the fireball yōkai are lumped together into one group, called *hi no tama*, which literally means "balls of fire."

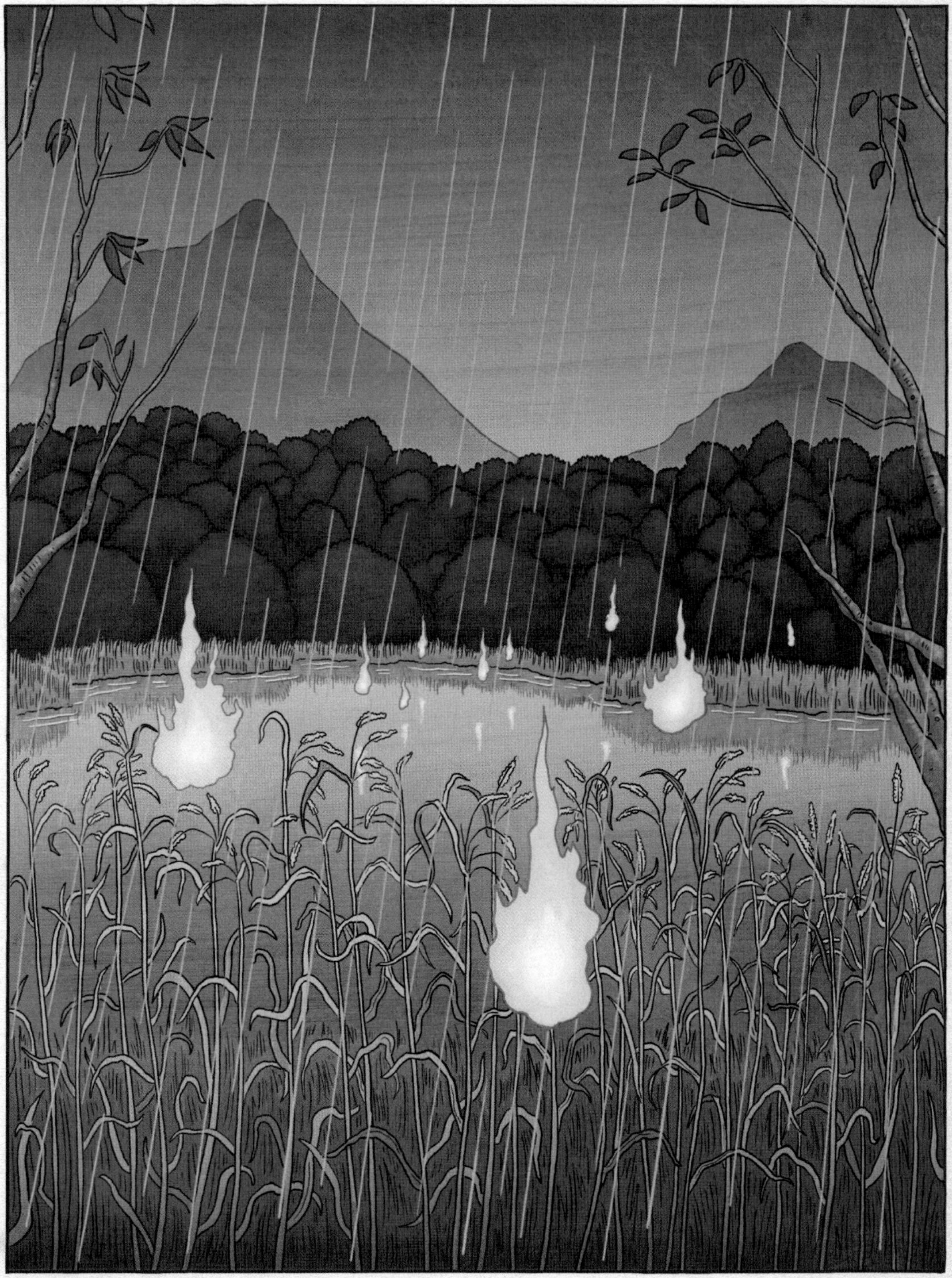

HITODAMA 人魂

TRANSLATION: human soul
HABITAT: graveyards and near the recently deceased
DIET: none

APPEARANCE: Hitodama are the visible souls of humans detached from their host bodies. They appear as red, orange, or blue-white orbs, and float about slowly not too far from the ground.

BEHAVIOR: On warm summer nights, these strange, glowing orbs can be seen floating around graveyards, funeral parlors, or the houses where people have recently died. Most often they are seen just before or after the moment of death, when the soul leaves the body to return to the ether. It is most common to see them at night, though they occasionally appear during the daytime. Rarely, hitodama materialize when a person loses consciousness, floating outside of the body, only to return when the person regains consciousness.

Hitodama are harmless, and it is important not to confuse them with other, potentially deadly fireball yōkai. Hitodama can be distinguished from other hi no tama by the distinctive tails of light which trail behind them.

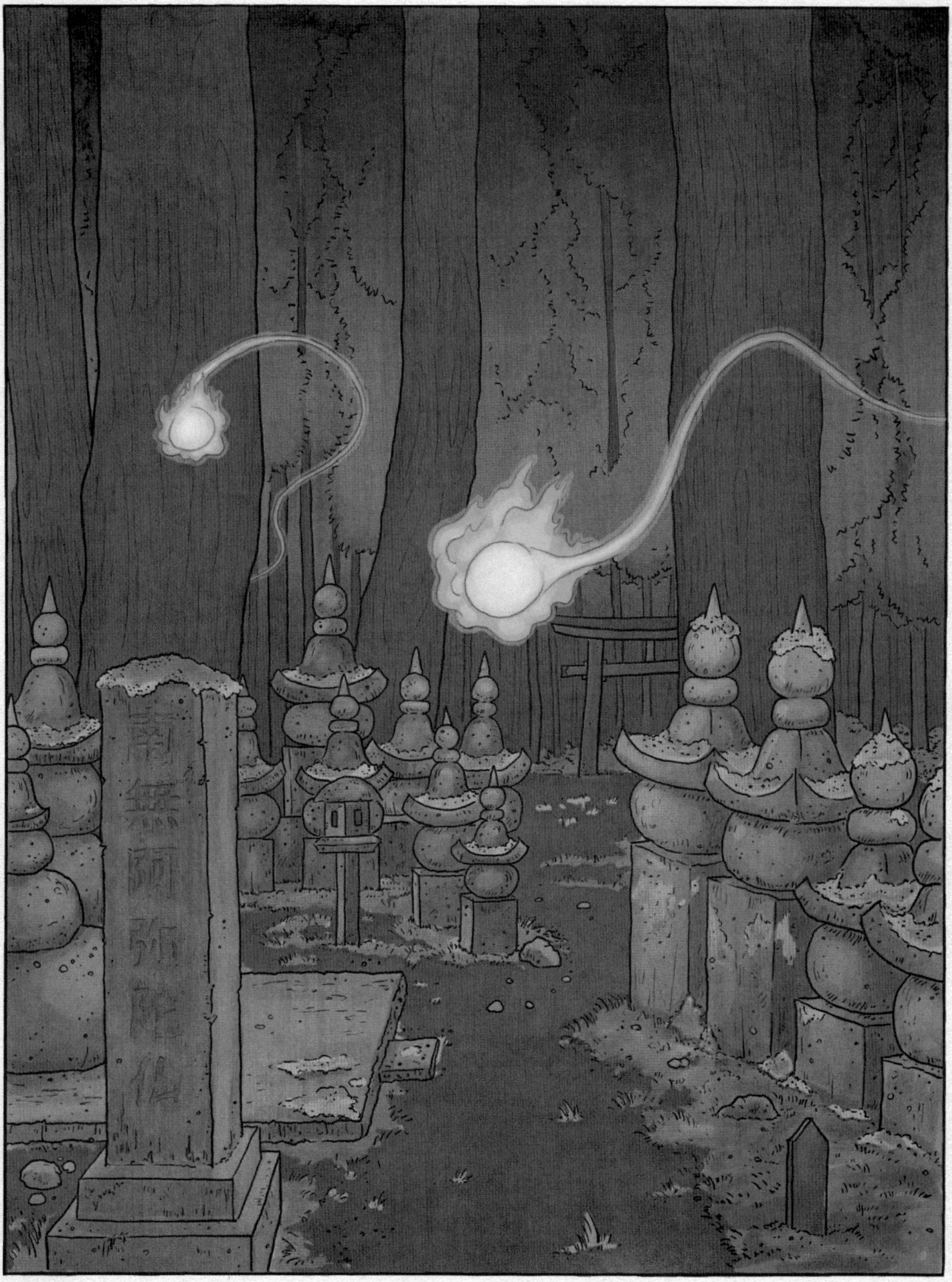
南無阿弥陀仏

Kodama 木霊

TRANSLATION: tree spirit
HABITAT: deep in untouched forests, inside very old tress
DIET: none; its life is connected to the life of its host tree

APPEARANCE: Deep in the mountainous forests of Japan, the souls of the trees are animated as spirits called kodama. These souls wander outside of their hosts, tending to their groves and maintaining the balance of nature. Kodama are rarely ever seen, but are often heard—particularly as echoes that take just a little longer to return than they should. When they do appear, they resemble faint orbs of light in the distance; or occasionally a tiny, funny shaped vaguely humanoid figure. A kodama's life force is directly tied to the tree it inhabits; if either the tree or the kodama dies, the other cannot live.

INTERACTIONS: Kodama are revered as gods of the trees and protectors of the forests. They bless the lands around their forest with vitality, and villagers who find a kodama-inhabited tree honor it by marking it with a sacred rope known as a shimenawa. Occasionally, very old trees will bleed when cut, and this is regarded as a sign that a kodama is living inside. Cutting down such an ancient tree is a grave sin, and can bring down a powerful curse, causing a prosperous community to fall into ruin.

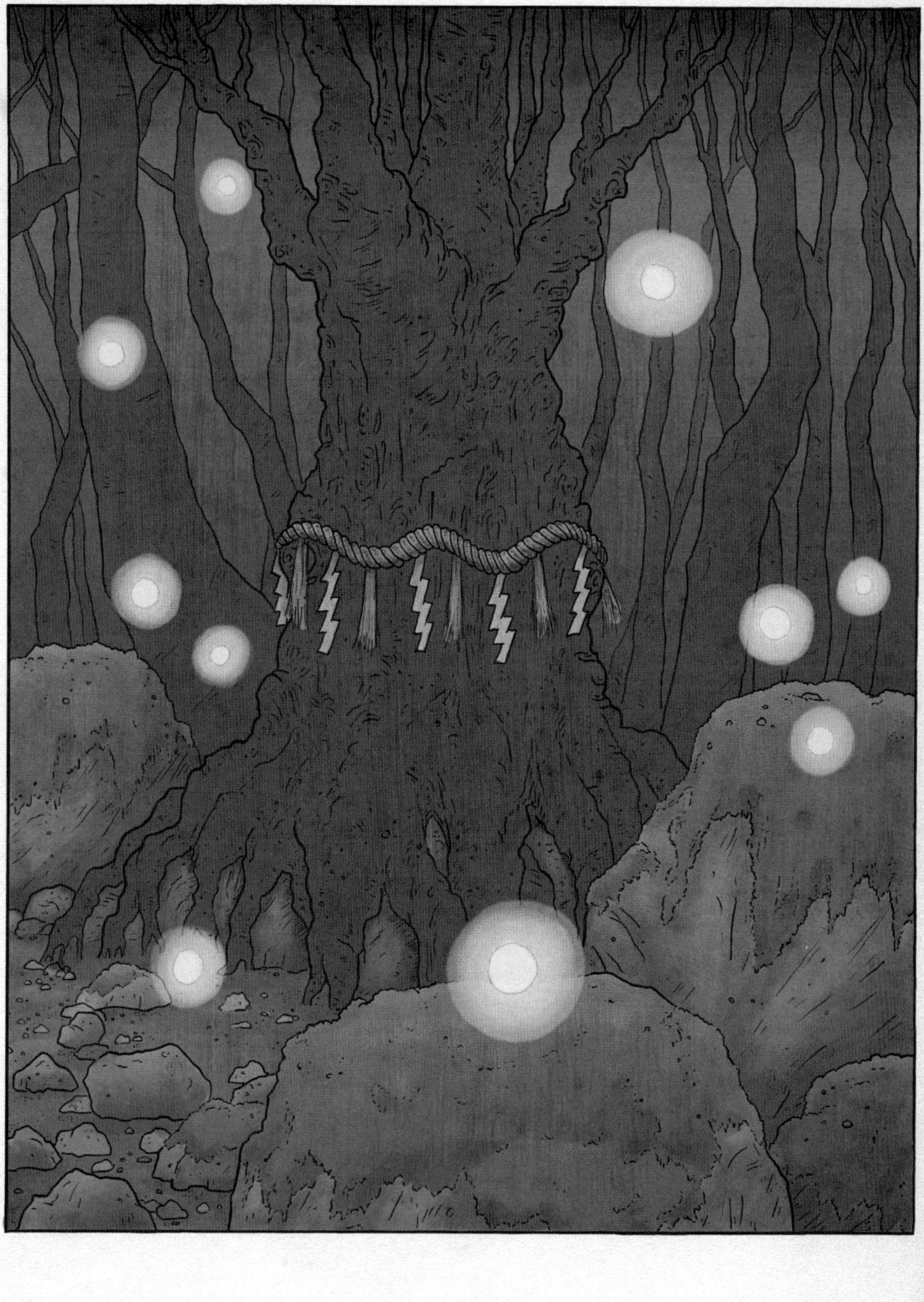

Yamabiko 山彦

TRANSLATION: echo; written with characters meaning mountain boy
HABITAT: forested mountains and valleys, inside camphor tress
DIET: unknown

APPEARANCE: The wilds of Japan are full of strange phenomena, like echoes that bounce back with more delay than they should, or that come back slightly different from the original sound. When the false echo comes from the forest, it is usually attributed to a kodama. When it comes from the mountains, it is due to something called a yamabiko. They are small, appearing like a cross between a dog and a wild monkey.

Yamabiko are known almost exclusively by their voices. They are skilled at mimicking any sound, including natural sounds, human language, and trains and cars. They occasionally unleash terrible and mysterious screams deep in the forests that can carry for long distances.

BEHAVIOR: Little is known about these yōkai due to their rarity and elusiveness. They live deep in the mountains and make their homes in camphor trees, in close proximity to (and sharing a common ancestry with) other tree and mountain spirits. For many centuries, their calls were speculated to be a kind of rare bird, or other kinds of yōkai, or even natural phenomena. It wasn't until the Edo period—when determined yōkai researchers like Sawaki Sūshi and Toriyama Sekien began making illustrated yokai bestiaries—that this creature's form was decided.

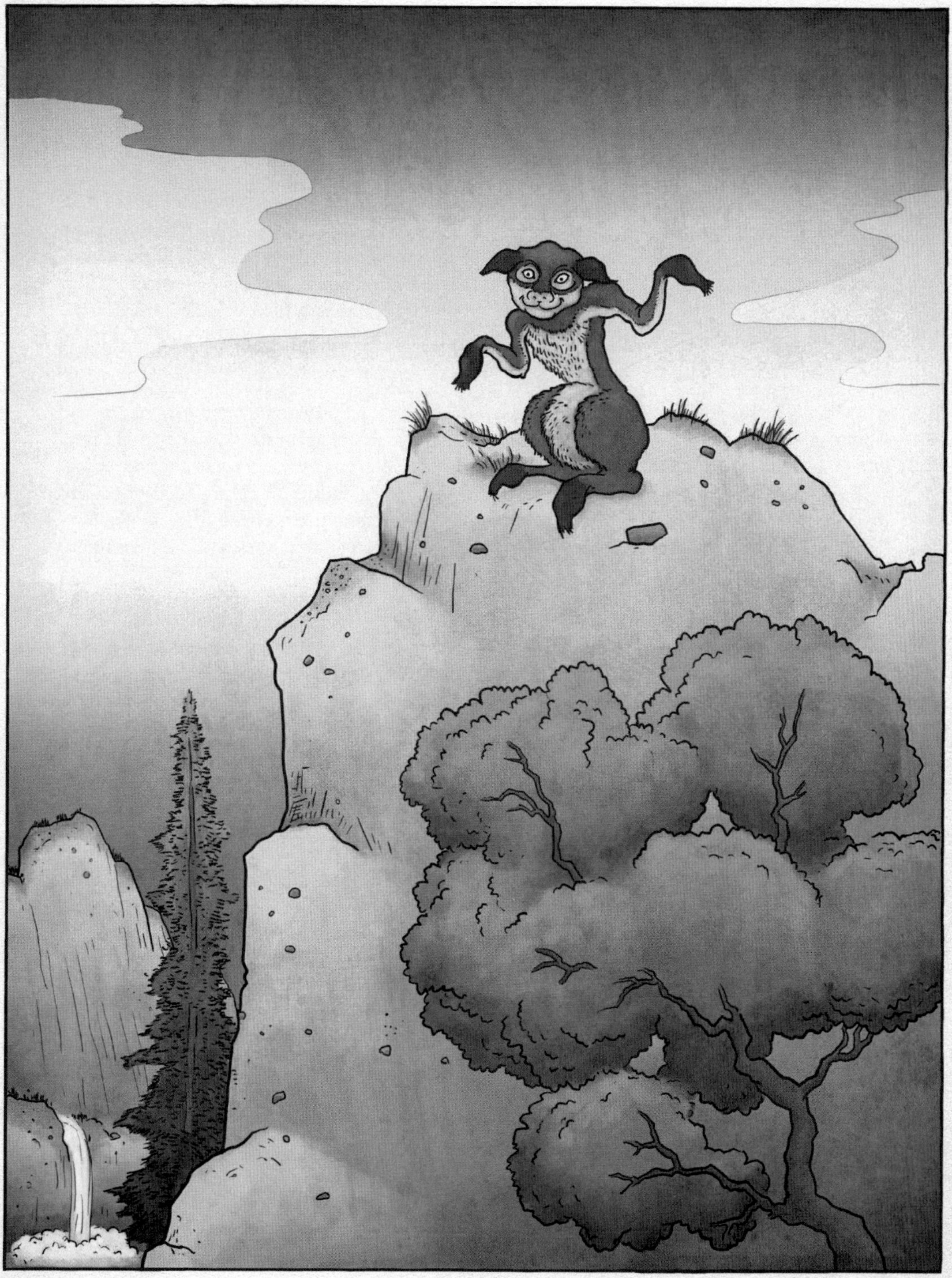

Kijimunā キジムナー

Translation: the name comes from an old Okinawan village, Kijimuka
Alternate names: sēma, bunagaya
Habitat: banyan trees on the islands of Okinawa
Diet: seafood; prefers fish heads and eyes

Appearance: The southern island chain of Okinawa is home to a number of unique yōkai that are not found anywhere else in Japan. One of these is the kijimunā: an elfin creature that makes it home in the banyan trees that grow all over the Ryukyu archipelago. Physically, kijimunā are about the same height as a child, with wild and thick bright red hair, and red tinted skin. They wear skirts made of grass, and move about by hopping rather than walking. Although kijimunā retain the appearance of child-like youthfulness into their adulthood, males are noted for their large and prominent testicles.

Behavior: The kijimunā lifestyle mimics humans in many ways. They fish along the shores, live in family units, get married, and raise children in much the same way as the native islanders. On rare occasions, they marry into human families. The kijimunā diet consists entirely of seafood. They are excellent fishers, and are particularly skilled at diving. Kijimunā use both these skills to catch their favorite dish: fish heads—specifically the head of the snapper species called the double-lined fusilier. They are especially fond of fish eyes, even preferring the left eye over the right. Okinawans attribute eyeless corpses of fish found on the beach to picky kijimunā.

Kijimunā have a number of peculiar fears and prejudices. They loathe chickens and cooking pots. They are extremely put off by people passing gas. However, the thing they hate above all else is the octopus. They avoid octopuses at all costs, despising them and fearing them at the same time.

Interactions: Kijimunā often help fishermen catch fish, or aid humans in other ways in return for a cooked meal. When they form friendships with humans, it can last for a lifetime. Kijimunā will often return to their human friends many times, even spending holidays with their adopted family.

Unprovoked kijimunā attacks on humans are rare. Cutting down the banyan tree in which they live is a sure way to earn their wrath. Kijimunā thus wronged have been known to murder livestock, sabotage boats so they sink while their owners are far out at sea, or magically trap people in hollow trees from which they cannot escape. Sometimes they press down on peoples' chests while they sleep, or snuff out lights during the night. Once earned, the enmity of a kijimunā can never be assuaged.

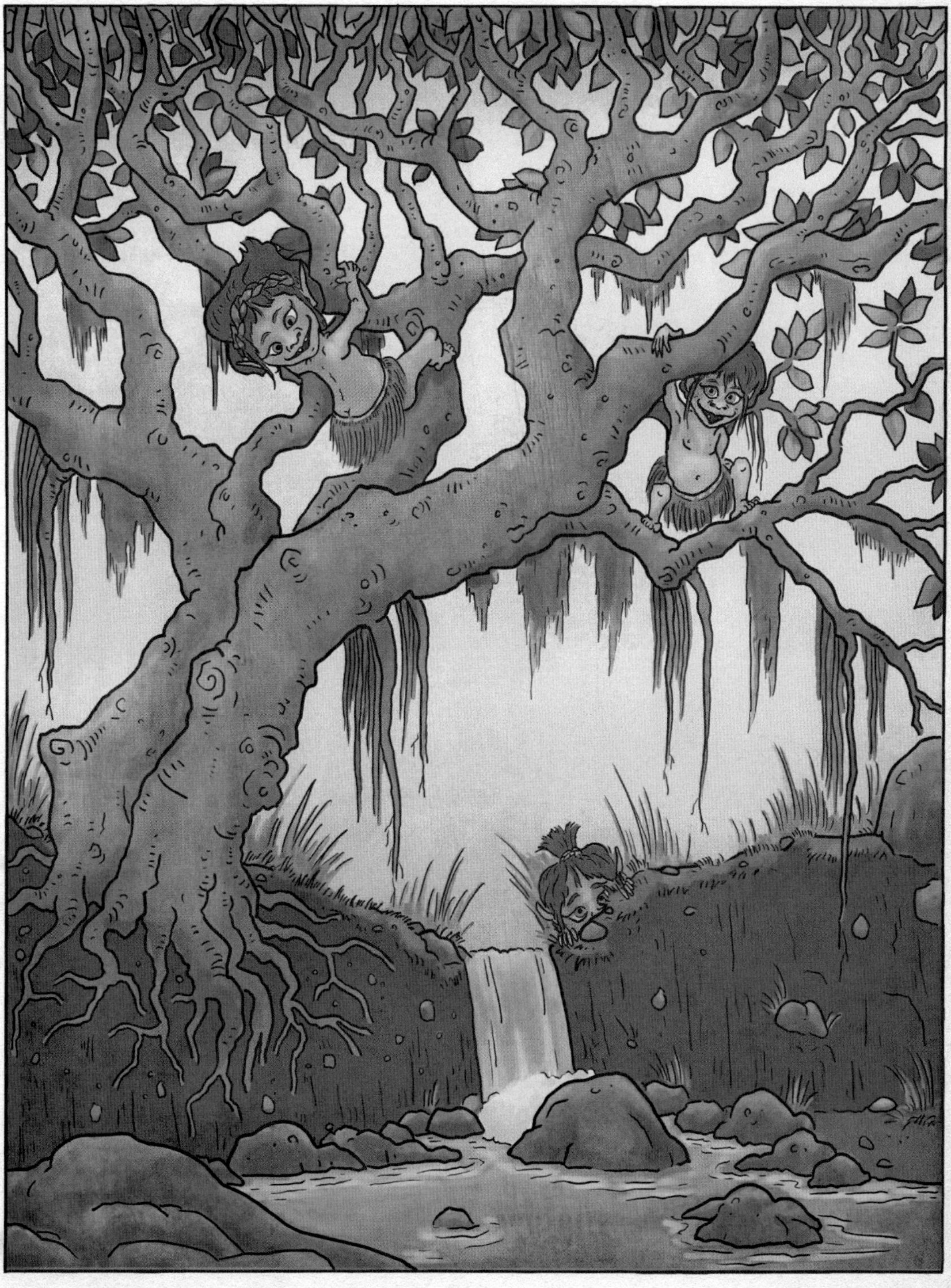

Nure onago 濡女子

TRANSLATION: wet girl
ALTERNATE NAMES: nure hanayome ("wet bride")
HABITAT: watersides, wetlands, fishing villages; anywhere near water
DIET: attention

APPEARANCE: Nure onago appear as disheveled-looking young girls with matted, wet hair. As the name implies, they are soaked with water from head to toe. Often, nure onago are covered with dead leaves and things stuck to their dripping bodies. They wander about dripping and sopping wet, and are encountered on roads near swamps, rivers, and coasts, or during nights of heavy rain.

INTERACTIONS: Travelers along the coasts and rivers of the islands of Shikoku and Kyūshū occasionally encounter young girls, lost and soaked to the bone. Most people who witness such a pathetic sight rush over to help the poor girls. When a human draws close to a nure onago, she looks up into their eyes and smiles. If the smile is returned, she will follow the helpful stranger human, sticking by him forever. This isn't as nice as it seems; nure onago continually drip water and stink of mildew and swamp water. Although she causes no particular harm, her constant presence is often enough to ruin the rest of a person's life.

Ignoring a nure onago and refusing to return her smile is the only way to avoid this yōkai. Unfortunately, by the time her true nature is discovered it is often too late.

ORIGIN: Nure onago are born from the strong feelings of loss and sadness shared by widows of drowning victims—particular widows of sailors lost at sea. These feelings build up and materialize into a nure onago, whose desire for attention is the amplified desire of heartbroken widows to see their husbands again.

Nure onago behave similarly to hari onago, although in a less violent form. The two are sometimes grouped together as waraionago, smiling girls. Both are also found on the island of Shikoku, suggesting a possible relation between them. They should not, however, be confused with the similarly named nure onna, a much larger and more dangerous yōkai.

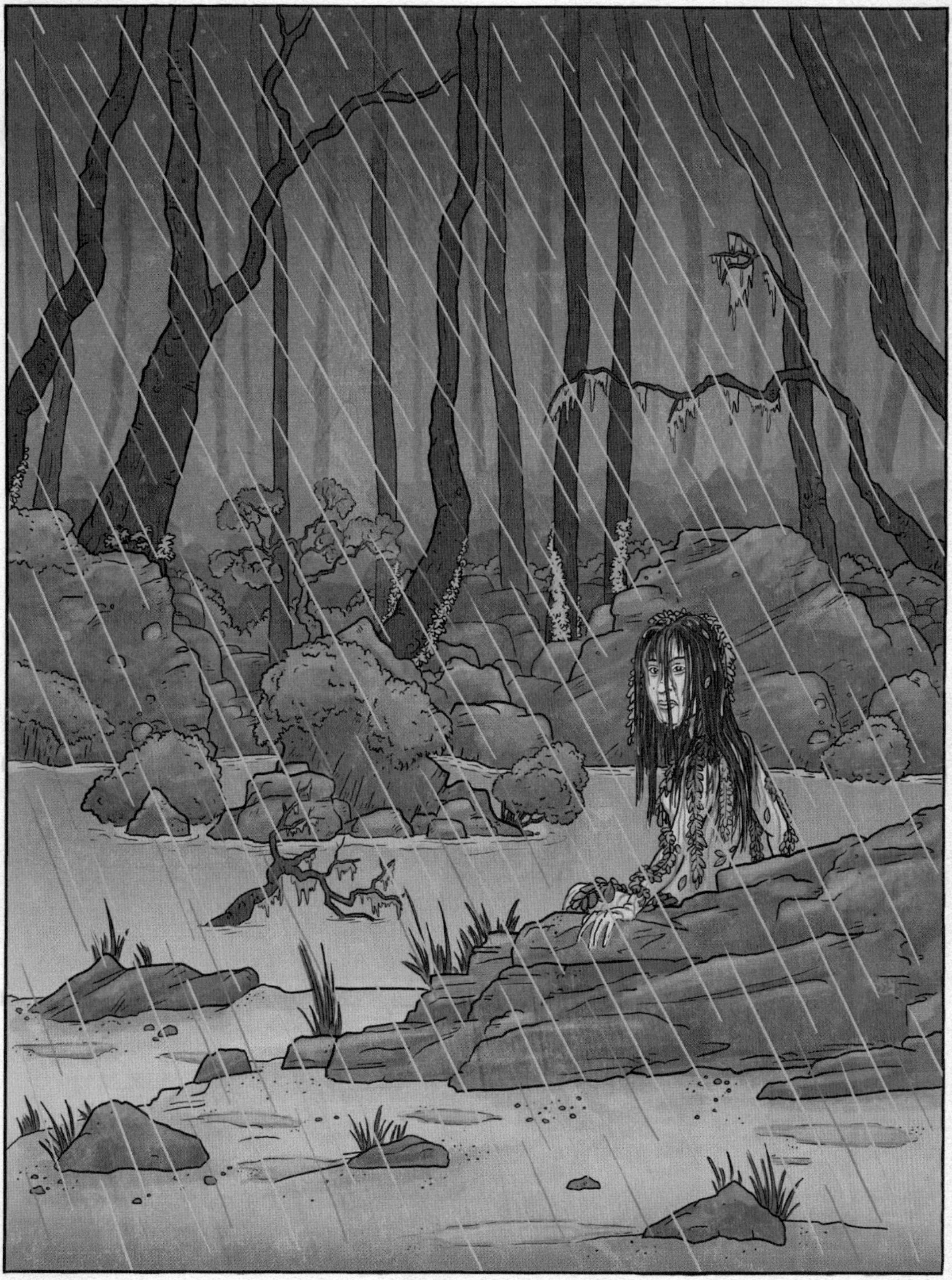

Jorōgumo 絡新婦

TRANSLATION: entangling bride; alternatively whore spider
HABITAT: cities, towns, rural areas, forests, and caves
DIET: young, virile men

APPEARANCE: In Japan, some spiders are known to possess amazing supernatural powers. One of these is the jorōgumo, known as the golden orb-weaver in English. The jorōgumo is the most well-known of the arachnid yōkai, and found all over the Japanese archipelago except for the northern island of Hokkaidō. Their body size averages between two to three centimeters long, but they can grow much larger; some are massive enough to catch and eat small birds. Renowned for their size, their vividly beautiful colors, and the large and strong webs they weave, the beautiful jorōgumo are also famous for the cruel destruction they wreak on young men. Written with modern kanji, their name means "entangling bride." However, these characters were added much later to cover up the original meaning of jorōgumo—"whore spider."

BEHAVIOR: Jorōgumo live solitary lives, both as spiders and as yōkai. When a golden orb-weaver reaches 400 years of age, it develops magical powers and begins to feed on human prey instead of insects. Jorōgumo make their nests in caves, forests, or empty houses in towns. Possessing a cunning intelligence and a cold heart, they see humans as nothing more than insects to feed on. They are skillful deceivers and powerful shape-shifters, usually appearing as young, sexy, and stunningly beautiful women.

INTERACTIONS: Jorōgumo's favorite prey are young, handsome men looking for love—or other favors. When a jorōgumo spots a man she desires, she lures him into her home with promises of affection. He is never seen again. Jorōgumo spin silk threads strong enough to ensnare a grown man so that he cannot escape. They also have powerful venom that can slowly weaken a man day by day, allowing the spider to savor her victim's long and painful death. Jorōgumo can control other, lesser spiders, even employing fire-breathing spiders to burn down the homes of any suspicious meddlers. They are such skillful predators that a jorōgumo can operate like this for years and years, even in the middle of a busy city, piling up hundreds of desiccated skeletons of foolish young men.

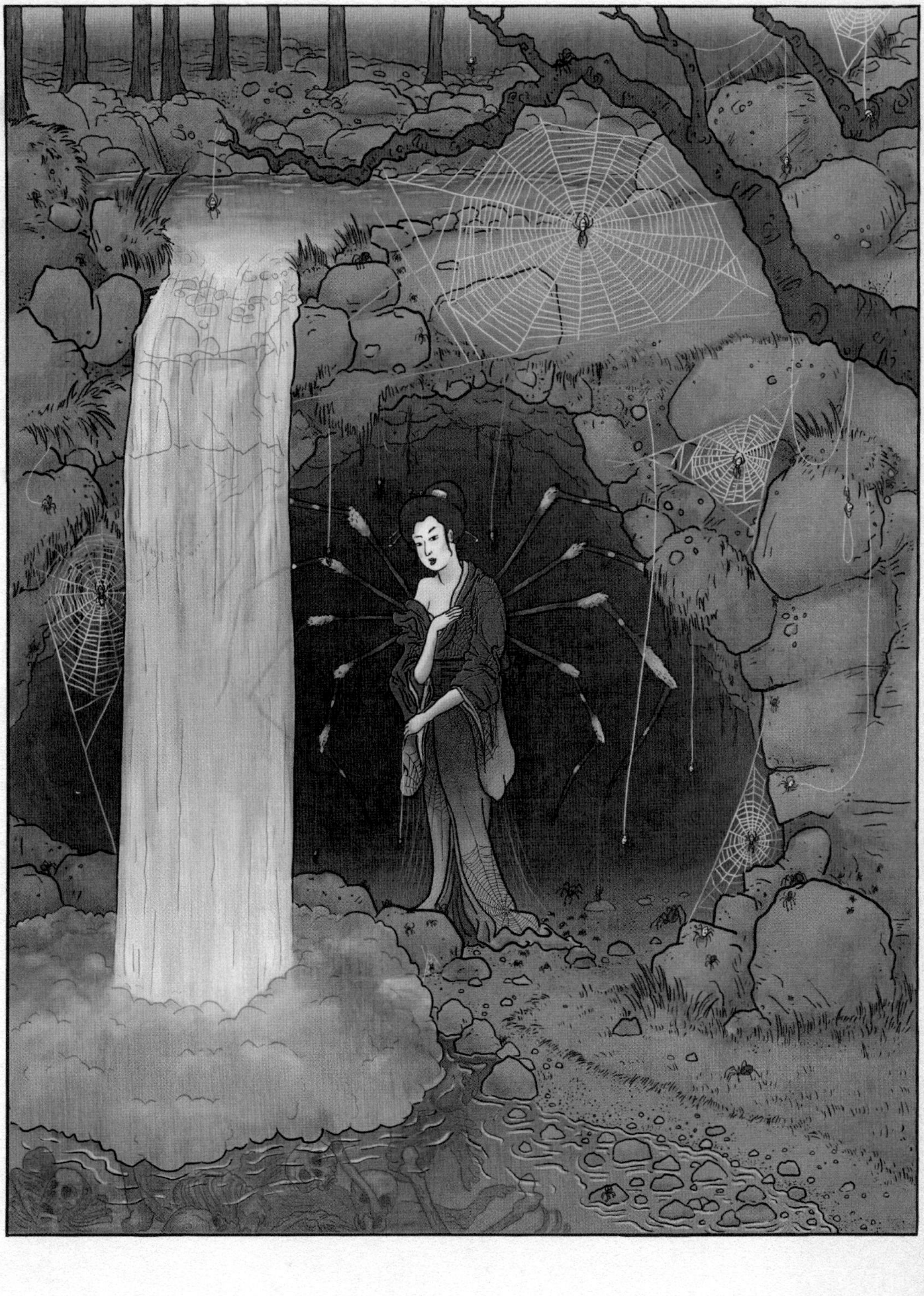

TSUCHIGUMO 土蜘蛛

TRANSLATION: ground spider
ALTERNATE NAMES: yatsukahagi, ōgumo ("giant spider")
HABITAT: rural areas, mountains, forests, and caves
DIET: humans, animals; anything that it can trap

APPEARANCE: Tsuchigumo, known as the purse web spider in English, are found all over the Japanese islands and throughout much of the world. Long-lived tsuchigumo can transform into yōkai. They grow to a monstrous size, able to catch much larger prey—particularly humans.

BEHAVIOR: Tsuchigumo live in the forests and mountains, making their homes in silk tubes from which they ambush passing prey. Like other spider yōkai, they rely on illusion and trickery to deceive people. While the jorōgumo use their sexuality to seduce young men, the tsuchigumo have a wider selection of deceptions—and often bigger ambitions.

LEGENDS: The accounts of the legendary warrior Minamoto no Yorimitsu contain numerous encounters with tsuchigumo. In one, a tsuchigumo changed itself into a servant boy to administer venom in the form of medicine to the famed warrior. When his wounds were not healing and the medicine didn't seem to be working, Yorimitsu suspected foul play. He slashed his sword at the boy, who then fled into the forest. The attack broke the powerful illusion which the spider had laid on Yorimitsu, and he found that he was covered in spider webs. Yorimitsu and his retainers followed the trail of spider's blood into the mountains, where they discovered a gigantic, monstrous arachnid—dead from the wound Yorimitsu had inflicted.

In another legend, a tsuchigumo took the form of a beautiful warrior woman and lead an army of yōkai against Japan. Yorimitsu and his men met the yōkai army on the battlefield. With his experience in such matters Yorimitsu attacked the woman general first. The blow struck, her army vanished—it was merely an illusion. The warriors followed the woman to a cave in the mountains, where she morphed into a giant spider. With one swing of his sword, Yorimitsu sliced her abdomen open. Thousands of baby spiders the size of human infants swarmed out from her belly. Yorimitsu and his retainers slew every one of the spiders and returned home victorious.

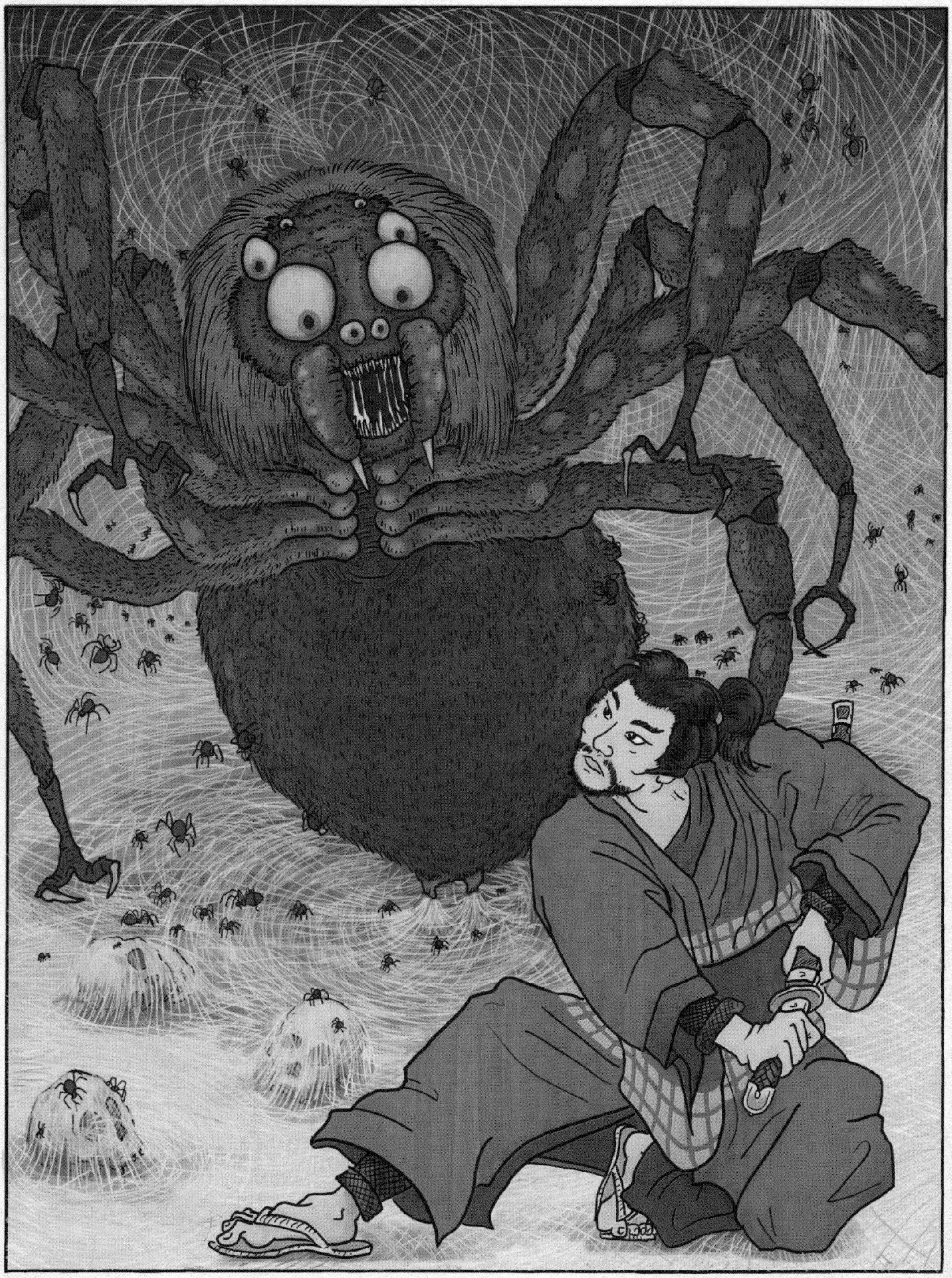

Aosagibi 青鷺火

TRANSLATION: blue heron fire
ALTERNATE NAMES: goi no hikari ("night heron light")
HABITAT: rivers, wetlands; wherever herons and other water birds can be found

APPEARANCE: When they reach an advanced age, many types of birds transform into magical yōkai with eerie powers. Aosagibi is the name for a bizarre phenomenon caused by transformed herons—particularly the black-crowned night heron. Found all along the islands and coasts, this heron prefers remote areas with heavy reeds and thick woods. Though aosagibi is most commonly attributed to this particular bird, other herons and wild birds such as ducks and pheasants are able to develop this manifestation. Aosagibi is most commonly seen at night, either in the trees where the herons roost, by the rivers where they hunt, or in the twilight sky as birds fly overhead.

BEHAVIOR: Long-lived herons develop shining scales on their breasts, which fuse together from their feathers. With each breath, they blow a yellow iridescent powder from their beaks that scatters into the wind. During the autumn nights, their bodies radiate a bluish-white glow. Their powdery breath ignites into bright blue fireballs, which they blow across the water or high in the trees. These fireballs possess no heat and do not ignite what they touch, but eventually evaporate in the wind.

INTERACTIONS: Like most wild birds, night herons are shy and flee from humans. Even after transforming into yōkai, they retain their shyness. While the sight of a colony of wild birds breathing blue flames and making strange calls on a cool autumn night can be rather disconcerting, aosagibi does not post any threat. However, because their fireball breath appears similar to other phenomena, caution should be taken to avoid confusing aosagibi with onibi or other supernatural lights.

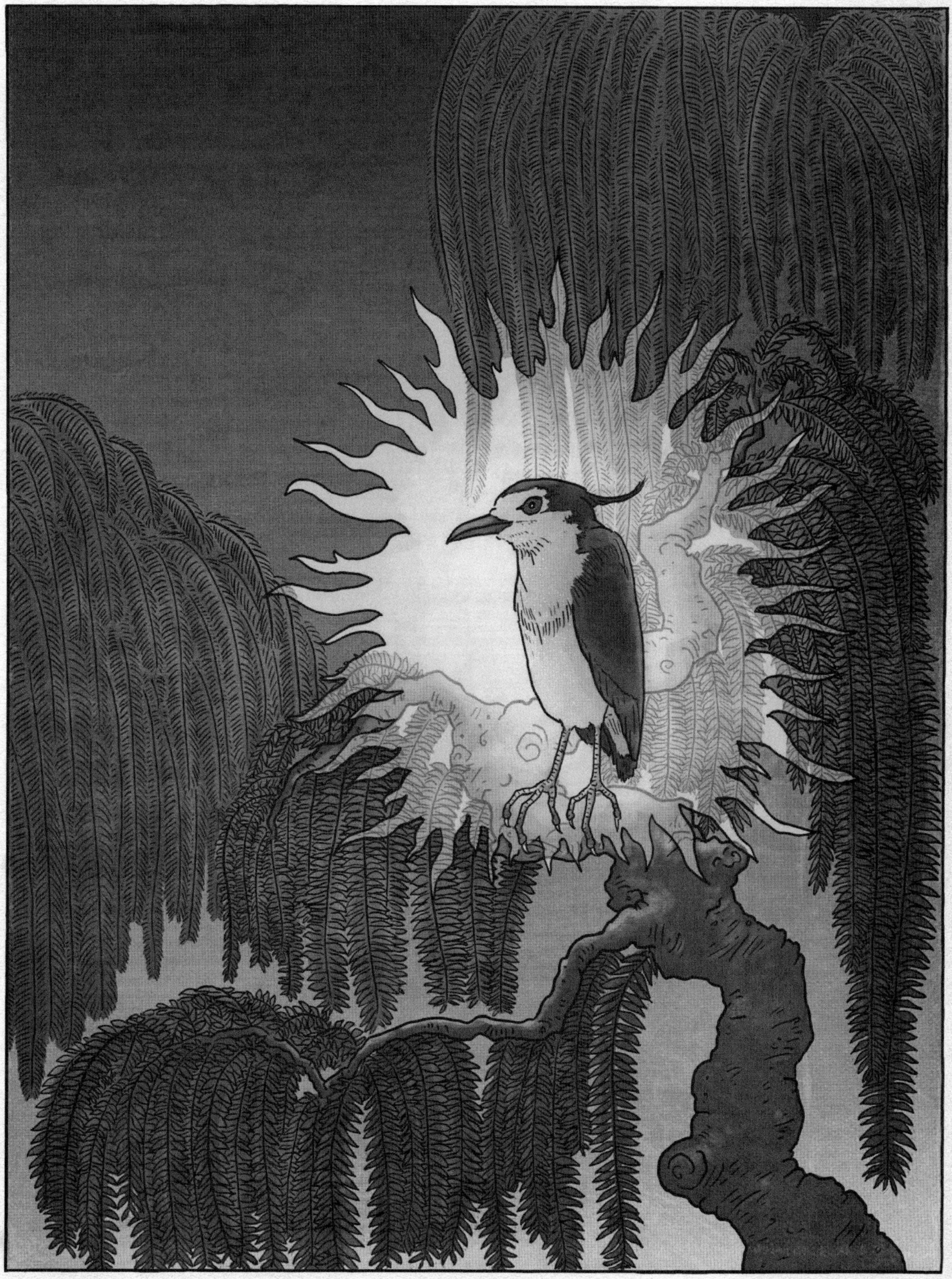

ITACHI 鼬

TRANSLATION: weasel
ALTERNATE NAMES: often referred to as ten, the Japanese marten
HABITAT: found all across Japan, particularly in mountainous areas
DIET: carnivorous; feeds on small wild animals

APPEARANCE: Like birds and spiders, many other animals develop into yōkai when they reach a certain age. Japanese weasels, known as itachi, are disconcerting animals. They bring ill omens, and people fear their particular brand of magic. Like most animals-turned-yōkai, they possess shape-shifting abilities in addition to a number of supernatural powers.

INTERACTIONS: Itachi are tricksters and pranksters, but generally shy away from interaction with humans. As a result, they are mistrusted and disliked. Itachi calls are also considered to be ill omens. After the yelping cries of a group of itachi are heard, misfortune and despair always follows. Though itachi can transform, they prefer to use other kinds of magic—usually with unfortunate results for their targets. When an itachi is seen standing on its hind legs it is said to be bewitching a human—perhaps hypnotizing them into leaving out food or performing some other task for the weasel's benefit. Itachi are dangerous in groups. They gather together at night, climb up onto each other's shoulders, and create huge columns of fire which erupt into whirlwinds. These are frequently blamed for starting conflagrations which can burn down entire towns.

ORIGIN: In the old days, weasels were believed to transform into *ten* (martens) or *mujina* (badgers or tanuki, depending on the region) after reaching an old age. Additionally, the names ten and itachi were often used interchangeably. As a result, there is confusion over which animal is being referred to in many stories.

OTHER FORMS: Itachi are often considered to be the most skilled shape-changing animals, possessing more forms than any other shape-changer. An old phrase about animal yōkai goes, *"Kitsune nanabake, tanuki hachibake, ten kubake"*—foxes seven forms, tanuki eight forms, martens (i.e. itachi) nine forms. When an itachi changes its shape, it usually adopts the form of a young priest boy dressed in clothes that are too big for him. This form is used chiefly to acquire alcohol, which the weasels cannot brew. Itachi also frequently adopt the forms of other yōkai in order to scare humans. One of their favorites is the ōnyūdō: a colossal, bald-headed giant who terrorizes villages, destroys houses, devours livestock and even eats people.

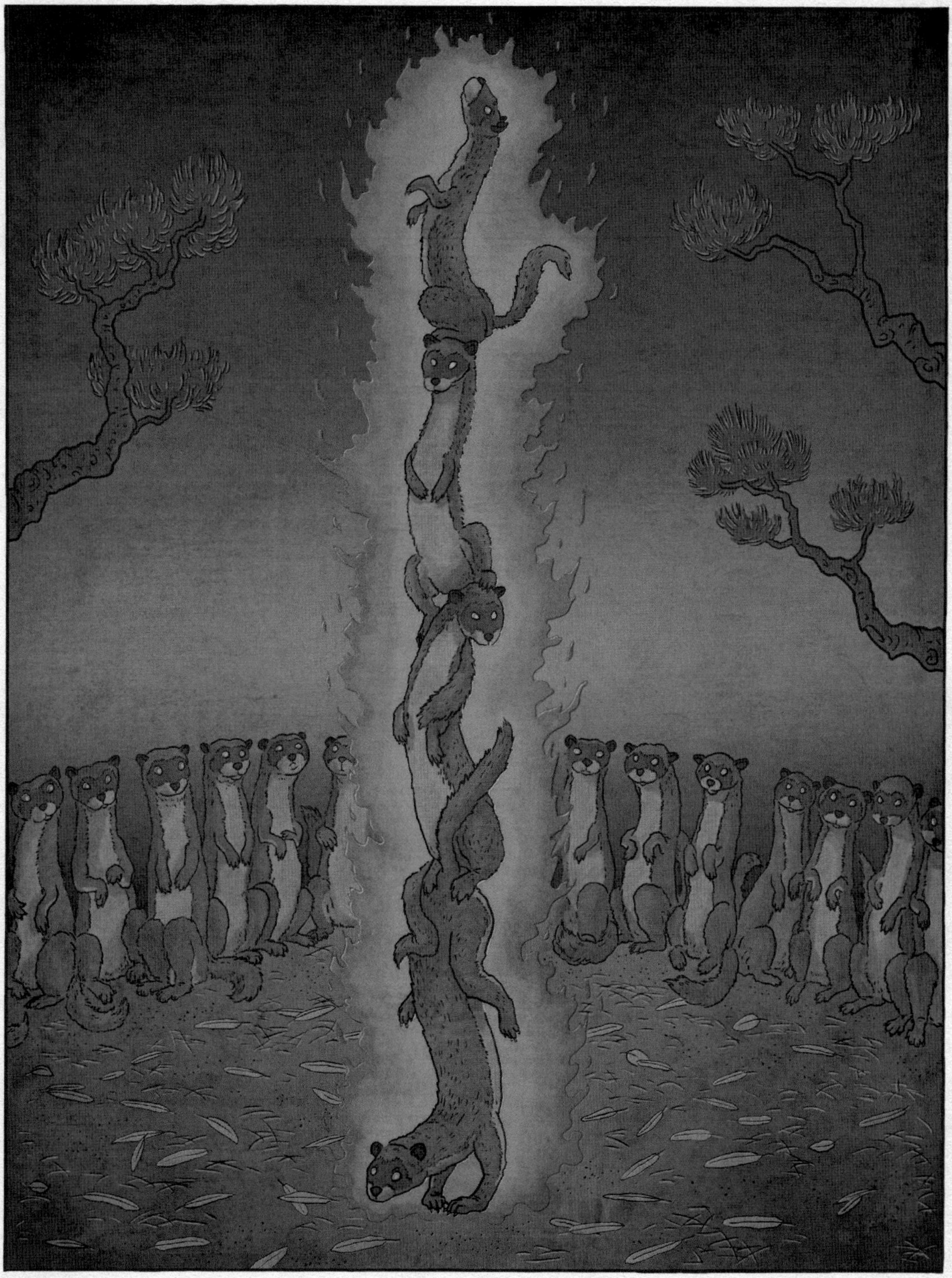

KAMA ITACHI 鎌鼬

TRANSLATION: sickle weasel
HABITAT: primarily the Japan Alps, but potentially anywhere that weasels are found
DIET: carnivorous; feeds on small wild animals

APPEARANCE: The mountainous regions of Yamanashi, Nagano, and Niigata are known for a particularly meddlesome kind of itachi. In these areas, grandparents warn their grandchildren to beware of kama itachi, or "sickle weasels." These itachi have learned to ride the swirling whirlwinds of this cold region. They have claws as strong as steel and as sharp as razors. Their fur is spiny like a hedgehog, and they bark like a dog. They move so quickly that they are invisible to the naked eye. They come and go with the wind.

INTERACTIONS: Kama itachi travel and attack in threes, striking out at people from thin air. The first kama itachi slices at its victim's legs, knocking him to the ground. The second one uses its fore and hind legs to slice up the prone victim with thousands of dreadful cuts. The third one then applies a magical salve which heals up the majority of the wounds instantly, so that none of them proves fatal. It is said that the kama itachi strikes with such precision that it can carve out entire chunks of flesh from its victims without spilling even a drop of blood. The attack and the healing happen so fast that the victim cannot perceive them; from his perspective he merely trips and gets up with a bit of pain and a few scratches here and there.

ORIGIN: One theory about the kama itachi's origin is that it is only a joke: a play on words based on a sword fighting stance known as *kamae tachi*. However, legends of invisible beasts that ride the wind and attack humans in a similar manner are found in all regions of Japan, and the sickle weasel remains a popular explanation.

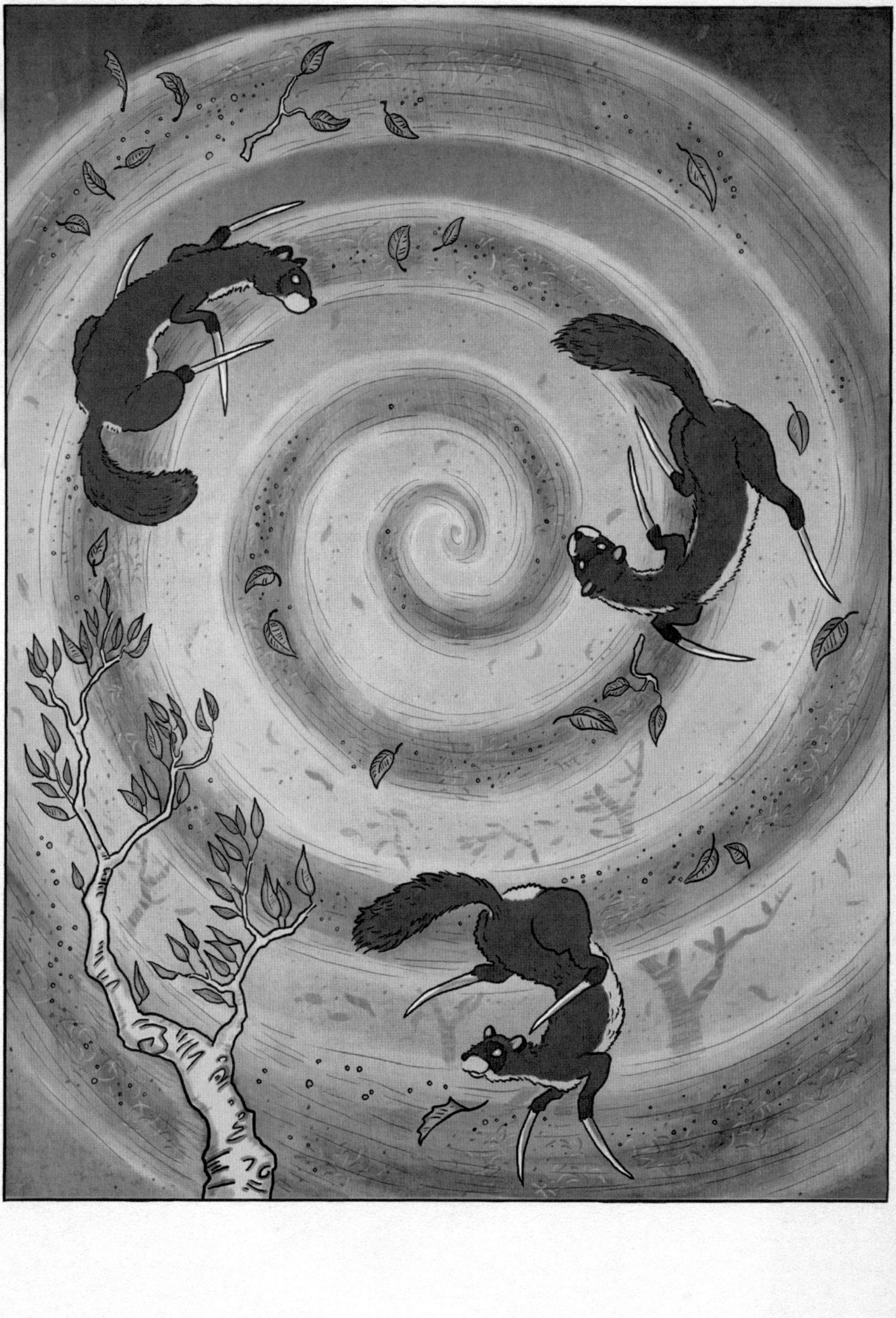

BASAN 波山

TRANSLATION: onomatopoeic; the sound of its flapping wings
ALTERNATE NAMES: basabasa, inu hōō ("dog phoenix")
HABITAT: mountainous forests; found only on Shikoku
DIET: charred wood and embers

APPEARANCE: Basan are rare birds found only on the island of Shikoku, in the mountains of Ehime. They are roughly the size of a turkey, and shaped like a chicken. Basan are easily recognized by their bright red comb and brilliantly colored plumage which appears like tongues of flame. Their most notable feature is their breath, which flows visibly from their mouth like a dragon's fire. However, the flame gives off no heat, nor does it ignite combustible material.

BEHAVIOR: Basan are entirely nocturnal, and little is known about their behavior. They make their homes in remote bamboo groves, far from human activity. Charred wood and embers make up their diet, and they have been known to wander into remote villages at night to feast on the remains of bonfires or charcoal. When pleased or startled, basan beat their wings creating the distinctive rustling *basabasa* sound from which they get their name. People who have witnessed this report that the birds vanish into thin air when they realize they have been seen.

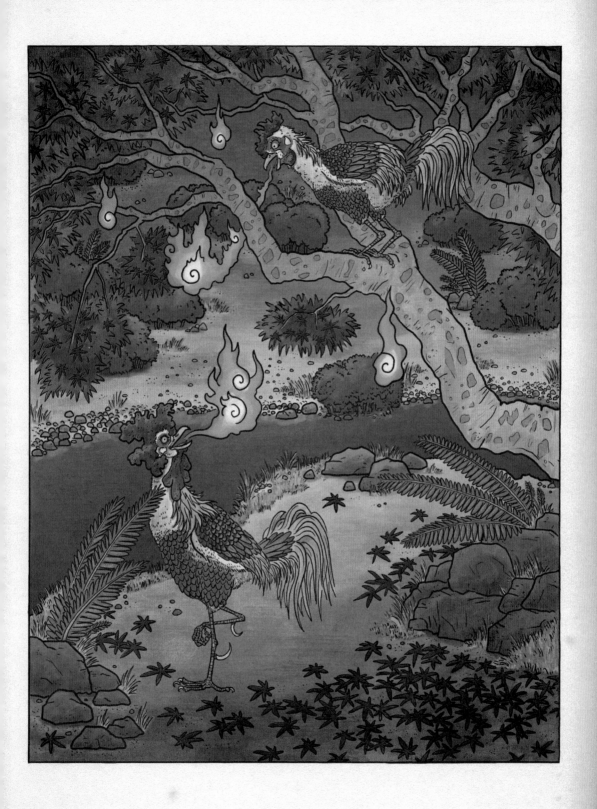

Yamawaro 山童

Translation: mountain child
Alternate names: yamawarawa
Habitat: mountains; commonly found throughout Kyūshū and West Japan
Diet: omnivorous

Appearance: Yamawaro are minor deities of the mountains, closely related to other nature spirits such as kappa, garappa, and hyōsube. Short creatures resembling boys of about 10 years of age, their heads are crowned in long brown hair and their bodies are covered in fine, light hair. They have a short torso and two long legs, on which they walk upright. A yamawaro's most distinguishing feature is the single eye in the middle of its head. They are skillful mimics, copying the sound of falling rocks, wind, dynamite, and tools. They can even learn to speak human languages and sing human songs.

Interactions: Like their cousins the kappa, yamawaro despise horses and cows, and attack them on sight. They love the sport of sumo, which they are better at than any human. Like hyōsube, they sneak into homes to nap and take baths, and leave behind a thick film of grease and hair when they are done.

Yamawaro are frequently encountered in the mountains by woodcutters, and are known to help with work. If properly thanked and offered food for their services, a yamawaro is likely to return to help again. However, care must be taken when feeding a yamawaro. If the amount of food is less than what was promised, it will grow angry and never return. If offered before the work is performed, the yamawaro will simply take the food and run.

Origin: One theory from Kumamoto Prefecture says that yamawaro and garappa are actually different forms of the same yōkai. During the cold months, these creatures live in the mountains as yamawaro (or yamawarawa, as they are known locally). During the warm months, they live in lakes and rivers as garappa. Every year on the autumn equinox, all of the country's garappa transform into yamawaro and travel from the rivers to the mountains in a mass migration. They return on the spring equinox and transform back into garappa. Villagers who build their houses in the pathway of these massive yōkai migrations are prone to find holes, gashes, and other damage caused by yamawaro angry at having their path blocked. People who witness the springtime return of the yamawaro often catch deadly fevers.

This theory is supported by the fact that these creatures share so many traits in common with one another, and because it is extremely rare to see garappa in the winter. However, it is also possible that these aquatic yōkai go into hibernation during the colder months, and that the similarities between garappa and yamawaro are simply coincidence.

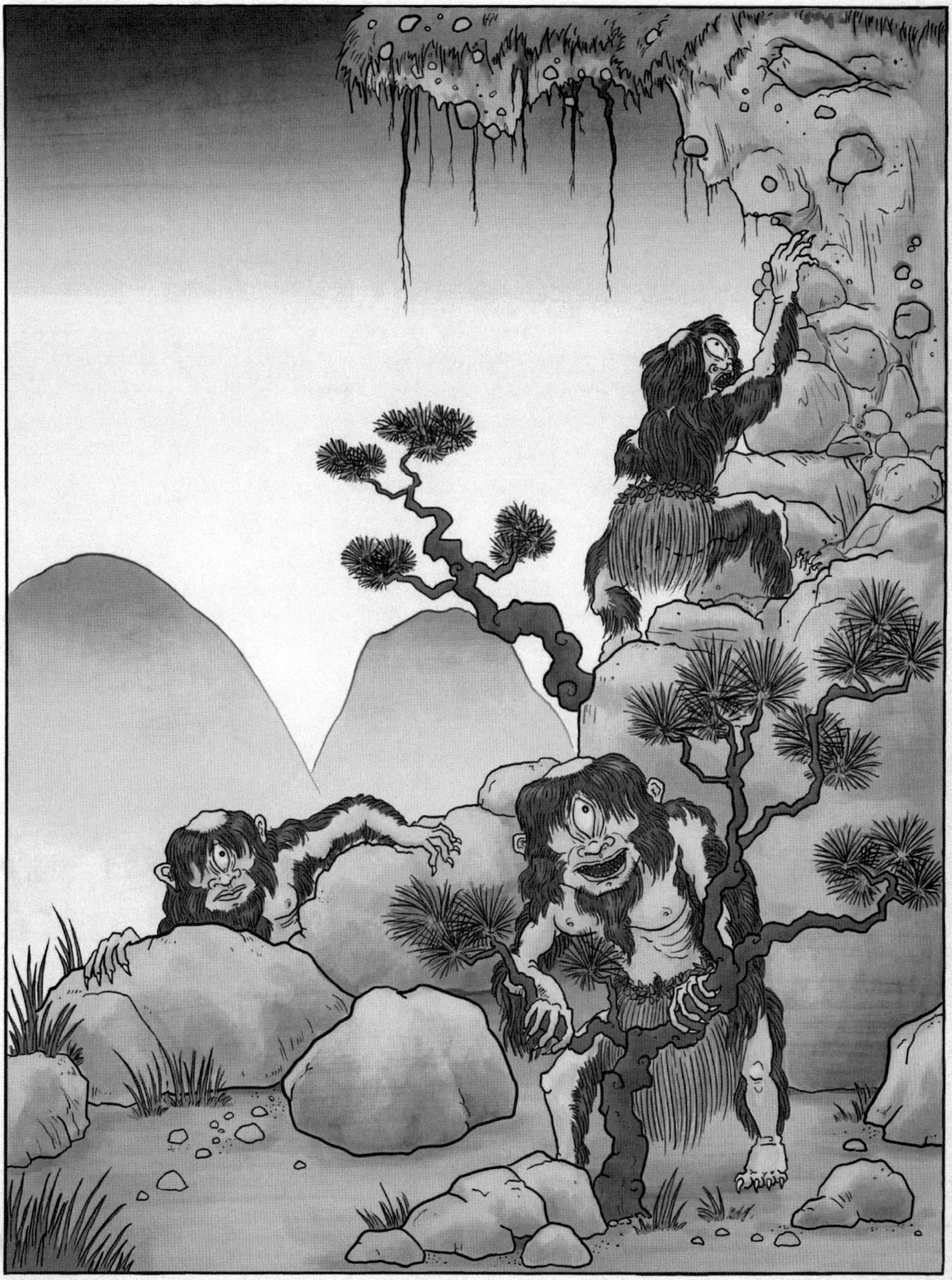

AZUKI ARAI 小豆洗い

TRANSLATION: the bean washer
ALTERNATE NAMES: azuki togi ("bean grinder")
HABITAT: remote forests; found throughout Japan
DIET: unknown, but probably includes azuki beans

APPEARANCE: Azuki arai are mysterious yōkai encountered in mountainous regions all across Japan. They have many regional nicknames, a common one being azukitogi. These yōkai live deep in forests and mountains, spending their time near streams. Few actual sightings have been recorded, but they are said to be short and squat, with big, round eyes, and overall resembling Buddhist priests. They appear full of mirth with silly smiles and large hands with only three fingers.

BEHAVIOR: Azuki arai are more often heard than seen. Their main activity seems to be washing red azuki beans by the riverside while singing a dreadful song interspersed with the "shoki shoki" sound of beans being washed in a basket:

Azuki araou ka? Hito totte kuou ka? (shoki shoki)
Shall I wash my red beans, or shall I catch a human to eat? (shoki shoki)

INTERACTIONS: Passersby who hear an azuki arai singing usually slip and fall into the river. The noise from the splash scares the yōkai away. Nearly all encounters with azuki arai are purely auditory; they are notoriously shy, and do all they can to avoid being seen. Their uncanny ability to mimic the sounds of nature and animals helps them to hide. Because of their elusiveness, spotting an azuki arai is supposed to bring good luck.

AZUKI YŌKAI

A number of yōkai share a connection to azuki, a red bean found in many Japanese dishes. In addition to the name, these yōkai share number of common traits and habits with each other. Whether they are related to one another or simply coincidentally connected is unknown. Some are dangerous and some are benign, but they are all incredibly shy—often heard, but almost never seen.

Due to their elusive nature, an accurate classification of this yōkai family is difficult to make. Stories of the azuki yōkai offer little clues to their true nature; some tales connect them with the ghosts of humans who drowned while washing beans at the riverbanks; others imply some connection with Shinto mountain gods and deities of good fortune; and still others attribute azuki yōkai to the magic of mischievous itachi or tanuki. With so few reliable observations, it is impossible to assign a proper taxonomy to these spirits.

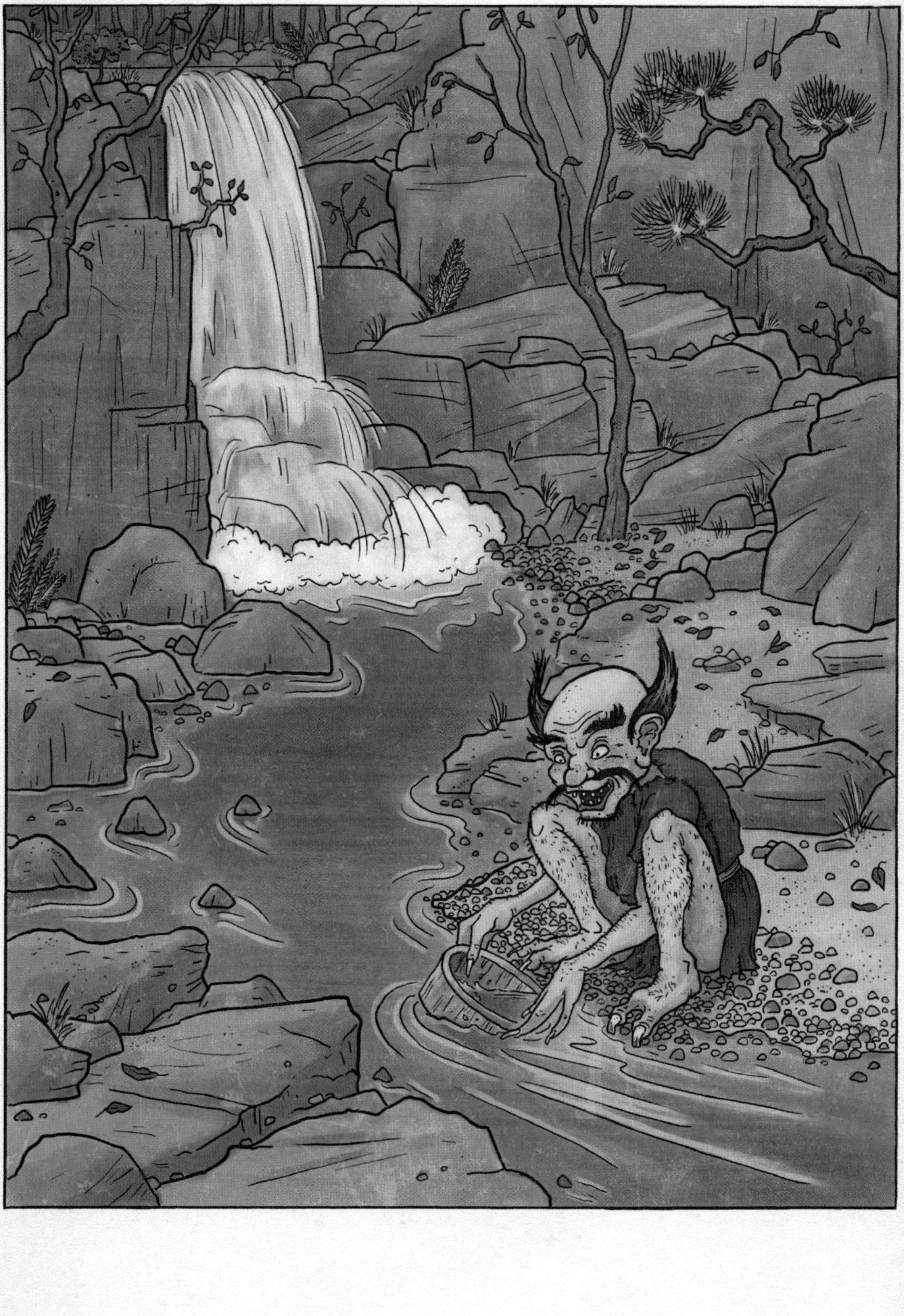

Azuki hakari 小豆はかり

TRANSLATION: the bean counter
HABITAT: rural villages, homes, attics, and gardens
DIET: unknown

APPEARANCE: A possible relative to azuki arai are the azuki hakari, or "the bean counters." A poltergeist found in some homes and temples, these yōkai are known only by the sounds they make. They are said to dwell in attics or gardens, and are most active at night. Azuki hakari have never been seen directly—only heard. Though similar in name and habit to their azuki-related cousins, azuki hakari have traits distinct enough to classify them as separate yōkai.

BEHAVIOR: Azuki hakari appear in homes late at night, after midnight. An encounter usually begins with the sound of heavy footsteps in the space between the attic and the roof. Shortly after, a rhythmic sound like dried azuki beans being scattered can be heard against the windows or sliding doors leading outside. The sound grows progressively louder, and gradually changes into the sound of splashing water, then finally to the sound of geta—Japanese wooden sandals—walking just outside the room. Opening the doors or windows causes the noise to stop, revealing no sign of any creature; nor any beans or puddles or markings

Because of the difficulty of direct observation of all azuki spirits, it is likely that some of the stories about azuki arai may in fact be about encounters with azuki hakari, especially those which take place near homes or away from rivers.

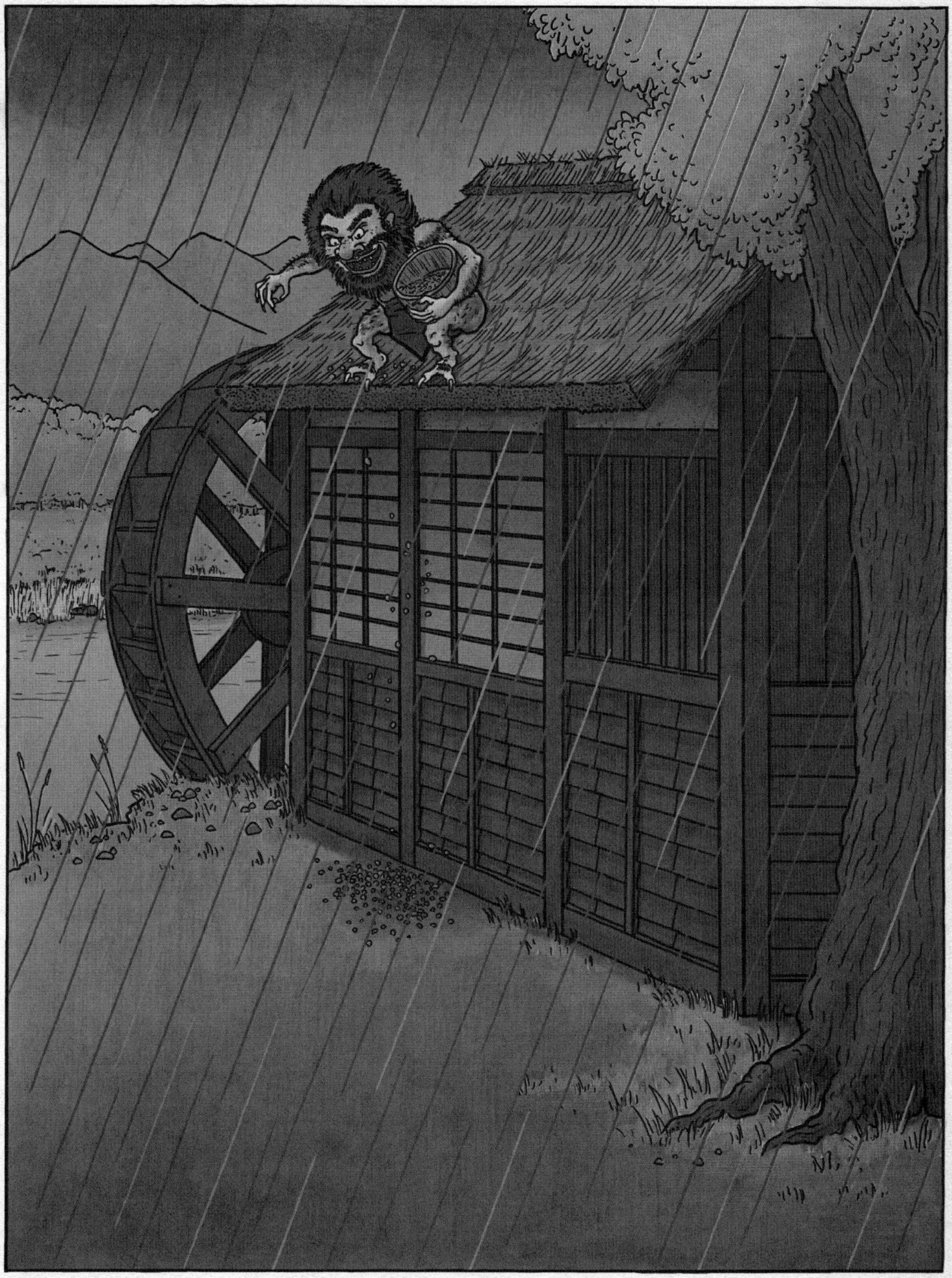

AZUKI BABĀ 小豆婆

TRANSLATION: the bean hag
ALTERNATE NAMES: azuki togi babā ("bean grinding hag")
HABITAT: forests and occasionally villages in Northeast Japan
DIET: humans, and probably also azuki beans

APPEARANCE: The people of Miyagi Prefecture tell of a much more sinister member of the azuki family of yōkai. Rather than the benign and cute azuki arai known throughout the country, this northeastern variation takes the form of a fearsome old hag dressed all in white, singing in a husky, ugly voice. Azuki babā appear only at twilight—particularly on rainy or misty autumn nights. Their song is similar to the azuki arai's, except that azuki babā follow through on the threat to catch and eat humans.

BEHAVIOR: Witnesses of azuki babā describe an eerie, white glow visible through a thick, white mist. From the mist, they hear the husky voice of an old hag singing her ghastly song and counting beans as she washes them in the river with a strainer. Those who don't turn away at this point never make it back.

INTERACTIONS: Azuki babā are rarer than their harmless, bean-washing counterparts. Despite their ferociousness, they are mostly found only in stories used to scare children into behaving properly. Of all the variations of azuki-related yōkai, this one is the most likely to be a shape-shifted evil itachi, tanuki, or kitsune imitating the harmless azuki arai to attract a curious child to catch and eat.

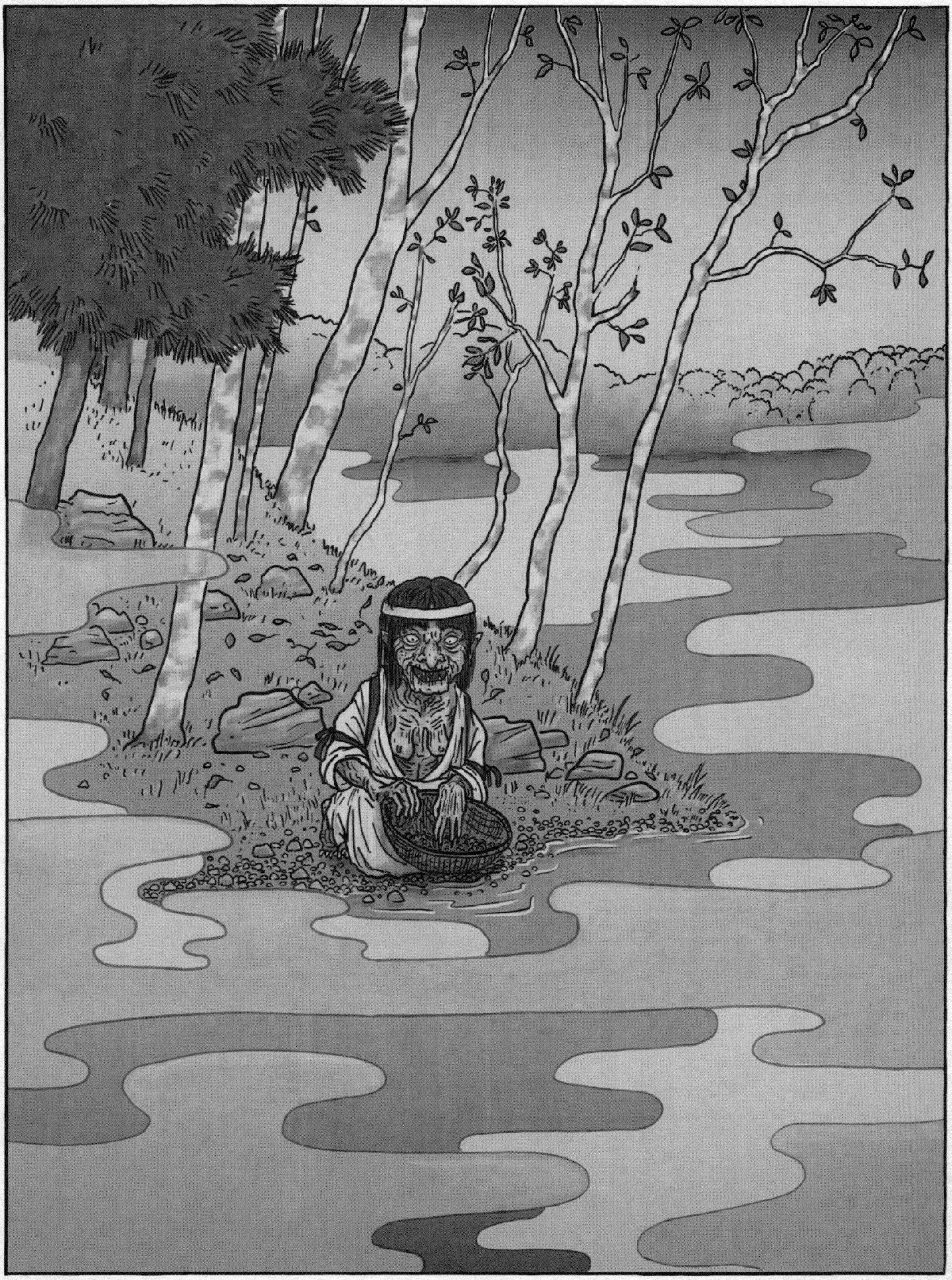

Wa nyūdō 輪入道

TRANSLATION: wheel priest
HABITAT: hell; encountered on roads, mountain passes, and occasionally villages
DIET: souls; occasionally snacks on babies

APPEARANCE: Wa nyūdō appear as giant, fearsome men's heads trapped within flaming ox-cart wheels. Their heads are shaved like monks' in penance for sins during life.

BEHAVIOR: Wa nyūdō are servants of hell, but spend most of their time on earth patrolling for the wicked. They are in constant suffering from the flames and the wheel, and take a sadistic pleasure in inflicting pain on others. When they capture a victim—ideally a wicked criminal or a corrupt priest, but often enough just an ordinary person—they drag their victim back to hell to be judged and damned. Then the wa nyūdō return to earth to continue their work, until the sins of their former lives have been redeemed.

INTERACTIONS: When a wa nyūdō is sighted, smart townspeople keep off the roads and stay away from all doors and windows to avoid any notice by this demon. The extra-cautious decorate their homes with prayer charms in hopes that the monster will be repulsed and stay away. Merely witnessing the wa nyūdō is enough to bring calamity upon a whole family. Their souls are torn from their bodies and brought to hell by the wheel.

LEGENDS: One famous story from Kyōto tells of a woman who peeked out her window at a wa nyūdō as he passed through town. The demon snarled at her, saying, "Instead of looking at me, have a look at your own child!" She looked back at her baby, who was screaming on the floor in a pool of blood—both of its legs had been completely torn from its body. When she looked back at the wa nyūdō, the child's legs were in its mouth, being eaten by the mad, grinning monster.

Katasharin 片車輪

In Buddhist cosmology, the souls of the damned are reborn in hell to be tortured until their sins have been atoned for. Sometimes, however, particularly wicked souls are enlisted as servants of hell. They are forced to work off their bad karma earned during their lives. One of these enlistments is reincarnation as a katasharin, or "single wheel," of which the males are known as wa nyūdō and the females as katawaguruma.

Only the most cruel lords, ladies, generals, and kings are transformed into katasharin. These crippled wagon wheels fly through the air, patrolling the highways and roads between earth and hell, searching for souls to drag back to their infernal masters.

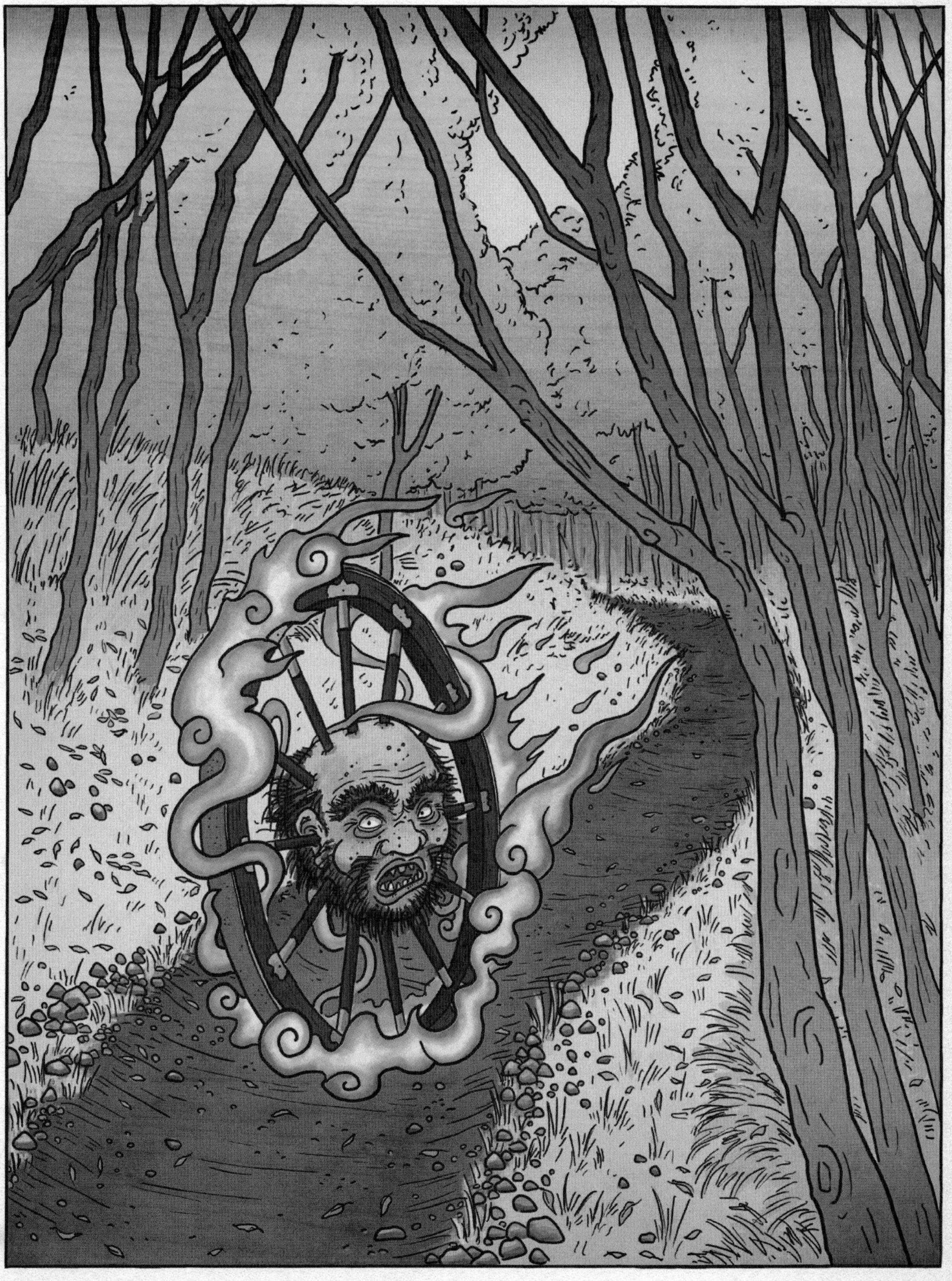

Katawaguruma 片輪車

Translation: crippled wheel
Habitat: hell; encountered on roads and mountain passes, and occasionally villages
Diet: souls

Appearance: Instead of a giant monk's head stuck in a wheel, a katawaguruma appear as tormented, naked women riding single, flaming, ox-cart wheels. They suffer eternally, burning in pain.

Behavior: Katawaguruma look and act in much the same manner as wa nyūdō, rolling along the roads of Japan, occasionally stopping in towns to hunt for impure souls to drag back to their hellish masters.

Interactions: These demons bestow powerful curses on any who see them. This curse spreads rapidly through town, traveling on the news and gossip about the katawaguruma. Eventually, this brings calamity upon an entire village. Despite this, there is evidence that the katawaguruma has a capacity for mercy alien to its male counterpart.

Legends: In a 17th century record, when a katawaguruma attacked a village in what is now Shiga, she abducted the child of a woman who dared to peek at her through a crack in her door, saying "Instead of watching me you should have been watching your child!" The distraught woman realized her own curiosity was responsible for the loss of her child. She composed a poem expressing her faults, and displayed it all around town, warning others to watch their children more carefully. The next night, the katawaguruma came again and saw that the woman was truly regretful. She returned the child unharmed. The katawaguruma was never seen in that village again.

Why Wheels?

The wheel is an important symbol in Buddhism. The hub of the wheel represents moral discipline, while the spokes represent wisdom to defeat ignorance. The rim of the wheel represents concentration, which holds the whole thing together. The revolving of the wheel represents the endless cycle of reincarnation.

Punishing evil by trapping it in a wheel was a way to express the supremacy of Buddhism over any evil. The katasharin demons may seem like tyrants to humans, but they were mere slaves in the greater scheme of things. They are forced to submit to Buddhism in order to attain their salvation. In this manner, the wheel plays a role in Buddhist symbolism analogous to the crucifix in Christian symbolism.

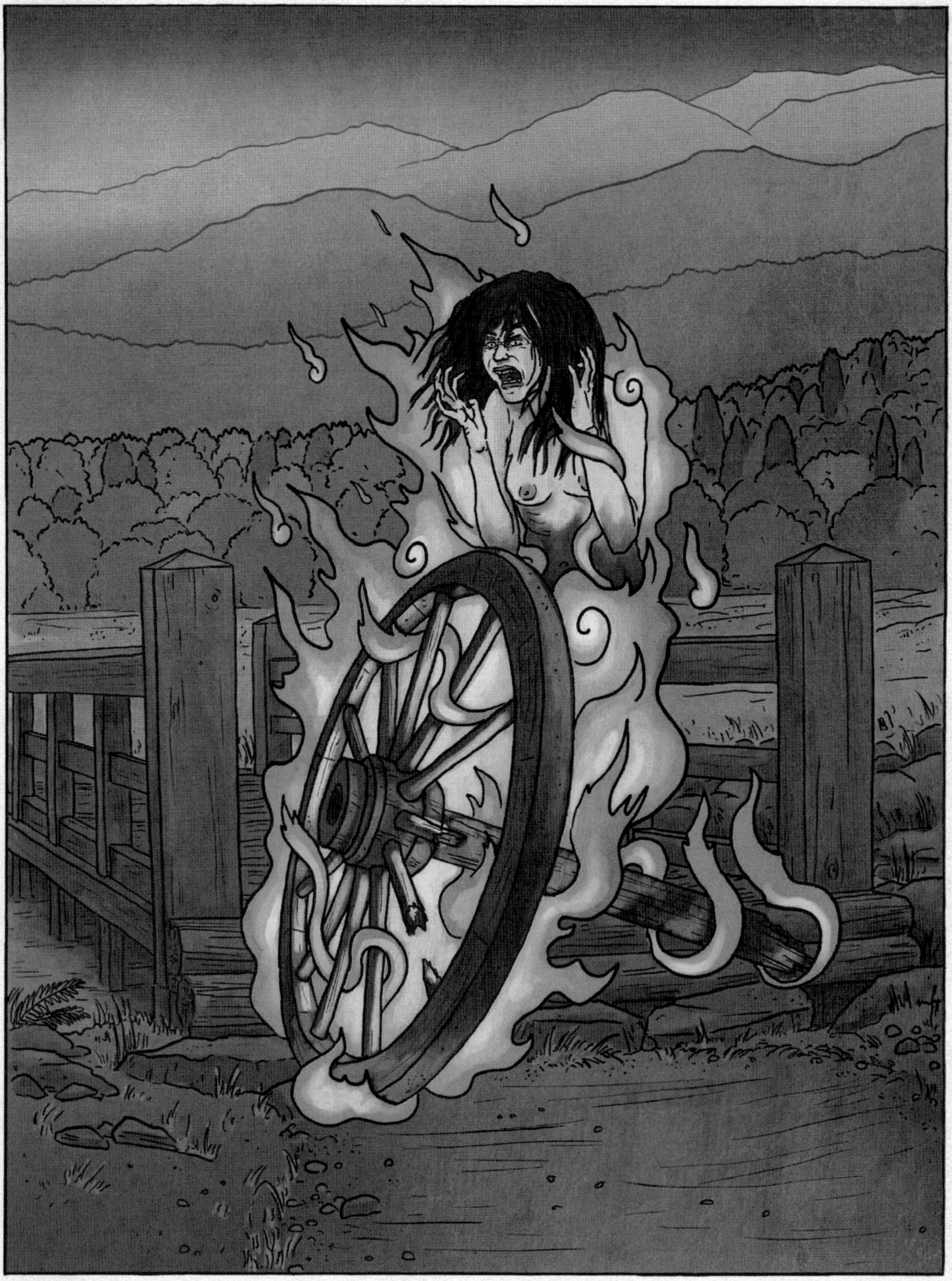

ONI 鬼

TRANSLATION: ogre, demon
HABITAT: hell; remote mountains, caves, islands, abandoned fortresses
DIET: omnivorous; especially livestock, humans, and alcohol

APPEARANCE: Oni are one the greatest icons of Japanese folklore. They are large and scary, standing taller than the tallest man, and sometimes taller than trees. They come in many varieties, but are most commonly depicted with red or blue skin, wild hair, two or more horns, and fang-like tusks. Other variations exist in different colors and with different numbers of horns, eyes, or fingers and toes. They wear loincloths made of the pelts of great beasts. All oni possess extreme strength and constitution, and many of them are accomplished sorcerers. They are ferocious demons, bringers of disaster, spreaders of disease, and punishers of the damned in hell.

BEHAVIOR: Oni are born when truly wicked humans die and end up in one of the many Buddhist hells. Transformed into oni, they become the ogreish and brutal servants of Great Lord Enma, ruler of hell. Wielding great iron clubs, they crush and destroy humans solely for enjoyment. An oni's job is to mete out horrible punishments such as peeling off skins, crushing bones, and rendering other torments too horrible to describe. All these tortures are for wicked sinners—but only those not quite wicked enough to be reborn as oni themselves. Hell is full of oni. They make up the armies of the great generals of the underworld.

Occasionally, when a human is so utterly wicked that his soul is beyond any redemption, he transforms into an oni while still alive. He then remains on earth to terrorize the living. These transformed oni are the ones most legends tell about, and the ones who pose the most danger to humankind.

INTERACTIONS: Oni are the stuff of legends and fairy tales. Japanese mythology is full of countless stories of oni encounters with lords and ladies, warriors and rogues. No two stories about oni are exactly alike except for one thing—oni are always the villains of mankind.

ORIGIN: Originally, all spirits, ghosts, and monsters were known as oni. The root of their name is a word meaning "hidden" or "concealed," and it was written with the Chinese character for ghost. In the old days of Japan, before the spirits were well-cataloged, oni could refer to almost any supernatural creature—ghosts, obscure gods, large or scary yōkai, even particularly vicious and brutal humans. As the centuries shaped the Japanese language, the definitions we know for the various kinds of monsters gradually came into being. Female demons are not called oni, but are known by another name: kijo.

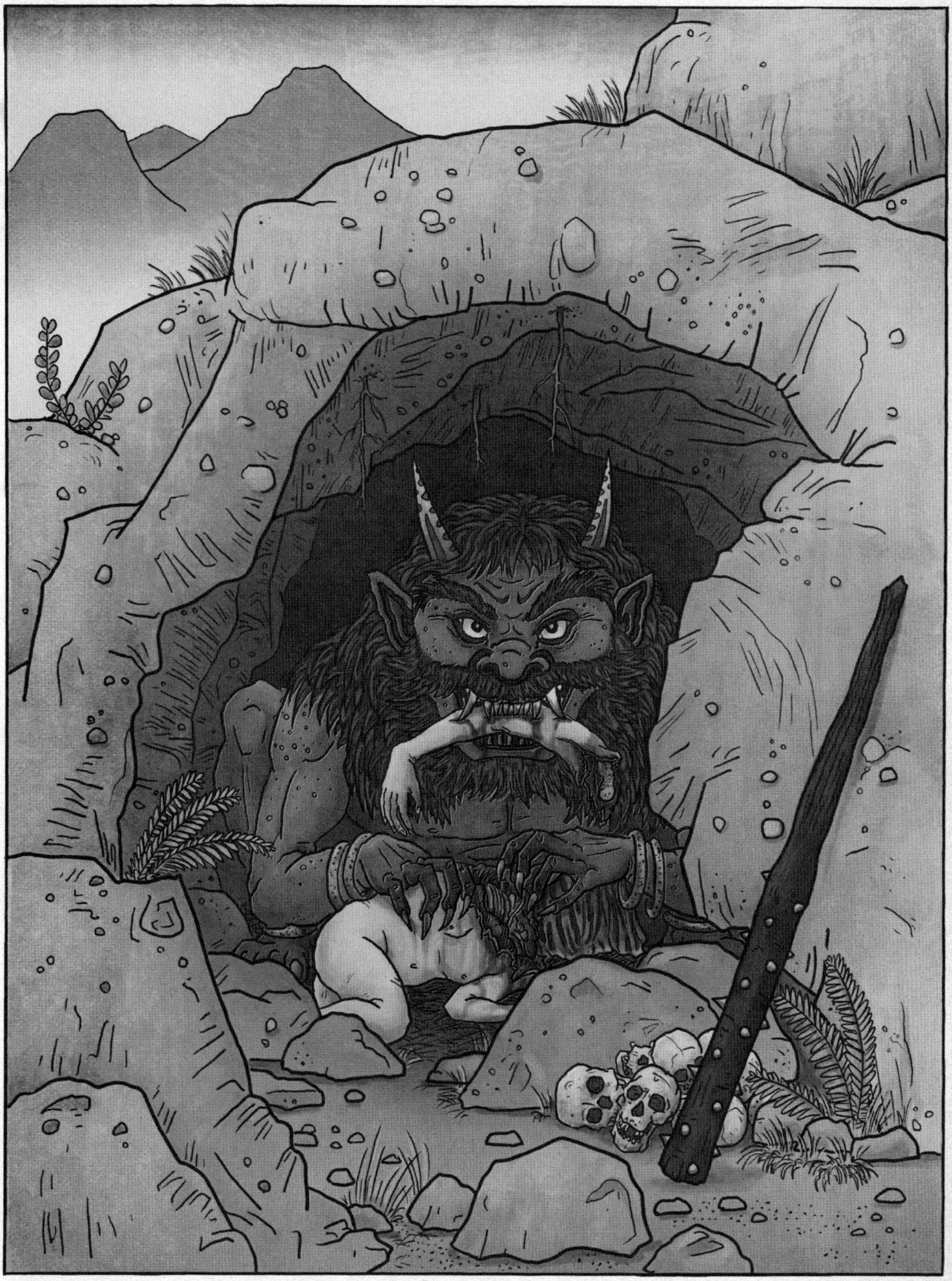

Kijo 鬼女

TRANSLATION: ogress, demoness
HABITAT: remote mountains, caves, islands, secluded huts
DIET: omnivorous; anything and anybody, particularly travelers

APPEARANCE: Kijo are female demons. They resemble human women in most ways, although they are hideously ugly to behold. Some have red or yellow eyes, blue skin, sharp horns, long claws, or other supernatural features. They usually dress in rags and wear their hair long and unkempt. They live like savages far from civilization.

BEHAVIOR: Kijo refers chiefly to women who have been transformed from humans into horrible monsters—either out of intense jealousy, wicked crimes, or a terrible grudge that twists the soul into pure hatred. These transformed women retreat from common society into more secluded places where they continue to perpetrate their wicked deeds. They can be found living in remote mountain caves, abandoned houses, or along mountain roads where they receive a steady supply of victims. Kijo are stronger than most humans, though their strength pales in comparison to oni. These demonesses excel in magic; they accumulate powerful spells over their long lives. Kijo are capable of bestowing hexes and curses, brewing poisons and potions, and weaving complex illusions. A few kijo dedicate themselves to personal vengeance or some political goal. But most just keep to themselves and go unnoticed by humankind for centuries.

INTERACTIONS: Like oni, kijo are the stuff of Japanese legends. Innumerable fairy tales, bedtime stories, kabuki plays, films, and so featuring kijo on have been created to entertain, to caution, and to preach morality. Women who do bad things might turn into kijo, and men who go after unscrupulous women might be heading to their deaths.

ORIGIN: Kijo is a broad term that in its most general sense encompasses any female demon, just as the term oni can technically refer to any male demon. Indeed, the name kijo is formed simply by combining the two kanji for oni and woman. Though their name might suggest that kijo are the female counterparts to the male oni, there is nothing to support this. Tales show oni working either as tormentors of the damned or as menaces to human society in the living world, but kijo do not seem to have any connection to hell or the afterlife. They work solo, and have their own motives. Further, kijo and oni are not commonly seen together. Little to nothing is known about how either creature reproduces (or if they even do). It is likely that kijo are entirely separate creatures from oni, other than the fact that both are born from corrupted human souls.

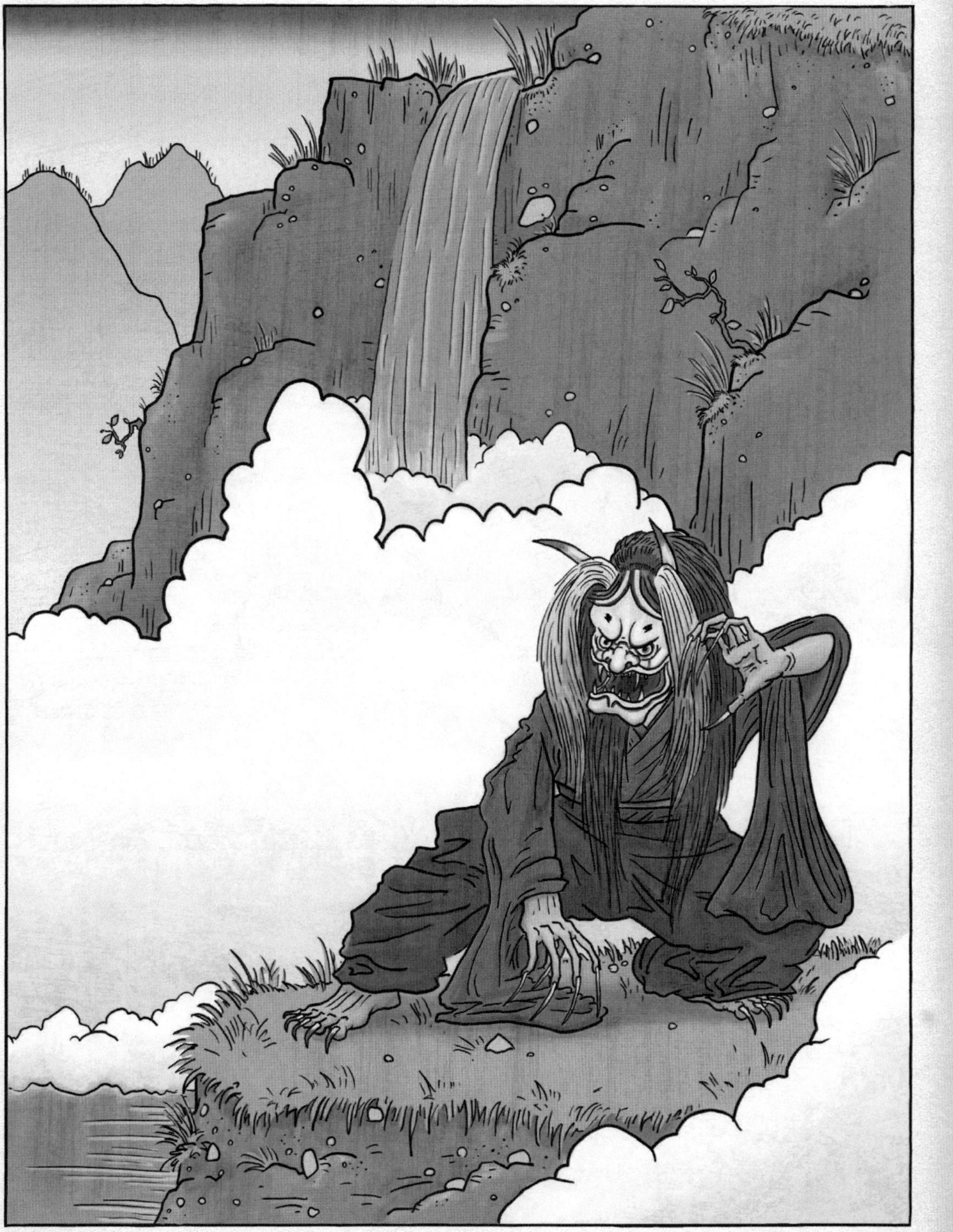

REIKI 霊鬼

TRANSLATION: demon spirit, demon ghost
HABITAT: any; usually haunts the area near its body
DIET: none

APPEARANCE: Some oni can be killed by manmade weapons, and others die of natural causes. But they do not always peacefully pass on to the next life. Some still have unfinished business or karma left to burn off, while others die such violent or passionate deaths that the soul becomes disjointed at the moment of death. They remain in the human world as a demon ghost. Reiki, written by combining the characters for spirit and demon, are the ghosts of oni unable to pass on to the afterlife. Reiki appear just as they did before death, but accompanied by an aura or an eerie glow. They are semi-transparent like ghosts, and often gain supernatural powers in addition to the magic they possessed in life.

BEHAVIOR: Reiki have only one motivation: revenge. They bring suffering to the person or people they feel are responsible for their death, or to those who stood against them in life. Reiki will either follow a target or attach themselves to a particular area—often their own grave site—and assault any who come near. They can haunt for centuries. Reiki persist until exorcised by a powerful Buddhist priest.

LEGENDS: There are fewer stories about reiki than about oni, but tales tell of powerful spirits even more fearsome than their living counterparts. One of the most well-known reiki legends takes place at Gangō-ji, a temple in Nara Prefecture. A mysterious force was haunting the temple's bell tower and murdering children every night. The force was so powerful that not even the most devout priests could identify it, let alone exorcise it. In a story reminiscent of the adventures of Hercules, only the son of a god was strong enough to track down and defeat the demon ghost, saving the children of the temple.

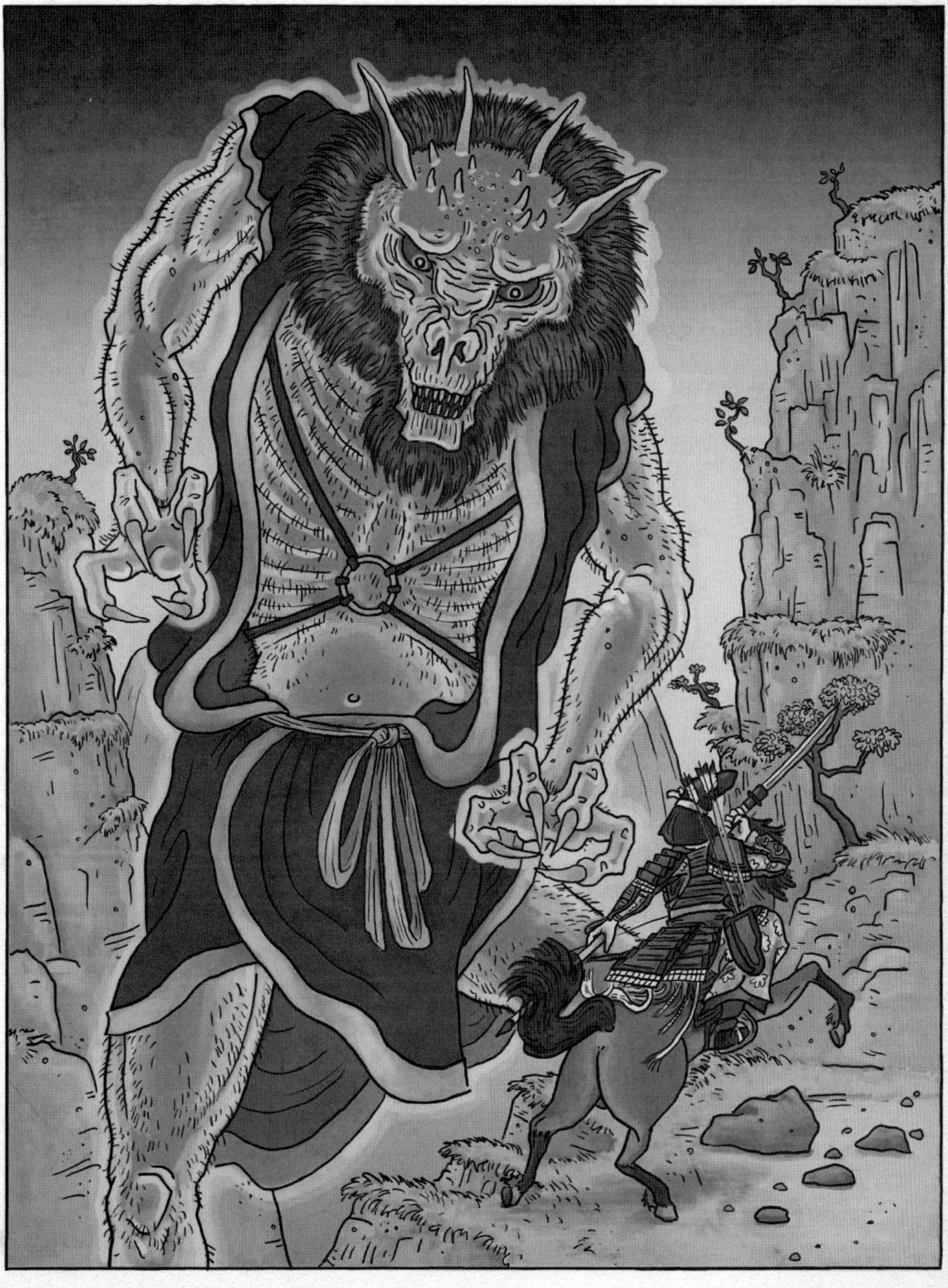

Jubokko 樹木子

Translation: tree child, shrub child
Habitat: battlefields, places where mass deaths occurred
Diet: blood

Appearance: On the fields of war and sites of vicious massacres, where the blood of thousands of warriors has saturated the soil, a strange kind of tree can be found. From afar, jubokko appear to be ordinary trees, indistinguishable from the various species that dot the landscape. It takes an observant eye to notice the slightly more fearsome features of its branches, or the piles of human bones buried in the undergrowth beneath the tree. In fact, they were once normal trees; but the vast amounts of human blood absorbed through their roots transformed them into yōkai. Thereafter, the trees thirst only for human blood.

Behavior: Jubokko wait for unsuspecting humans to pass underneath their branches. When somebody gets close enough, they attack, snatching their prey with long, jagged, finger-like branches, and hoisting it into their boughs. These branches pierce the skin of their victims, sucking out all of the blood with special tube-like twigs. After the body is drained, the flesh and organs are consumed by birds, insects, and other animals. Only the dry bones fall back to earth. By the time most people are close enough to notice the heaps of bleached bones at the base of the trees, it is too late to escape.

The Battle of Sekigahara

October 21st, 1600. The Battle of Sekigahara is one of the most important battles in Japanese history. Considered the decisive battle of the warring states period, it marked the beginning of the unification of Japan under the Tokugawa shogunate. This bloody battle was the culmination of centuries of civil war, fought between various lords, armed peasant uprisings, and religious conflicts that took the lives of countless Japanese. The Battle of Sekigahara saw the deaths of roughly 40,000 soldiers in a single day—it is no exaggeration to say that the rivers and fields ran red with blood. Because of the impact this battle had on Japanese history, it has remained a popular subject for ghost stories and legends about the past.

Today, visitors to Sekigahara talk of strange and unique local vegetation, born from the tainted soil soaked with the blood of tens of thousands of warriors. Ghosts and evil spirits still wander the fields. Could any jubokko have been born on the fields of Sekigahara after that great combat? Take care not to wander too close to any strange trees in the area.

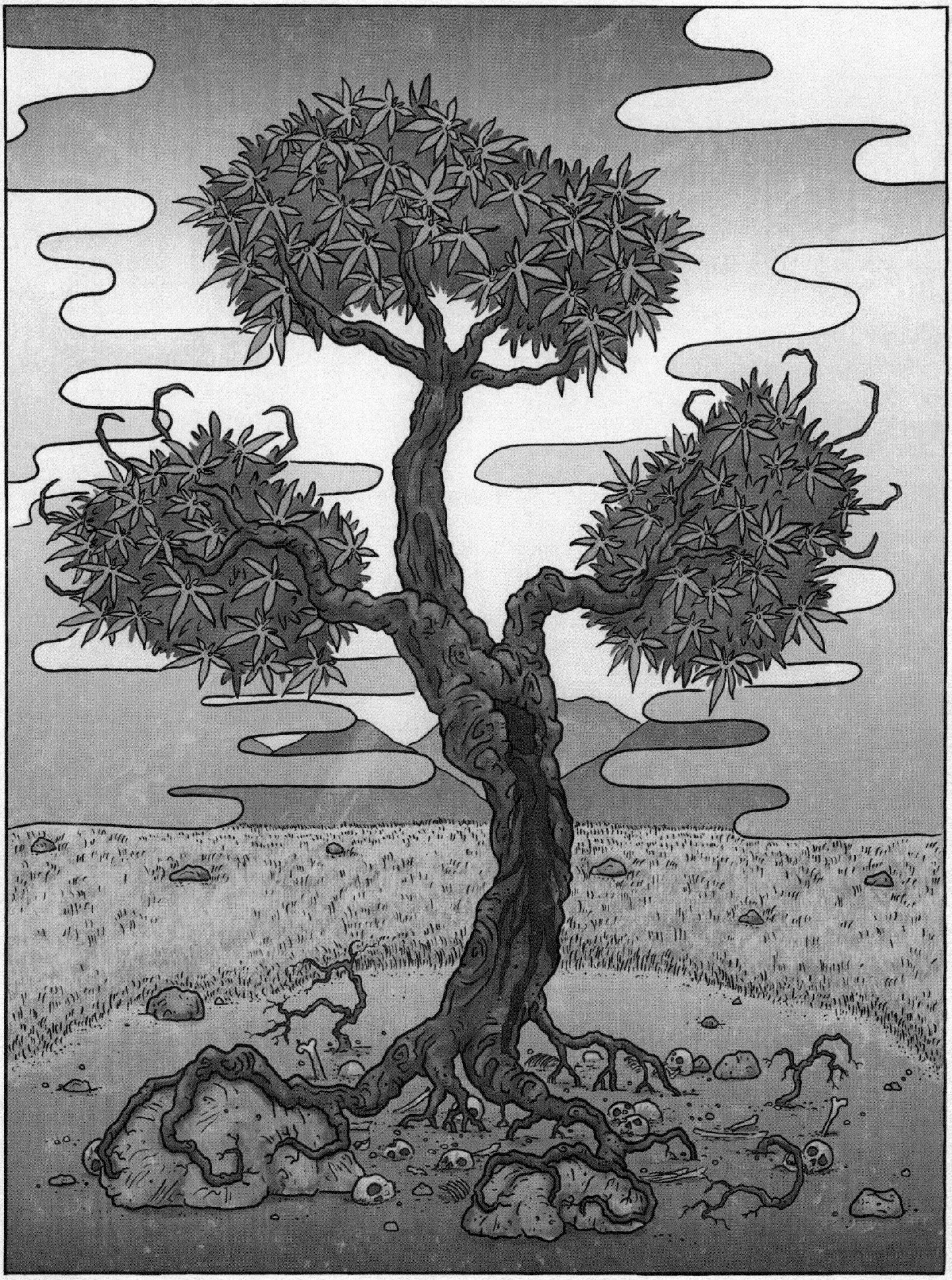

Tsurube otoshi 釣瓶落とし

TRANSLATION: a dropping well bucket
HABITAT: heavily wooded areas; particularly coniferous trees
DIET: carnivorous; large ones prefer humans, crushed or mashed

APPEARANCE: Tsurube otoshi are a gigantic disembodied heads of either a human, a tengu, or an oni. Sometimes they appear wreathed in flames like large fireballs with facial features. Spending most of their lives high in the trees (preferring pine, kaya, and other conifers for their height), they live deep along paths in the forest, or just outside of town where travelers are likely to pass. Tsurube otoshi range in size from an ordinary human head to up to two meters in diameter.

BEHAVIOR: Tsurube otoshi lurk in the treetops late at night and wait for unsuspecting creatures to pass underneath. When they need to feed, they drop quickly to the ground like a stone. This is the reason for its name, which means "falling well bucket." The goal is to trap and eat an animal, or a human if the head is large enough. Then they slip back into the trees, sometimes singing a monstrous taunt, challenging others to pass underneath. They enjoy this style of killing, letting out a horrible, guffawing laugh as they hunt and devour their prey. When they are not hungry, tsurube otoshi will sometimes drop down and crush people just for fun. They also drop large rocks or even well buckets (they have a sense of humor) on their victims from up high, laughing at the damage they inflict. Travelers passing under tall trees late at night would be wise to keep their heads up. They may be crushed by a falling tsurube otoshi.

Tsurube otoshi encountered in the Kansai region are most often solitary, gargantuan heads. In the Tohoku region, tsurube otoshi are usually encountered in larger groups of slightly smaller heads.

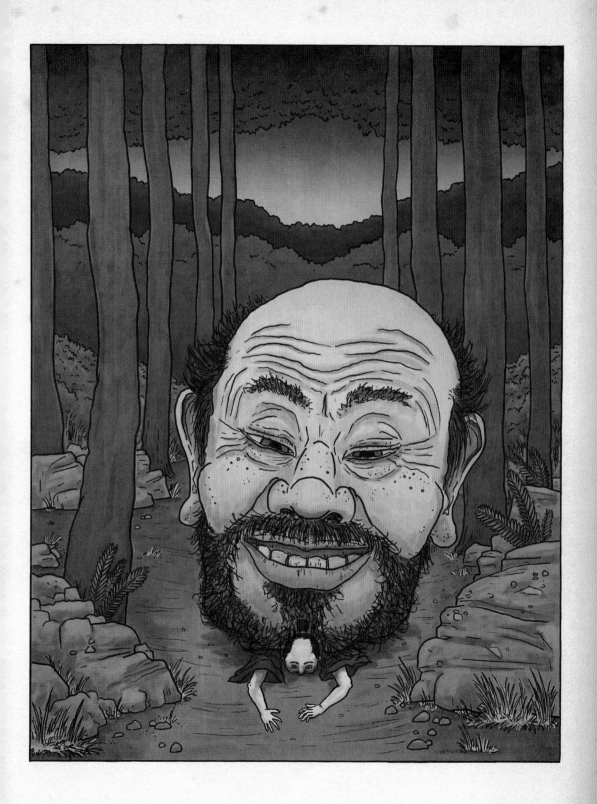

GASHADOKURO がしゃどくろ

TRANSLATION: onomatopoeic; rattling skull
ALTERNATE NAMES: ōdokuro ("giant skeleton")
HABITAT: any; usually found near mass graves or battlegrounds
DIET: none, but enjoys eating humans anyway

APPEARANCE: Gashadokuro are skeletal giants which wander around the countryside in the darkest hours of the night. Their teeth chatter and bones rattle with the "*gachi gachi*" sound of this yōkai's namesake. But they are not always noisy. If they should happen upon a human out late on the roads, the gashadokuro will silently creep up and catch their victims, crushing them in their hands or biting off their head.

ORIGIN: Soldiers whose bodies rot in the fields and victims of famine who die unknown in the wilderness rarely receive proper funerary rites. Unable to pass on, their souls are reborn as ghosts, longing eternally for that which they once had. These people die with anger and pain in their hearts. That energy remains long after their flesh has rotted from their bones. As their bodies decay, their anger ferments into a grudge against the living, which twists them into a supernatural force. When the bones of hundreds of victims gather together into one mass, they form the humongous, skeletal monster known as the gashadokuro.

Too large and powerful to be killed, gashadokuro maintain their existence until the energy and malice stored up in their bodies has completely burnt out. However, because of the large amount of dead bodies required to form a single one, these abominations are rarer today than they were in the past, when wars and famine were a part of everyday life.

LEGENDS: The earliest record of a gashadokuro goes back over 1000 years to a bloody rebellion against the central government by a samurai named Taira no Masakado. His daughter Takiyasha hime was a famous sorceress. When Masako was eventually killed for his revolt, his daughter continued his cause. Using her black magic, she summoned a great skeleton from the bodies of dead soldiers to attack the city of Kyōto. Her monster is depicted in a famous print by Utagawa Kuniyoshi.

JAPANESE FUNERALS

Japanese funerary rites are complex. As with Western customs, the body is carefully prepared, a wake is held, and finally a funeral. The body is cremated, and the bones are removed from the ashes by the family and interred in a grave. After the funeral, a number of memorial services are held. These occur on the 7th, 49th, and 100th days after death, and during the Obon festival. Other services are repeated on the 3rd, 5th, 7th, and 13th anniversaries, and many more times for up to 50 years after the person's death. These ceremonies help ensure that the deceased pass on to the proper realm of afterlife and do not dwell among the living, or suffer in one of the many Buddhist hells. Services are performed and family graves are tended to by their progeny for as long as the family line exists. Those who are not given proper rites might not pass on, and are often said to turn into yōkai. Or worse...

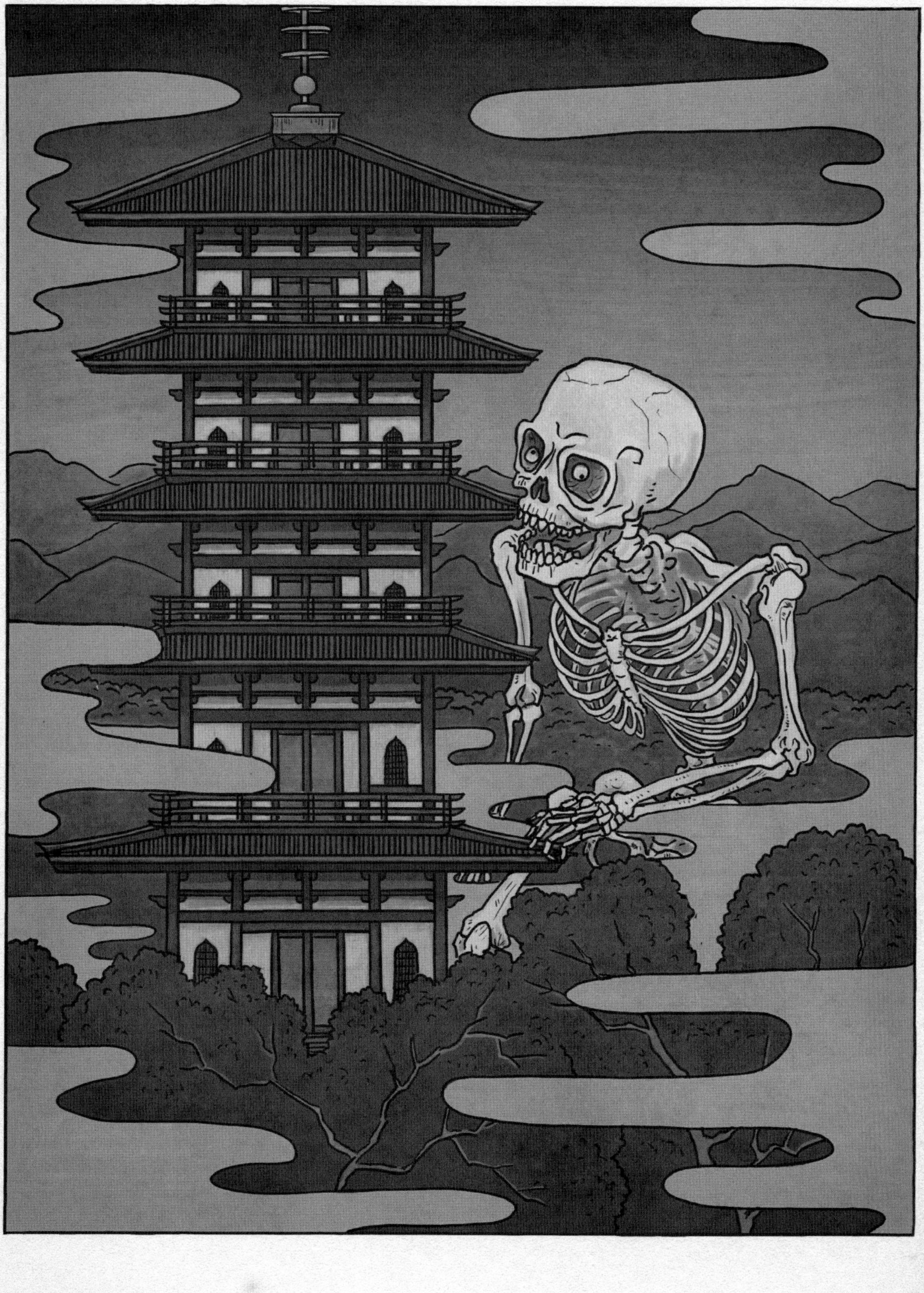

Yamauba 山姥

TRANSLATION: mountain hag, mountain crone
ALTERNATE NAMES: yamanba, onibaba
HABITAT: isolated huts or caves, deep in the mountains
DIET: generally eats human food, but will cook anything available

APPEARANCE: Yamauba are the old hags and witches of the Japanese mountains and forests. They were once human but became corrupted and transformed into monsters. Some sport horns or fangs, but most often yamauba look just like ordinary kind old ladies with no sign of their evil nature—until they attack.

INTERACTIONS: Yamauba live alone in huts by the road, where they occasionally offer weary travelers shelter, food, and a place to sleep. Late at night when their guests are fast asleep, yamauba transform into their true shape—an ugly, old, demonic witch. Thus revealed, they try to catch and eat their guests, often using powerful magic. Stories of encounters with yamauba have been spread by those few travelers lucky enough to escape. These tales were then passed along for generations until they came to be told as bedtime stories to disobedient children: "Be good or yamauba will come to get you!"

ORIGIN: Sometimes yamauba are created when young women accused of crimes or wicked deeds flee into the wilderness and live in exile. The women transform gradually over many years into mountain witches. In some cases, their origin can be explained by an old custom from times of famine or economic hardship. When it became impossible to feed everyone, families had to make a hard choice: remove one member so that the rest can survive. Often the sacrifice chosen was the newly born or the elderly. Some families led their mothers deep into the woods and left them there to die. These abandoned old women, either out of rage or desperation, transformed into horrible monsters that fed on humans and practiced black magic.

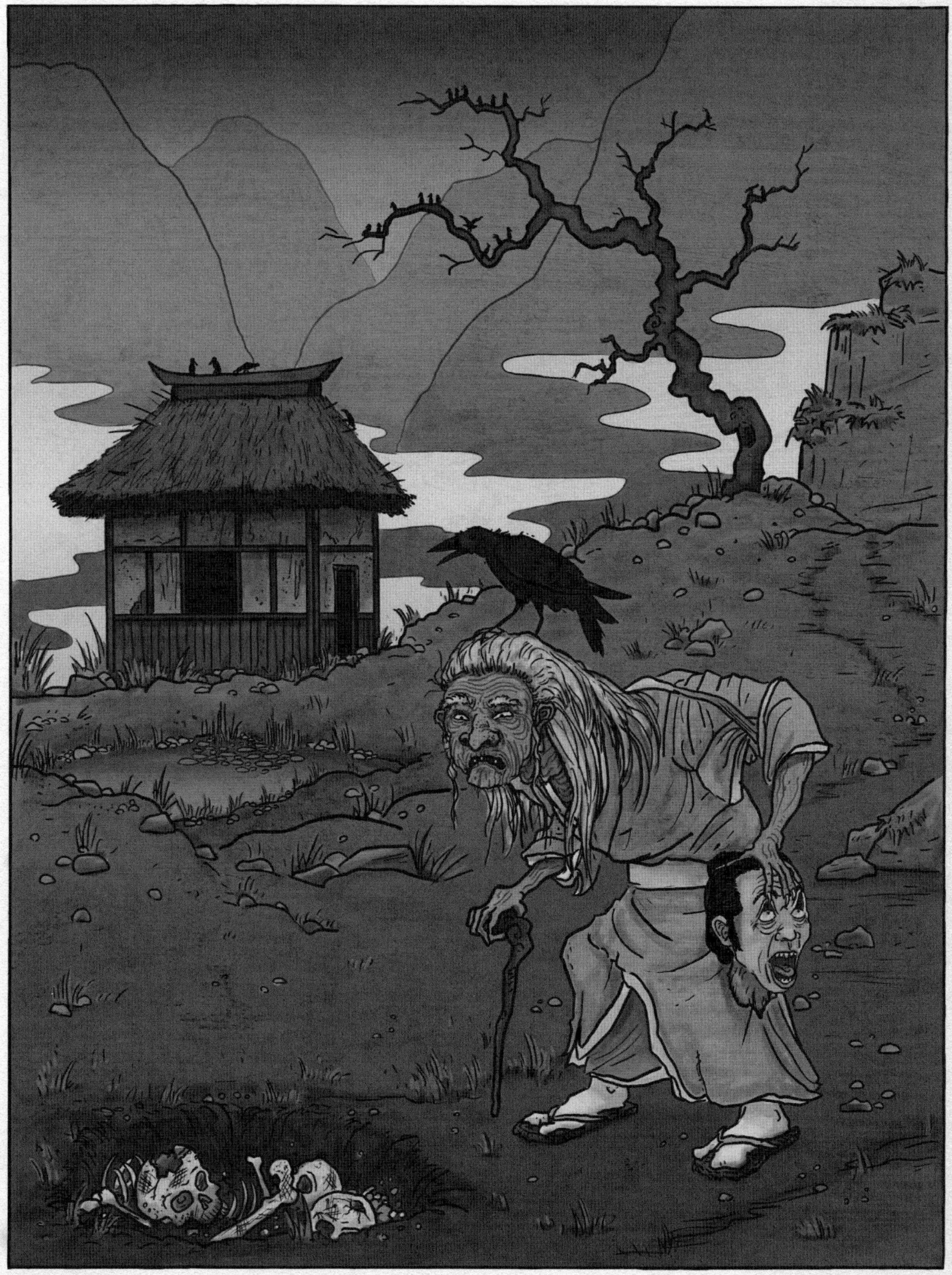

KOTENGU 小天狗

TRANSLATION: lesser tengu ("lesser divine dog")
ALTERNATE NAMES: karasu tengu ("crow tengu")
HABITAT: mountains, cliffs, caves, forests, areas surrounded by nature
DIET: carrion, livestock, wild animals, humans

APPEARANCE: Kotengu resemble large birds of prey with human-like characteristics. They often wear the robes of the ascetic and mystical hermits called yamabushi, and sometimes carry fine weapons or other items stolen from human homes or temples.

BEHAVIOR: Kotengu behave like savage monsters. They live solitary lives, but on rare occasions band together or with other yōkai to accomplish their goals. They accumulate hoards. Kotengu collect and trade trinkets and valuable magical items. When angered they throw tantrums and go on destructive rampages, taking out their anger on anything near them.

INTERACTIONS: Kotengu have little respect for humans. They feast on human flesh, and commit rape, torture, and murder for fun. Some of their favorite games are abducting people to drop them from great heights deep into the woods, or tying children to the tops of trees so all can hear their screams but none can reach them. Kotengu kidnap people and force them eat feces until they go mad. They especially revel in sacrilege. They torment monks and nuns, rob temples, and try to seduce clergy.

Kotengu's greatest weakness is overconfidence. There are countless folk stories about kotengu being duped into trading powerful magical items or giving up valuable information in exchange for worthless trinkets. Foolish kotengu overestimate their own intelligence when trying to trick humans, and end up being tricked themselves.

TENGU 天狗

No yōkai is as ubiquitous in Japan as the mighty tengu. They hold a singular place in Japanese folklore—worshiped as gods, reviled as demons, and revered as reincarnations of great heroes and wise men. Tengu are noble warriors, honorless thieves, wise sages, wicked villains, prophets, protectors of nature, and harbingers of war. Tengu are feared and honored for their vast knowledge and mystical secrets. They know magical spells, and keep the secrets of heaven and earth. Fierce martial artists, tengu are skilled in multiple forms of combat.

According to Buddhist lore, tengu are born when a person dies who is not wicked enough to go to hell, but is too angry, vain, proud, or heretical to go to heaven. The tengu is a personification of those excessive vices, magnified and empowered in a new, demonic form. Tengu are divided into two castes: daitengu and kotengu. Of these, the daitengu are more powerful and wiser—and more likely to be known by name and revered by humans. The kotengu are vicious, savage, and cruel.

During the Edo period, scarier tengu stories were gradually supplanted by amusing folk tales, dampening the vicious images of earlier lore. By the 19th century, the warlike nature and martial demeanor of the tengu came to be seen as honorable traits unique to these powerful bird-like spirits. Their knowledge and skills were popularized in the arts like ukiyoe prints and noh and kabuki theater. From then on, tengu have remained one of the most well-known and beloved subjects of Japanese folklore.

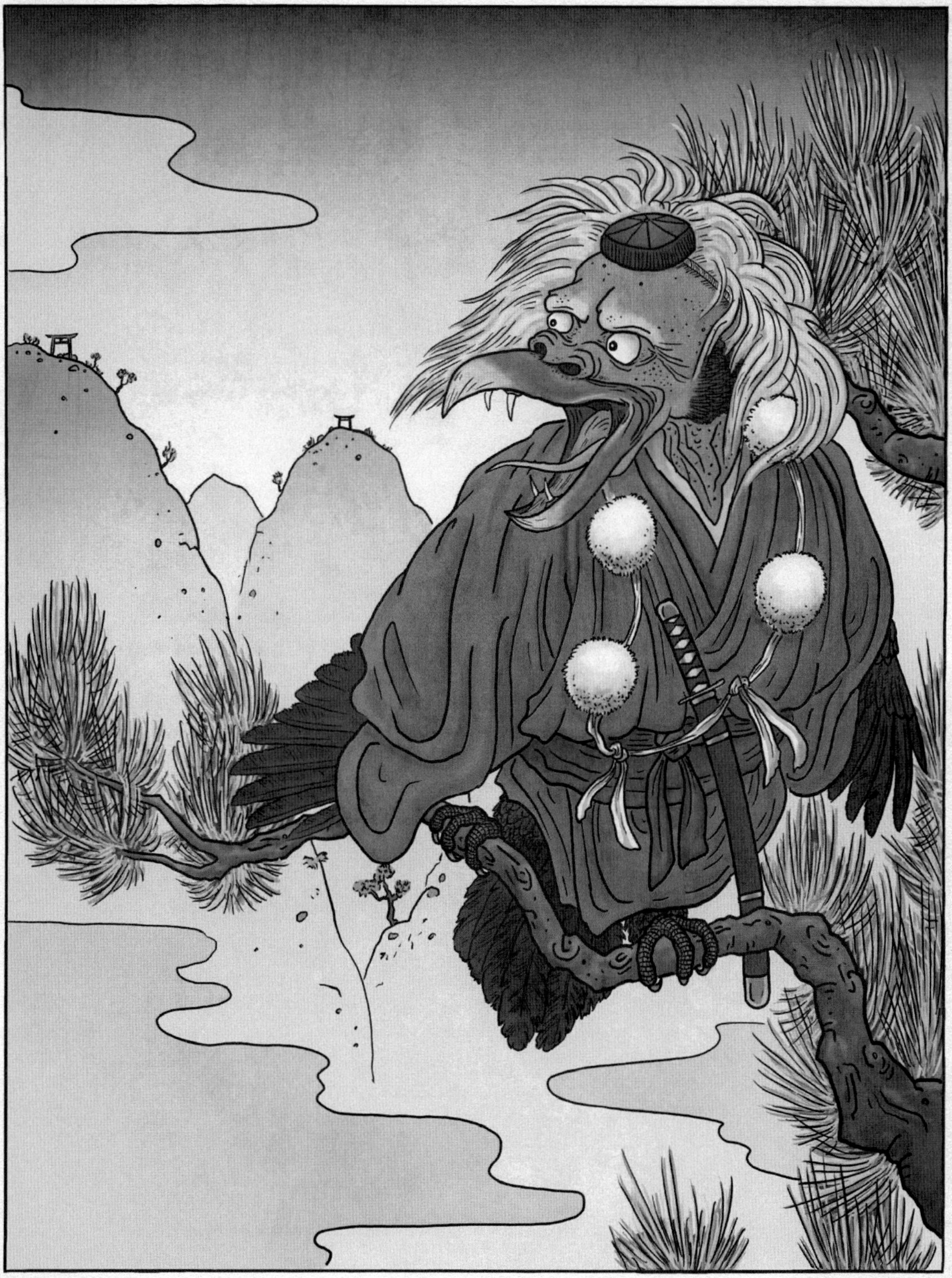

Daitengu 大天狗

TRANSLATION: greater tengu ("greater divine dog")
ALTERNATE NAMES: they usually go by their individual names
HABITAT: high, remote mountaintops
DIET: many individuals have preferred foods or strict religious dietary regimens

APPEARANCE: Daitengu are much larger and more imposing than kotengu. They appear in a more human-like form; usually that of a man dressed in the robes of an ascetic monk, with a red face, an incredibly long and phallic nose (the longer the nose, the more powerful the tengu). Large, feathered wings sprout from their backs. Only rarely do they appear in the more primitive avian form of the lesser tengu.

BEHAVIOR: Daitengu live solitary lives on remote mountaintops, far removed from humanity. Their lives are spent in thoughtful meditation, intent on perfecting themselves. Daitengu possess greater pride, wisdom, and power than their kotengu cousins, although they can also be just as savage and unpredictable. This savagery combined with intelligence makes daitengu more dangerous. In fact, natural disasters and other great catastrophes are sometimes attributed to the wrath of a powerful daitengu. However, daitengu also possess more self-restraint; there are stories of daitengu giving aid to worthy humans.

INTERACTIONS: While kotengu terrorize people whenever they could, over the centuries daitengu were viewed less as the enemy of mankind and more as a race of god-like sages living deep in the mountains. Daitengu became closely connected with the ascetic mountain religion of Shugendō. The mountain mystics grew close to the tengu, seeking their wisdom and worshiping them as divine beings. It is perhaps through this mystic religion that humankind was eventually able to earn the respect of the tengu. Brave men ventured into the unknown wilds in hopes of gaining some of the tengu's wisdom. Occasionally, tengu would teach secrets and impart magical knowledge to the worthiest of these men. One of Japan's most famous warriors, Minamoto no Yoshitsune, is said to have learned swordsmanship from the tengu king Sōjōbō.

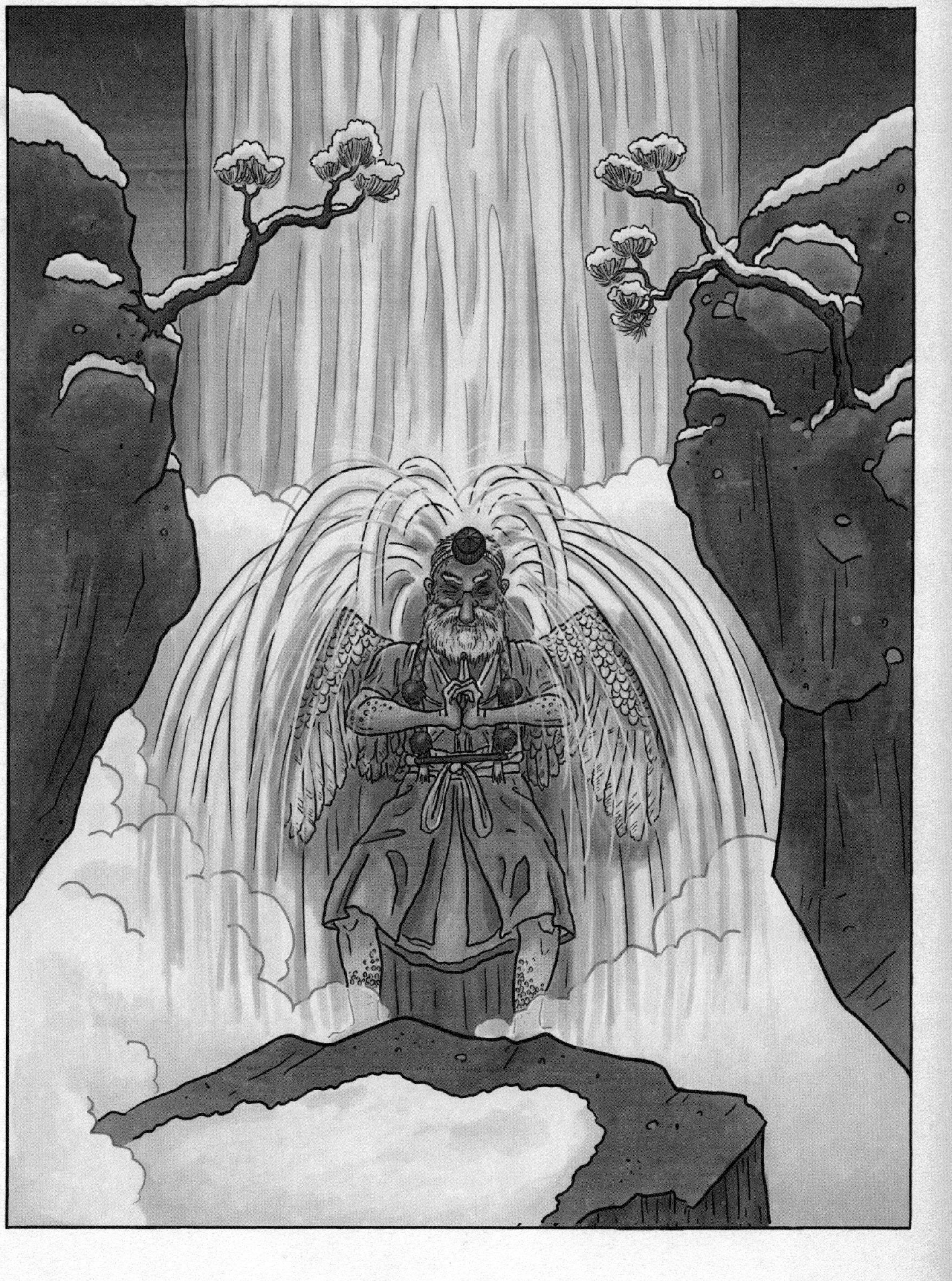

Ōnyūdō 大入道

TRANSLATION: giant priest
ALTERNATE NAMES: many variations and different kinds exist
HABITAT: any; usually found in mountainous regions
DIET: varies; most commonly livestock or humans

APPEARANCE: Ōnyūdō is a catch-all term for a number of giants found throughout Japan. The name is used in a euphemistic way; while some ōnyūdō bear a strong resemblance to Buddhist priests and monks, most have no actual relation to the clergy. Size, appearance, and mannerisms vary from region to region and account to account. Some giants are only slightly larger than a human while others are as big as a mountain. Some are saviors of men, while others are man-eaters.

BEHAVIOR: Ōnyūdō can be separated into four general groups: those that harm humans; those that help humans; transformations of other yōkai; and other, truly unique ōnyūdō that do not fit into any of these categories.

Ōnyūdō that harm humans are by far the broadest category. Among them are well-known yōkai, such as hitotsume nyūdō, mikoshi nyūdō, and the ocean going umi bōzu. These giants delight in terrorizing humans— sometimes hunting them to eat, sometimes pillaging and destroying villages out of rage, and other times terrifying lone travelers just for the fun of it.

Ōnyūdō that help humans are much rarer. They have been known to perform good deeds such as turning stuck waterwheels, moving heavy objects, or doing other things that require incredible amounts of strength. Though helpful, they are not always friendly. Ōnyūdō can change from benevolent to violent with little warning.

Helpful or harmful, true ōnyūdō are actually rare. Transformed yōkai—especially tanuki and itachi—make up a large percentage of the giant population. Shape-shifting yōkai take on giant form in order to scare people and cause mischief, though they rarely kill. There is no easy way to identify if a giant is a true ōnyūdō or just a shape-shifter. The two are functionally indistinguishable.

And then there are the remainder of the ōnyūdō—enigmatic and mysterious. They are only evidenced by their footprints or discarded trash. Regardless of how good or evil at heart a particular ōnyūdō is, they are by nature extremely dangerous. It is generally wise to leave them be. Better to avoid all contact with them than risk enraging an ōnyūdō and bringing destruction upon nearby villages.

WHY PRIESTS?

Many yōkai have names ending with nyūdō, bō, bōzu, kozō, and other terms for priests, monks, and so on. These yōkai are also often depicted with priestly robes, shaved heads, and other iconic Buddhist traits. It could be assumed that old Japan did not have a very high opinion of the Buddhist clergy....

While a few of these yōkai do actually have connections to religion, the majority do not. In ancient Japan, these words were used as endearing nicknames, humorous euphemisms, or colloquialisms to refer to strangers. Just as the English "sir" and "madam" actually refer to nobility but are used as polite terms of address in daily life, these Japanese words for the clergy have broader meanings outside of their religious context.

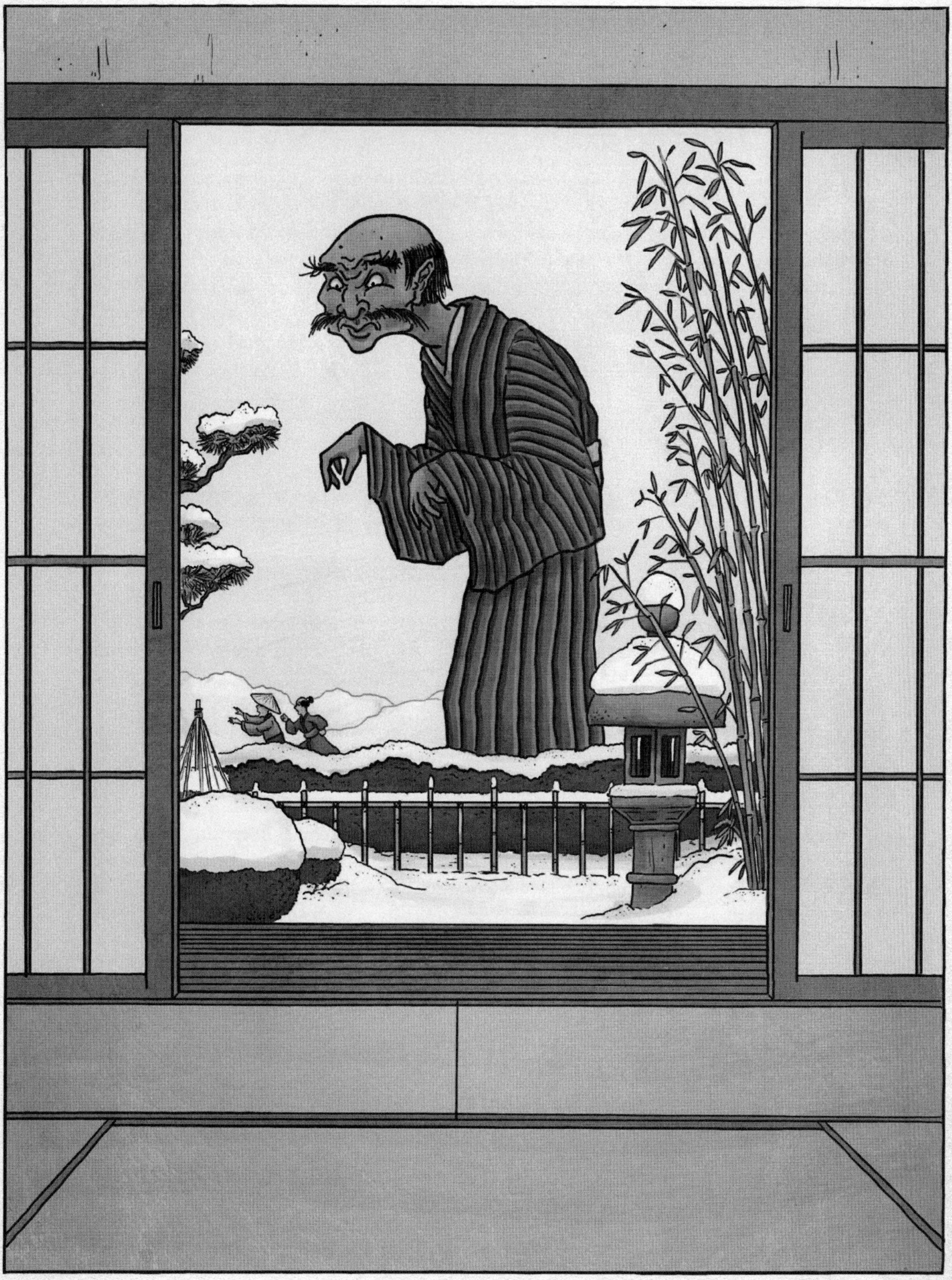

Hitotsume nyūdō 一つ目入道

TRANSLATION: one-eyed priest
HABITAT: roads and highways
DIET: omnivorous; occasionally humans

APPEARANCE: Hitotsume nyūdō could pass for really tall human priests if not for the large, single eye in the center of their faces. They dress in luxurious robes and travel in enormous, ornate palanquins carried by lesser yōkai or human slaves. Their palanquins are surrounded by a splendid precession fit for a corrupt abbot or a rich lord. The fantastic procession is enough to make most travelers stop and stare, speculating about what nobleman or lady might be riding inside. But when the palanquin stops and a hitotsume nyūdō comes strolling out, it means trouble for any curious gawkers.

BEHAVIOR: Hitotsume nyūdō are one of the most demonic types of ōnyūdō. They roam the roads and highways outside of the cities, assaulting lone travelers unfortunate enough to get in their way. Like many giants, they are able to increase and decrease their size at will. They can grow taller than the highest trees and trample forests to crush any who might be hiding within. With their long legs they are faster than any human. Running away is impossible. Like many ōnyūdō, hitotsume nyūdō attacks are blamed on mischievous kitsune or tanuki disguised by transformation magic; and occasionally this is true.

LEGENDS: A legend from Wakayama tells how a man, traveling along a wooded road, came across a splendid procession unlike any he had ever seen. Entranced, he climbed a tree to get a better look. As the procession approached, it stopped just as it reached his tree. There was a frighteningly large palanquin, and out from it stepped a giant, one-eyed monster. The creature went after the man, climbing the tree he was hiding in. In a panic the man swung his sword at the creature. At the moment he did so, the hitotsume nyūdō and the entire procession vanished.

Another hitotsume nyūdō, frequently seen outside of Kyōto, was said to be the reincarnation of a particularly fierce abbot of Enryaku-ji. Renowned for his strict discipline, in life he was known for expelling lazy monks from his temple. He saw the world as growing increasingly secular and wicked, and he constantly lamented and criticized the corruption and sin of the monks of his day. After his death, it is said he was reincarnated into a yōkai. This allowed him to continue punishing the wicked and impious clergy.

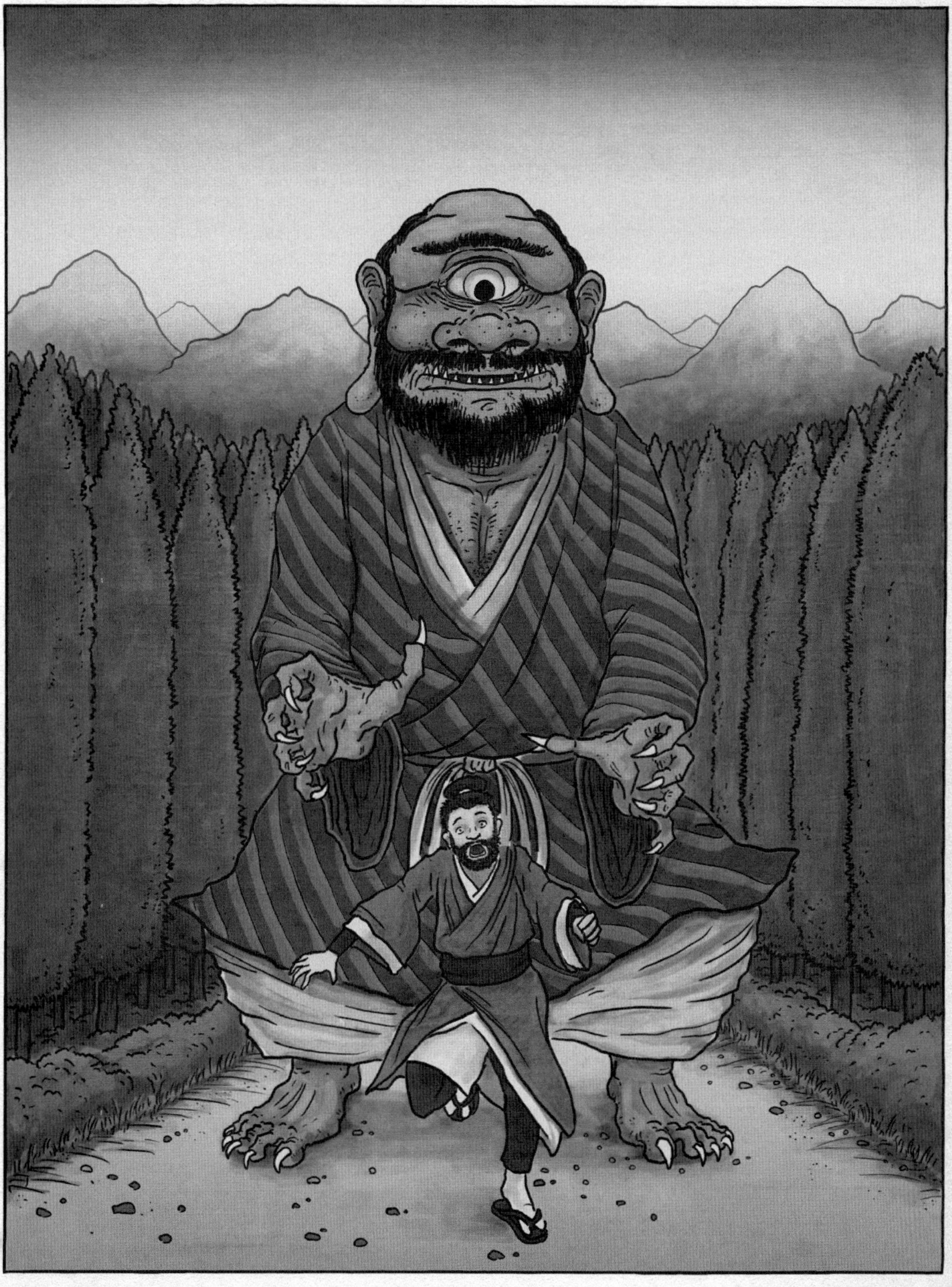

MIKOSHI NYŪDŌ 見越入道

TRANSLATION: anticipating priest
ALTERNATE NAMES: mikoshi, miage nyūdō, takabōzu
HABITAT: bridges, roads, streets; especially at night
DIET: omnivorous; prefers travelers

APPEARANCE: Mikoshi nyūdō are fearsome yōkai who appear late at night to lone travelers on empty streets, intersections, or bridges. They appear to be harmless traveling priests or monks, no taller than an ordinary person; but in an instant they grow abnormally tall, with long claws and hair like a wild beast.

BEHAVIOR: As soon as a person raises his eyes to look upon a mikoshi nyūdō, the giant grows to an immense height—as tall the observer is able to raise his eyes, and just as fast. This causes the person to look up so high and fast that they lose their balance and tumble backwards. That's when the mikoshi nyūdō lunges forward and bites their throat out with its teeth.

INTERACTIONS: Those unfortunate enough to meet this cruel yōkai usually do not live to tell the tale. Much depends on the person's reaction. If they try to ignore and walk past the mikoshi nyūdō, the angry giant will crush them or pierce them with bamboo spears and branches. The same fate is met by those who turn and try to run away. People who stare at the mikoshi nyūdō frozen in fear will drop dead on the spot, overcome by its presence.

The only possible escape is to anticipate the mikoshi nyūdō (thus its name). Meet it face-to-face, eye-to-eye, and show no fear. Then, look from its head down to its feet, rather than starting at the feet and looking up. If done properly, the giant's power to grow will be sapped. Telling the giant, "You lost! I anticipated your trick!" causes it to vanish in anger, leaving the traveler to pass safely along.

OTHER FORMS: Mikoshi nyūdō is a popular form of some shape-shifting animals. In particular, itachi and tanuki transform into these giants in order to hunt humans. Kitsune and mujina are known to occasionally take this form as well, though less often. When a mikoshi nyūdō is result of a transformation, it carries a bucket, a lantern, or some other tool. This tool is where the shape-shifter's true body is stored. If you can snatch the object away from the giant before it attacks, the spell is broken and the transformed yōkai will be at its captor's mercy.

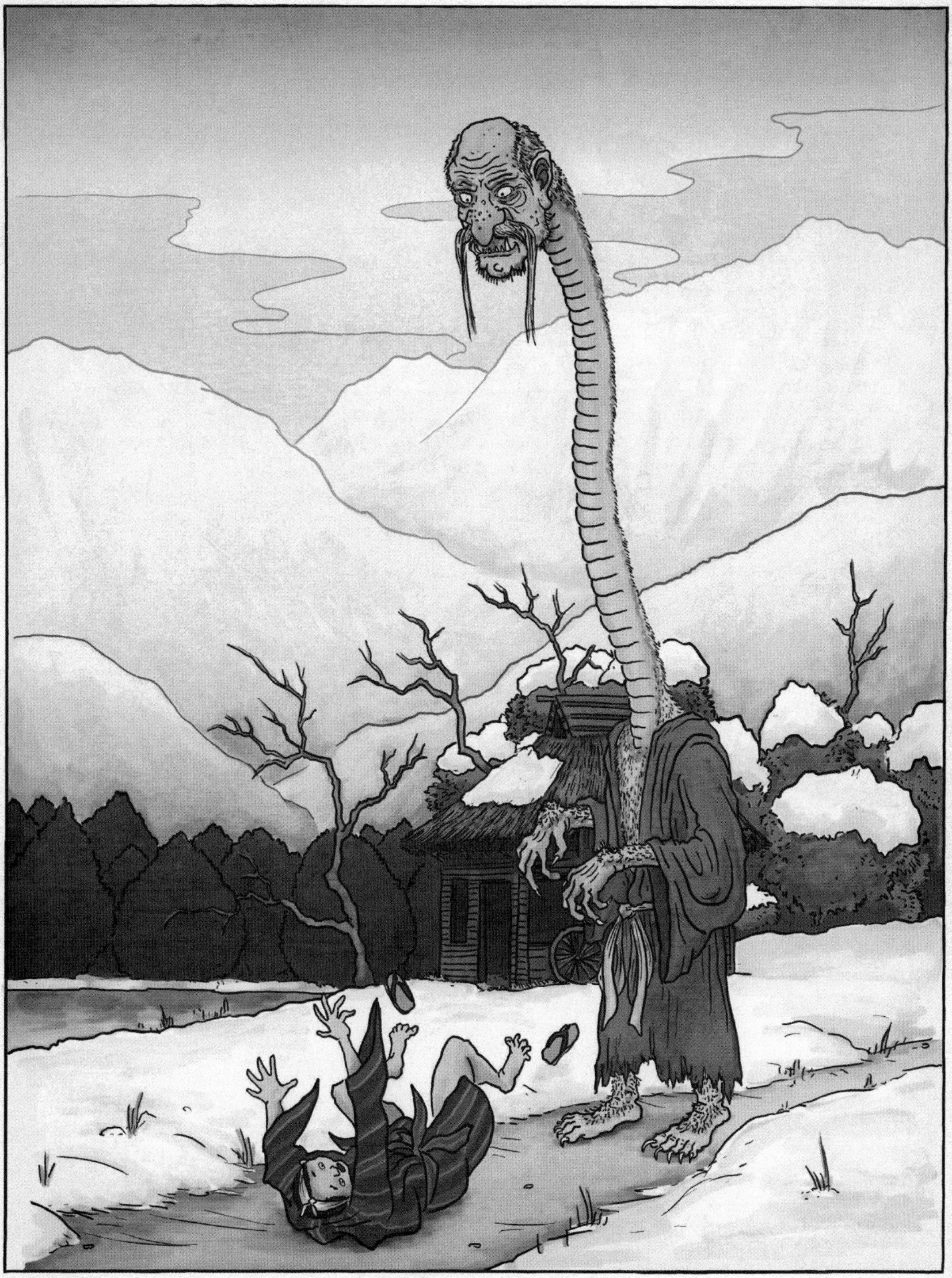

Taka nyūdō 高入道

Translation: tall priest
Alternate names: frequently confused with mikoshi nyūdō
Habitat: alleys, roads, mountains; native to Shikoku and the Kinki region
Diet: omnivorous

Appearance: The taka nyūdō is a close relative of the mikoshi nyūdō. Because of the similarity in regional names and appearance, taka nyūdō and mikoshi nyūdō are often confused with one another. Taka nyūdō are usually encountered in alleyways, suddenly appearing before unsuspecting humans. Like the mikoshi nyūdō, they increase their height at the same speed as their victim's gaze.

Interactions: Taka nyūdō can be defeated in a similar manner as the mikoshi nyūdō—by demonstrating courage in the face of death, showing no fear, and refusing to raise your head and denying them the chance to grow. Some say they can also be outsmarted by carrying a ruler or other measuring utensils and attempting to calculate their height before it can react. The confused giant usually leaves in disgust and will not bother the same person again.

Taka nyūdō are generally less violent than other giants. They are content with simply scaring its victims instead of ripping their throats out or crushing them with trees. Its true form is often a tanuki, kitsune, or kawauso.

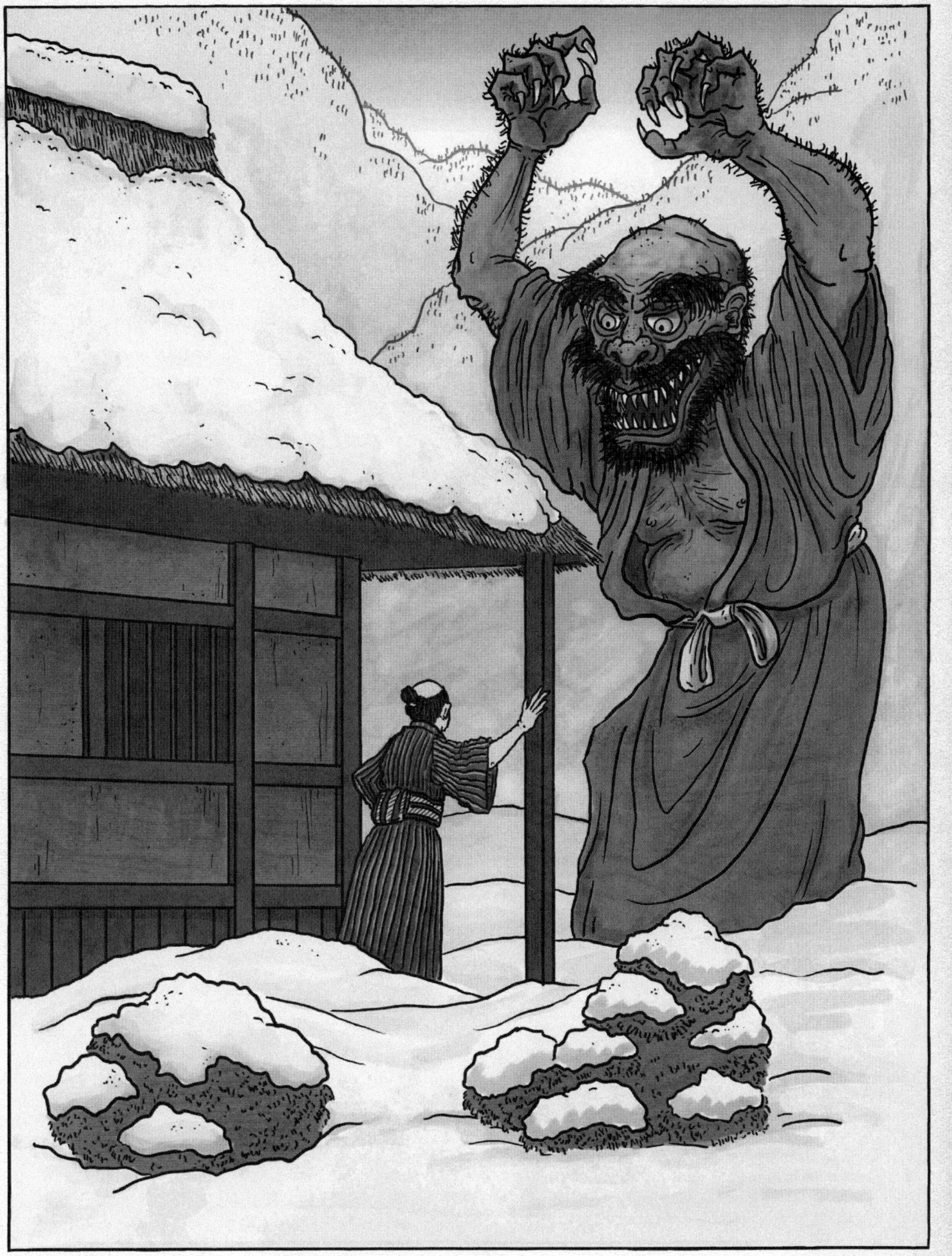

ABURA SUMASHI 油すまし

TRANSLATION: oil presser
HABITAT: mountain passes; native to Kumamoto Prefecture
DIET: unknown

APPEARANCE: The abura sumashi is a rare yōkai native to Kumamoto Prefecture. It looks like a squat humanoid with a large, ugly head like a potato or a stone. It wears a straw-woven raincoat. Abura sumashi are extremely rare, only found deep in the mountains or along mountain passes in the southern parts of Japan—throughout the range where wild tea plants grow.

BEHAVIOR: Very little is known about the lifestyle and habits of this reclusive yōkai. The most well-known abura sumashi lives in the Kusazumigoe Pass in Kumamoto, but only ever appears briefly to travelers. Occasionally, an old grandmother walking the pass with her grandchildren will say, "You know, a long time ago, an abura sumashi used to live in these parts." A mysterious voice will call out in reply, "I still do!" On rare occasions the abura sumashi will appear to the travelers, materializing out of thin air.

ORIGIN: The name abura sumashi means "oil presser," and comes from the act of pressing oil out of the seeds of tea plants which grow in Kumamoto. Though its origins are a mystery, it is commonly believed that abura sumashi are the ghosts of oil thieves who escaped into the woods. Oil was a difficult and expensive commodity to make. It required time and hard work to extract it from tea seeds, so its theft was a serious crime. Oil thieves who went unpunished in life reincarnated as abura sumashi—a divine punishment for their sins.

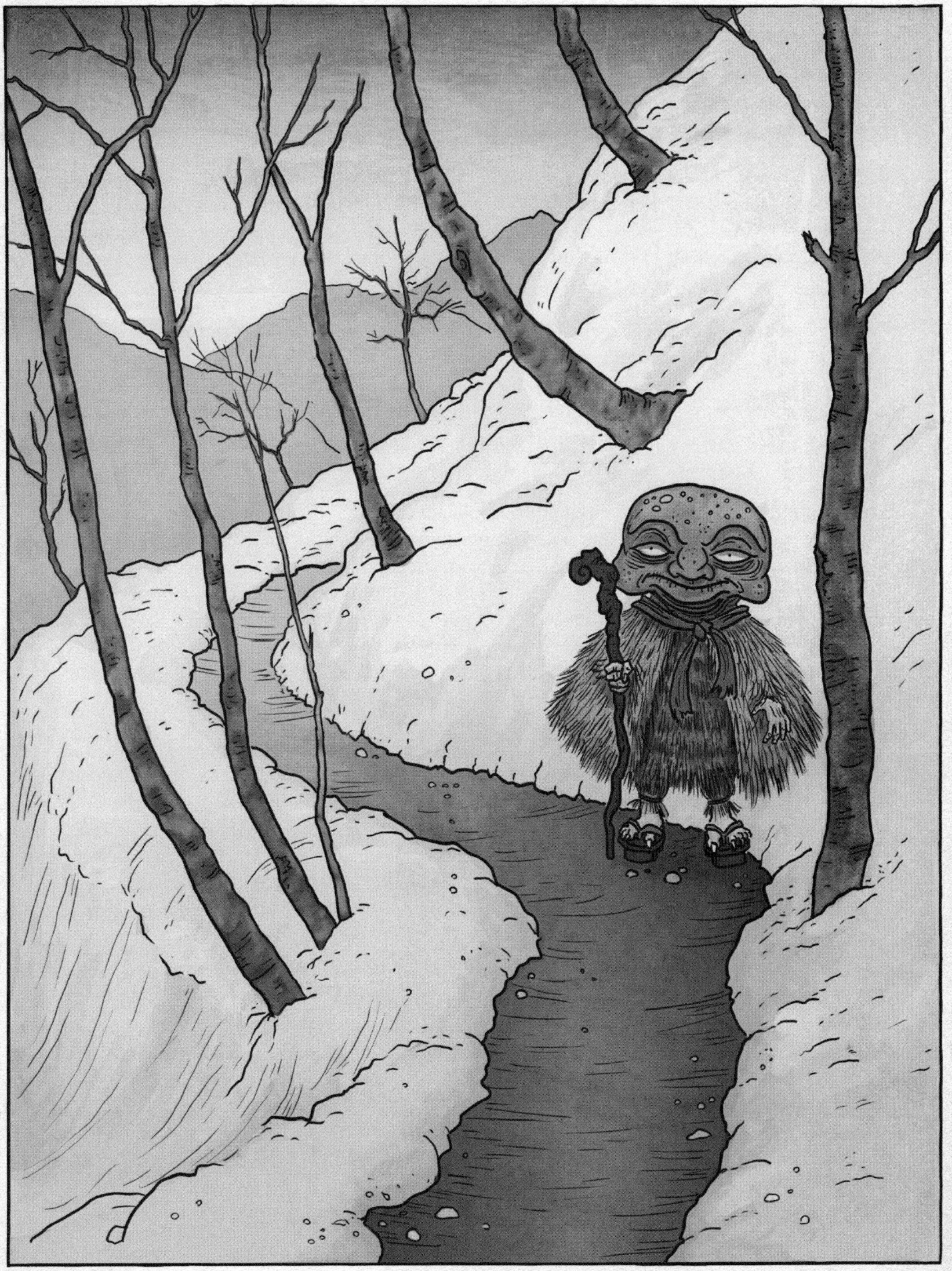

Yuki onna 雪女

TRANSLATION: snow woman
HABITAT: mountain passes; anywhere there is snow
DIET: life energy; can also eat ordinary food

APPEARANCE: Yuki onna prey on travelers lost in the heavy snowstorms that blanket the Japanese Alps in winter. They have an otherworldly beauty, with long black hair and dark, piercing eyes. Their skin is ageless and as white as snow, but their bodies are as cold as ice. A mere touch is enough to give a human a deep, unshakable chill. They feed on life force, sucking it from human's mouths with an icy breath that freezes their victims solid.

INTERACTIONS: Yuki onna spend their lives hunting humans in the snow. They stay near mountain roads and prey on the travelers coming and going, or break into homes and flash-freeze the inhabitants during the night. While they are killers, Yuki onna are not entirely cold blooded. Legends say they can fall in love with their intended prey and let them go free. Some go so far as to marry humans and live happily together. As supernatural spirits never age, however, their husbands inevitably discover their true identities. This revelation usually ends these happy marriages.

LEGENDS: In Niigata Prefecture, an elderly man operated an inn on a mountain trail with his wife. One snowy night, the inn was visited by a young lady traveling alone. She warmed herself by the fire and ate with the innkeeper and his wife. She was sweet and charming and extremely beautiful. So it was even more of a surprise when, in the middle of the night during a fierce blizzard, she stood up and made to leave the inn. The innkeeper begged her not to go outside, and took her hand to hold her back. It was as cold as ice. Merely touching it sucked all the warmth from the innkeeper's body. As he tried to keep the girl in the house, her entire body turned into a fine icy mist, and shot up the chimney and out into the night.

A man from Yamagata Prefecture claimed that he had been married to a yuki onna. His wife was beautiful, with piercing eyes and skin as white as a marble statue. While he loved to take long hot baths every night, his wife always refused to bathe. This puzzled him greatly. One particularly cold and snowy night, he insisted that his wife take a bath. Otherwise she would freeze to death in the cold, he said. She protested, but there was no reasoning with the man. Finally she acquiesced. When he went in to check on her a few minutes later, all he found in the tub were half-melted icicles.

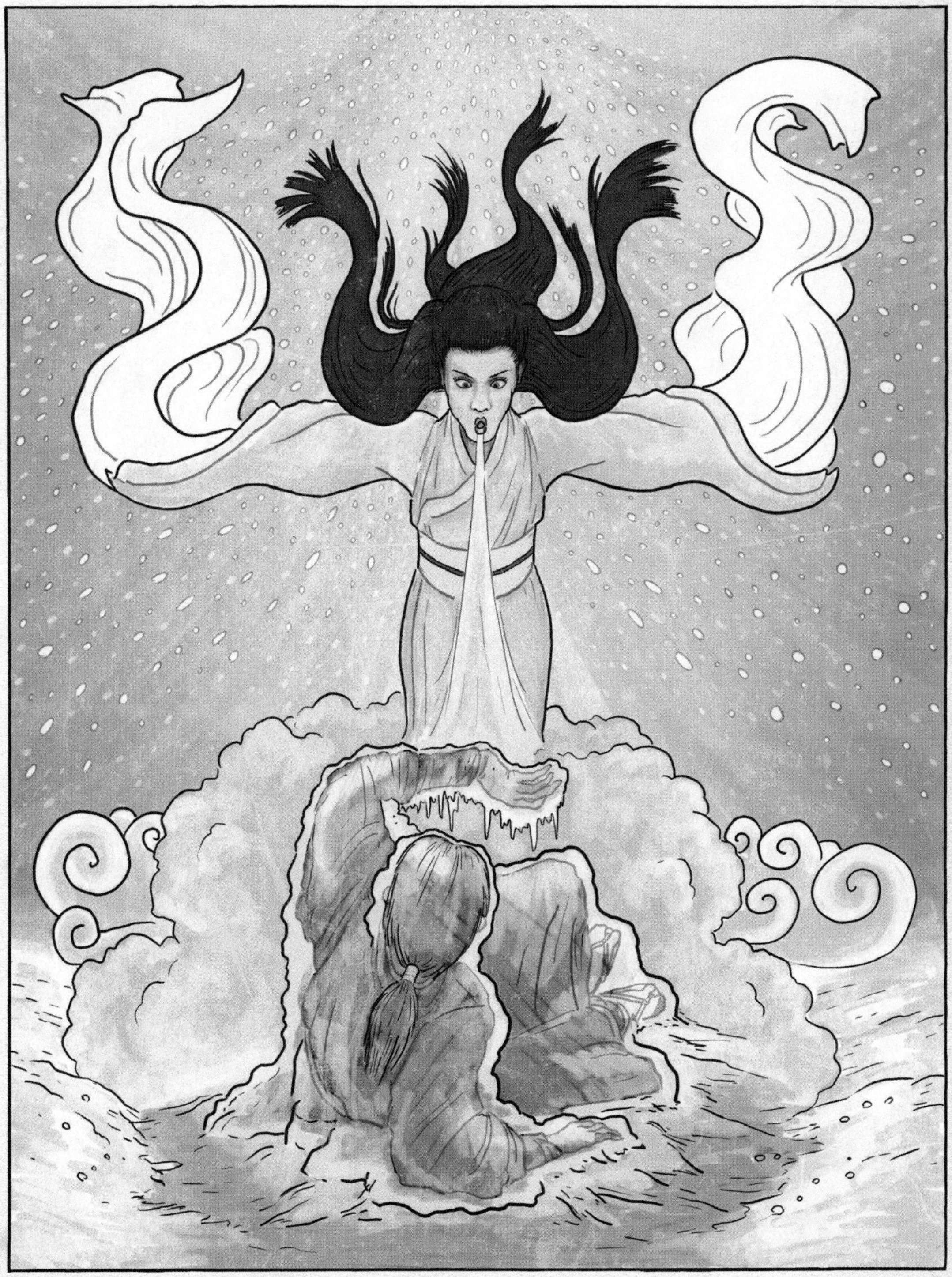

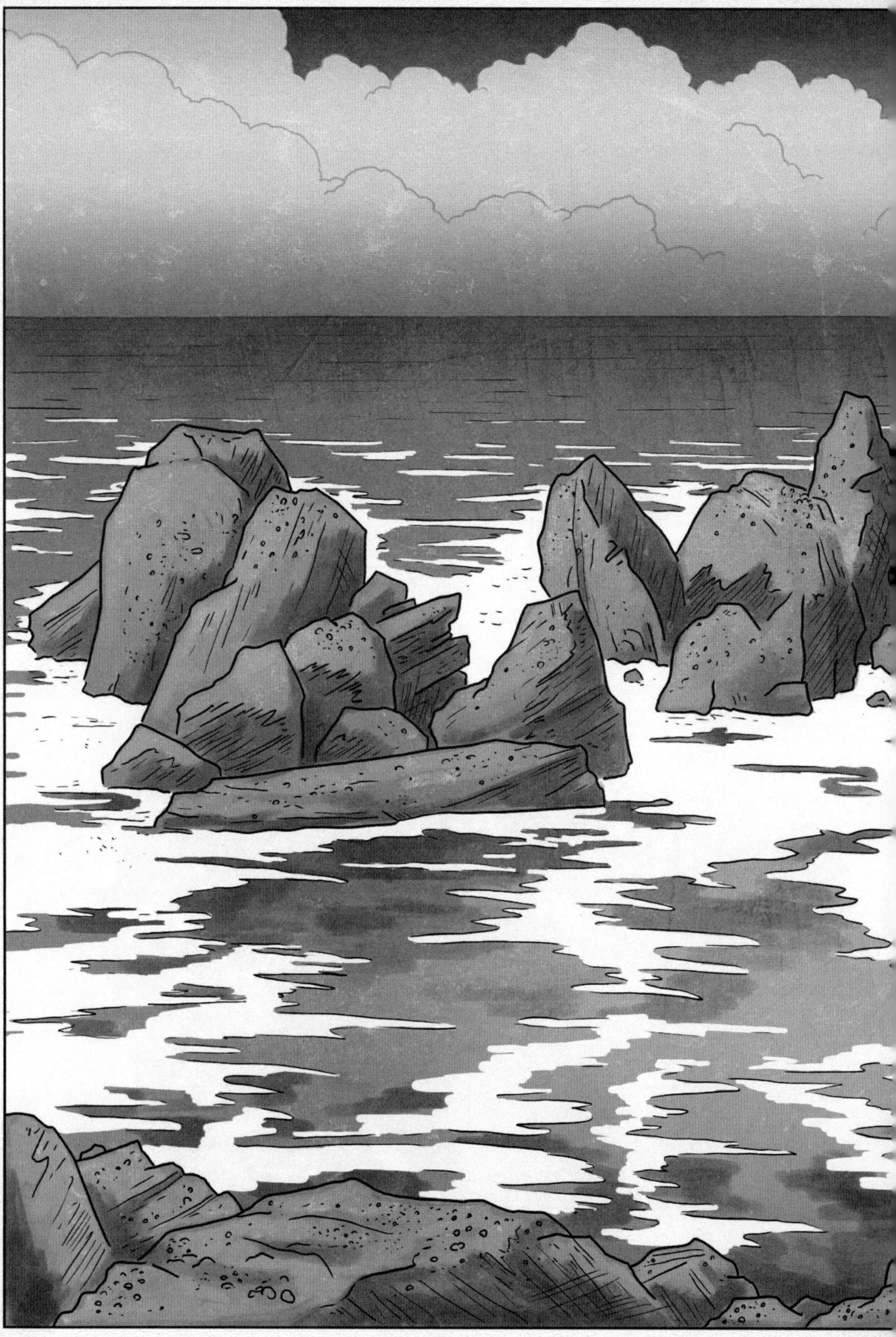

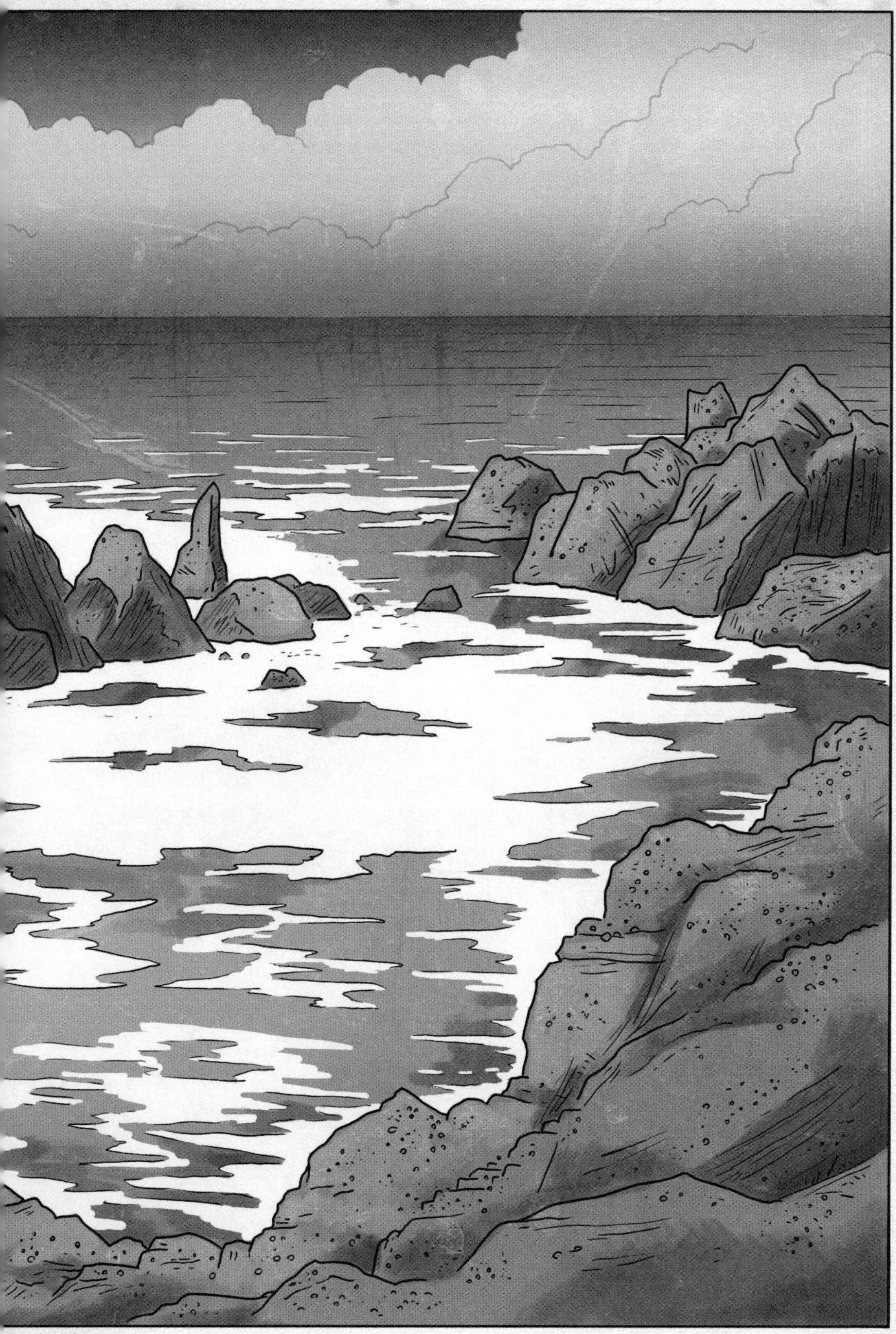

Sнōjō 猩々

TRANSLATION: none; based on the Chinese name for the same creature
HABITAT: coasts, islands, and shallow waters; found throughout Japan
DIET: omnivorous; extremely fond of sake

APPEARANCE: Along the mountainous coasts of Japan lives a race of intelligent sea spirits known as shōjō. They look like man-sized apes, with long, shaggy red hair. Their faces are also reddish and blushed as if drunk. Shōjō are bipedal like humans, and occasionally wear clothes or skirts made of seaweed.

BEHAVIOR: Shōjō spend their lives drinking large quantities of alcohol and playing in the sea and sand of secluded beaches. They revel in drunken silliness, singing, dancing, and enjoying life. Despite their silly appearance and demeanor, they are said to be wise. Extremely fond of sake and other types of alcohol, they are excellent brewers themselves and can distil a powerful brine wine from seawater. The taste of the wine varies depending on the imbiber. If he is a good person, the wine will be delicious. However, if he is a wicked person it will taste like a foul poison. The wine may even kill him if he does not change his evil ways.

INTERACTIONS: Shōjō can understand human languages and even parrot a number of words. They are curious and gentle towards friendly humans. Generally peaceful, shōjō keep to themselves, preferring to remain apart from the world of mankind. Occasionally there have been stories of groups of shōjō harassing sailors and ships which stray too close to their homes. These stories are rarely violent; usually the shōjō flee into the water after stealing a few barrels of sake.

ORIGIN: The name shōjō is the Japanese version of the Chinese name for these ape-like spirit, *xīng xīng*. The name connotes liveliness, a fitting match for the personality of this creature. Due to the orangutan's physical resemblance to this yōkai, the name shōjō is applied to that species of great ape in both Japan and China. Additionally, shōjō can be used to refer to a person who is a heavy drinker. The famous artist and yōkai painter Kawanabe Kyōsai jokingly referred to himself as a shōjō in this way.

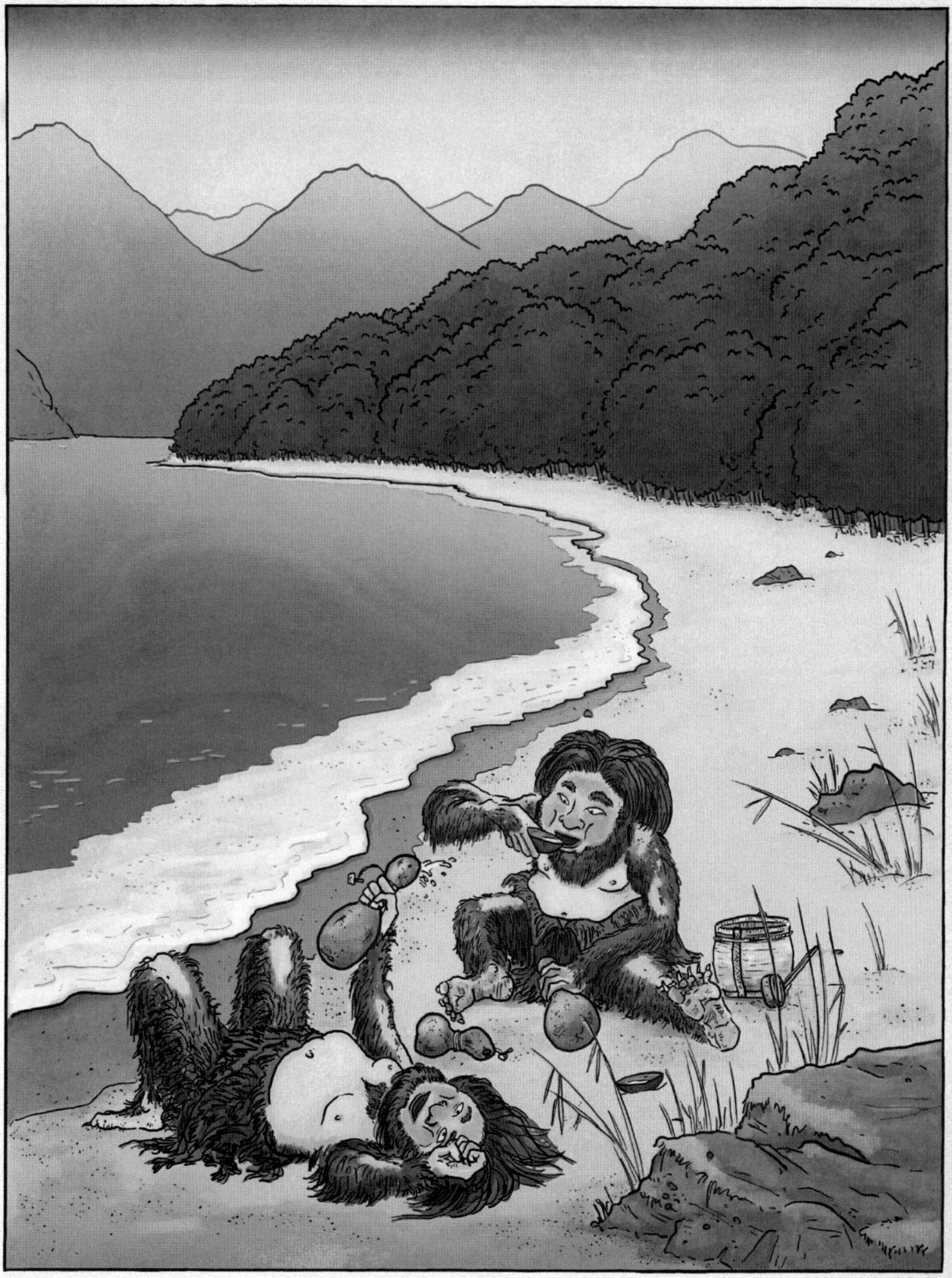

Ushi oni 牛鬼

TRANSLATION: ox demon
ALTERNATE NAMES: gyūki
HABITAT: usually along the coast or near bodies of water; found in West Japan
DIET: varies from type to type, but always carnivorous

APPEARANCE: A terror from Western Japan, ushi oni is a class of monster that lives near water. The name literally means "ox demon," and it refers to a number of different monsters with bovine traits. Most Ushi oni resemble an ox from the head up and a demonic horror below. Many variations are known to exist; the body of an ox with a head like an oni's; the head of an ox on a body like a spider's or a cat's; or even an ox's head on the body of a kimono-clad human (a Japanese version of the minotaur).

BEHAVIOR: Despite their unique and varying morphology, all ushi oni share a number of characteristics, pointing to a common origin. They are exceedingly cruel and savage. They breath toxic poison, and eat humans. Some ushi oni are lurkers, attacking people who draw too close to their lairs; others are hunters, roaming the coasts seeking prey. The cruelest ushi oni ravage the same towns over and over, inflicting terrible curses or bringing diseases. Although a few roam the mountains of the island of Shikoku, most ushi oni live along the rocky coasts and beaches of Western Japan.

Ushi oni frequently work together in cooperation with other yōkai. The spider-like version from the coasts of the islands of northern Kyūshū and western Honshu frequently partners with nure onna and iso onna. These siren-like yōkai use their charms to lure unsuspecting men towards the water's edge. When they approach, the ushi oni pounces and bites the victims to death. The meal is then shared between the yōkai.

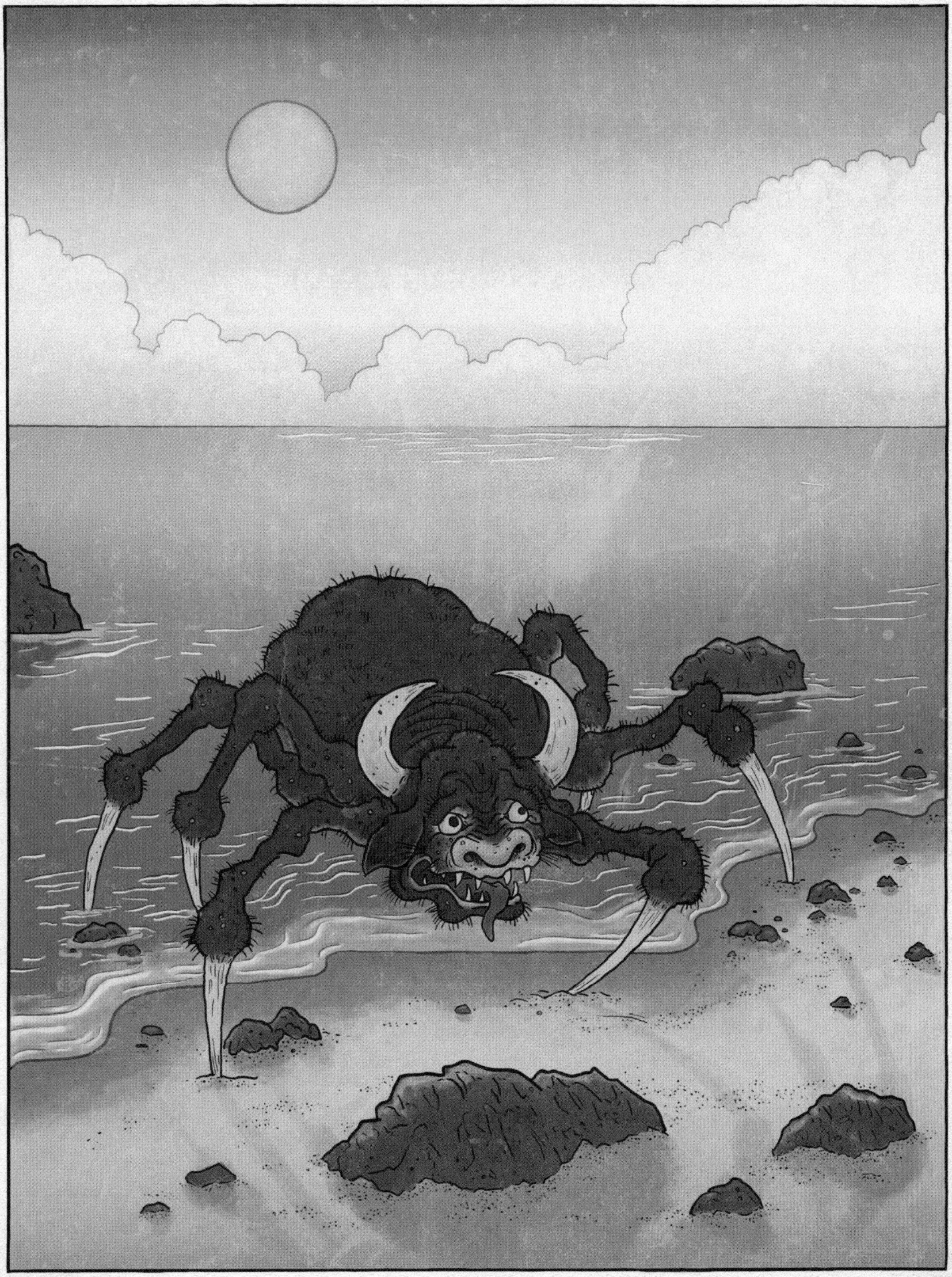

Nure onna 濡女

TRANSLATION: wet woman
ALTERNATE NAMES: nure yomejo
HABITAT: coasts, rivers, and other bodies of water; native to Kyūshū
DIET: blood

APPEARANCE: Nure onna are vampiric sea serpents who haunt shores and rivers looking for humans to eat. They are most commonly found on the shores of the island of Kyūshū, but there are stories of nure onna encounters as far north as Niigata Prefecture and as far east as Fukushima Prefecture. There are two variations of this yōkai: one without arms, which resembles an enormous sea serpent with a woman's head, and one with human-like arms. Aside from this difference, the two look and act in exactly the same manner. Their faces are hideous and betray serpent-like features such as a forked tongue. They have long black hair which sticks to their dripping bodies. Their name comes from the fact that they always appear soaking wet.

INTERACTIONS: While physically much stronger than a human, nure onna prefer not to rely on brute force and use trickery and guile to catch their prey. They most often appear near the water, on a coast or by a riverbank. Nure onna magically disguise themselves as a distressed woman carrying a bundled up baby. They cry out for help from fishers, sailors, or anybody passing by. When the prey approaches, a nure onna will plead with their victim to hold her baby for just a moment so that she can rest. If he agrees and takes the bundle, the "baby" becomes as heavy as a boulder. The victim is unable to move. The nure onna is then free to attack her helpless victim, feeding by draining his blood with her long, serpentine tongue.

Nure onna frequently appear together and cooperate with ushi oni, as they inhabit the same environments and share the same diet.

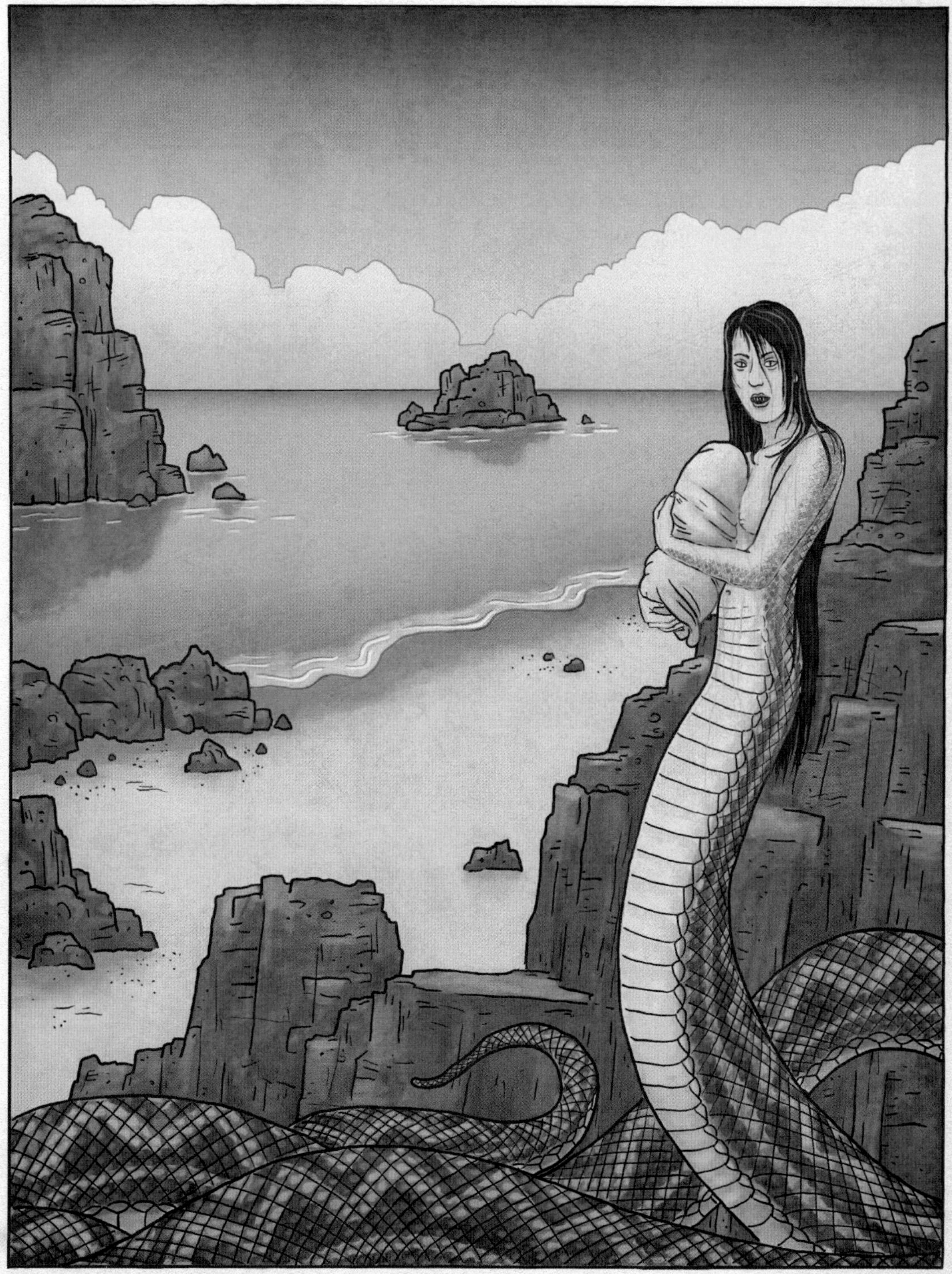

Iso onna 磯女

TRANSLATION: coast woman
HABITAT: coasts, particularly rocky ones; native to Kyūshū
DIET: blood

APPEARANCE: Iso onna are dangerous vampires from the Kyūshū islands and Western Japan. They hunt for fisherman and travelers to feed upon. Despite having no serpentine features, Iso onna are closely related to nure onna. Iso onna wander rocky beaches, hunting for prey.

Individual accounts of iso onna vary when it comes to their appearance. In most cases, they appear as beautiful women who have just come out of the water, dripping wet. Their hair is long and matted, reaching almost all the way down to the sand. Their eyes are heavy with sultry, sexual energy, and their nearly transparent wet clothes stick to their skin. From the waist up, they appear like ordinary human women. But from the waist down, they are blurry and slightly transparent, betraying their otherworldly nature. In some regions they are said to be large enough to crush ships out at sea, like umi bōzu. They also have the ability to disguise themselves perfectly as large beach rocks when they don't want to be seen.

INTERACTIONS: When iso onna appear on sandy beaches, they look like beautiful women, staring far out to sea. When somebody approaches and tries speaking to them, they turn around and let out an ear-piercing shriek. This stuns their victim. Then they lash out with their long hair and drag their prey into the sea. Once in the water, they drain their victims' blood with their hair.

On rocky coasts without sandy beaches, iso onna appear sitting on the cliffs and calling out to passersby in an eerie voice. Their victims are mesmerized, and walk straight towards them, ignoring the dangers posed by the rocky cliffs. They walk off the cliffs and fall to their deaths, leaving the iso onna free to feed on their bodies.

Iso onna are occasionally encountered far out at sea. They act much the same as they do on land, capturing their human prey with their long hair and draining their blood.

Iso onna are most commonly encountered during the holiday seasons of Obon and New Year's Eve, when the border between the realm of the living and the spirit world can be more easily crossed. They occasionally cooperate with ushi oni to catch their prey.

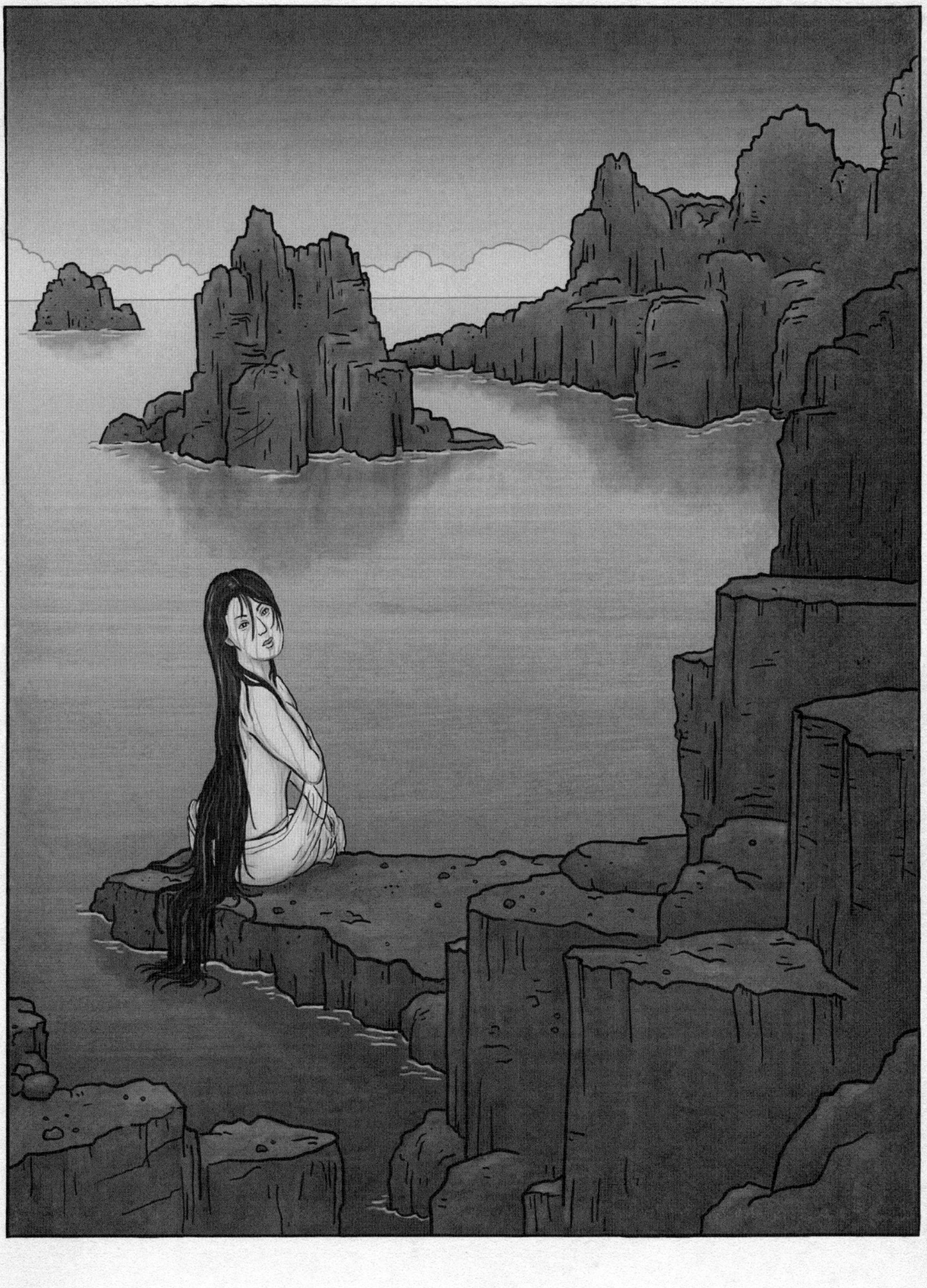

FUNAYŪREI 船幽霊

TRANSLATION: ship ghosts
ALTERNATE NAMES: ayakashi
HABITAT: seas, oceans, bays
DIET: none

APPEARANCE: When the ghosts of people who have died at sea transform into vengeful spirits, they become a particular type of ghost called a funayūrei. These are the shades of drowned sailors which remain in this world, hunting for their former friends and comrades to take them down into the sea. Like many ghosts, funayūrei appear as dead bodies wearing white funerary robes. They can be seen at night, either when the moon is new or full, on particularly stormy or foggy nights, or during the festival of Obon. Funayūrei appear as an eerie, luminescent mist, which gets closer and closer until it forms into a ship with a ghostly crew.

INTERACTIONS: Funayūrei ghost ships attack in different ways. Sometimes they charge headlong towards the other ship, causing it to steer away so sharply that it capsizes. Other times they pull alongside the other ship and the ghostly crew tries to drag it down under the water. The ghosts themselves carry large ladles and buckets which they use to fill ships with seawater, sinking the ships and adding more souls to the funayūrei crew. Occasionally funayūrei strike not as a large crew of man-sized ghosts, but as one very large ghost who rises out of the water to capsize a ship immediately. This ghost often demands a barrel from the crew, which it uses to flood the deck and sink the ship. Giant funayūrei are often confused with umi bōzu, which appear and attack in a similar manner.

It is said that a clever crew can outsmart the funayūrei by carrying buckets and ladles with holes in the bottom. Despite their efforts the ghosts will not be able to flood the human ship with such tools. Encounters with ghost ships can also be avoided by boldly sailing directly through the phantasm instead of turning to avoid a collision—though this runs the risk that the other ship may actually be real and not a phantasm. Some crews have also escaped the wrath of the funayūrei by throwing food and provisions overboard as offerings to the hungry ghosts, who chase after the food instead of the crew.

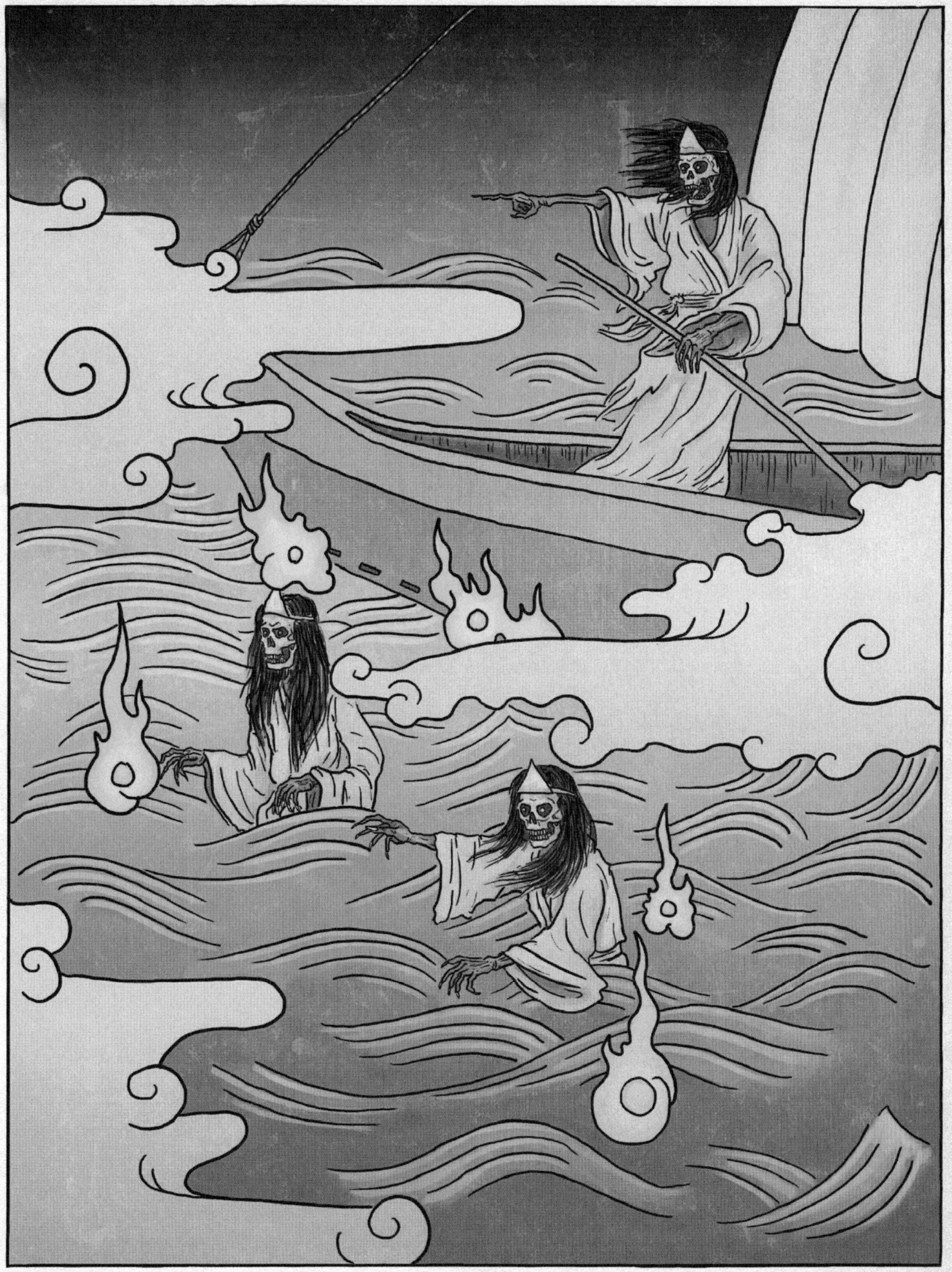

NINGYO 人魚

TRANSLATION: human fish; mermaid, merman
HABITAT: seas, oceans, and other large bodies of water
DIET: omnivorous; fish, seaweed, and other aquatic foods

APPEARANCE: Mermaids are known as ningyo in Japanese, but they are very different from the mermaids of Western tradition. Unlike the mermaids of the Atlantic Ocean and Mediterranean Sea, ningyo from the Pacific Ocean and the Sea of Japan are hideous to behold. Instead of seductive sirens, they are otherworldly nightmares. Ningyo are more fish than human. They can have anything from ugly, deformed fish-like faces, to entire human torsos with long, bony fingers and sharp claws. Ningyo range in size from a human child to a large seal.

These days, mermaids resembling the breeds known throughout the West—with an attractive human torso and a piscine lower body—are not unheard of in the Japanese islands. Since the end of the Edo period and the opening of Japan to the West, ningyo that resemble Western-style Atlantic mermaids have become popular in Japan. However, the traditional Japanese mermaid is more beast than beauty.

INTERACTIONS: Ningyo sightings go back to the earliest written histories of Japan. The first recorded mermaid sightings in Japan are found in the *Nihon Shoki*, which is one of the oldest books of classical Japanese history and dates back to 619 CE. The flesh of a ningyo is believed to grant eternal life and youth to those who eat it, and thus it is the subject of many folk tales. However, this meal carries a danger that most people unwilling to risk; ningyo can place a powerful curse on humans who try to wound or capture them. Some legends tell of entire towns that were swallowed by earthquakes or tidal waves after a foolish fisherman brought home a ningyo in one of his catches.

While their grotesque appearance and supernatural powers make them an intriguing subject, ningyo are best avoided at all costs.

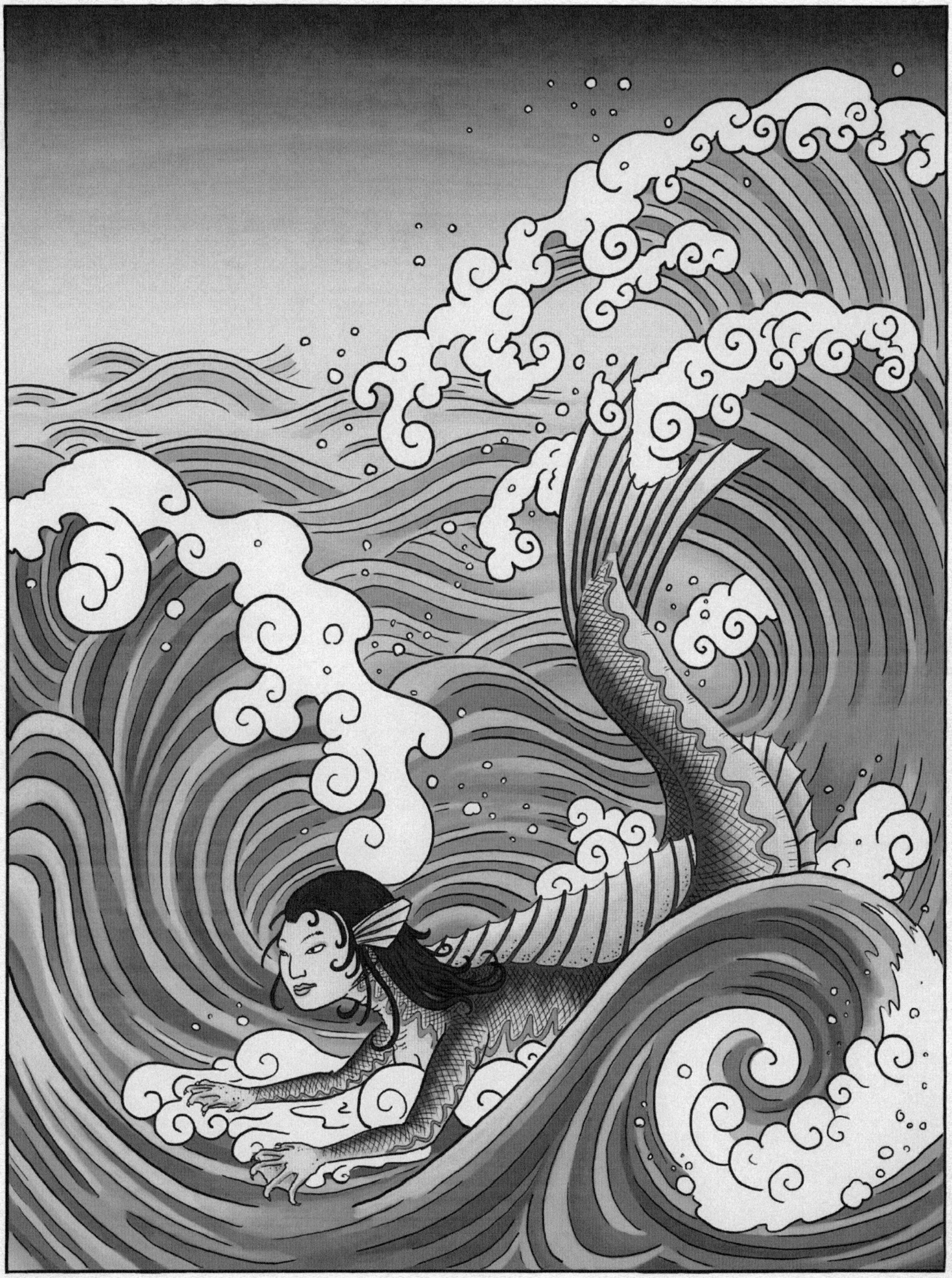

Isonade 磯撫で

TRANSLATION: beach stroker
ALTERNATE NAMES: ōkuchi wani ("giant mouthed sea monster")
HABITAT: shallow seas and coastal waters of West Japan

DIET: carnivorous

APPEARANCE: Isonade are mysterious, shark-like sea monsters which scour the rocky coastlines searching for boats to scuttle and fishermen to snatch. Their bodies are enormous, and their fins are covered with countless, tiny metallic barbs like a grater. They use these barbs to hook their prey, dragging them deep into the water to be eaten. Isonade are said to appear when the north winds blow and the sea currents change.

BEHAVIOR: Despite their size, isonade are incredibly elusive. They move through the water with unparalleled grace and can swim without creating so much as a splash. This makes them difficult to spot. By the time most sailors have noticed that the winds have changed and a strange color is upon the sea, it is too late—a huge tail is already rising out of the water, above their heads. When isonade strike, they do not thrash about violently like a hungry shark. Instead they hook their prey on their fins or tail with a gentle stroking motion, dragging them into the depths almost peacefully. They do this without a sound and without ever showing their bodies, making them all the more dangerous for their stealth.

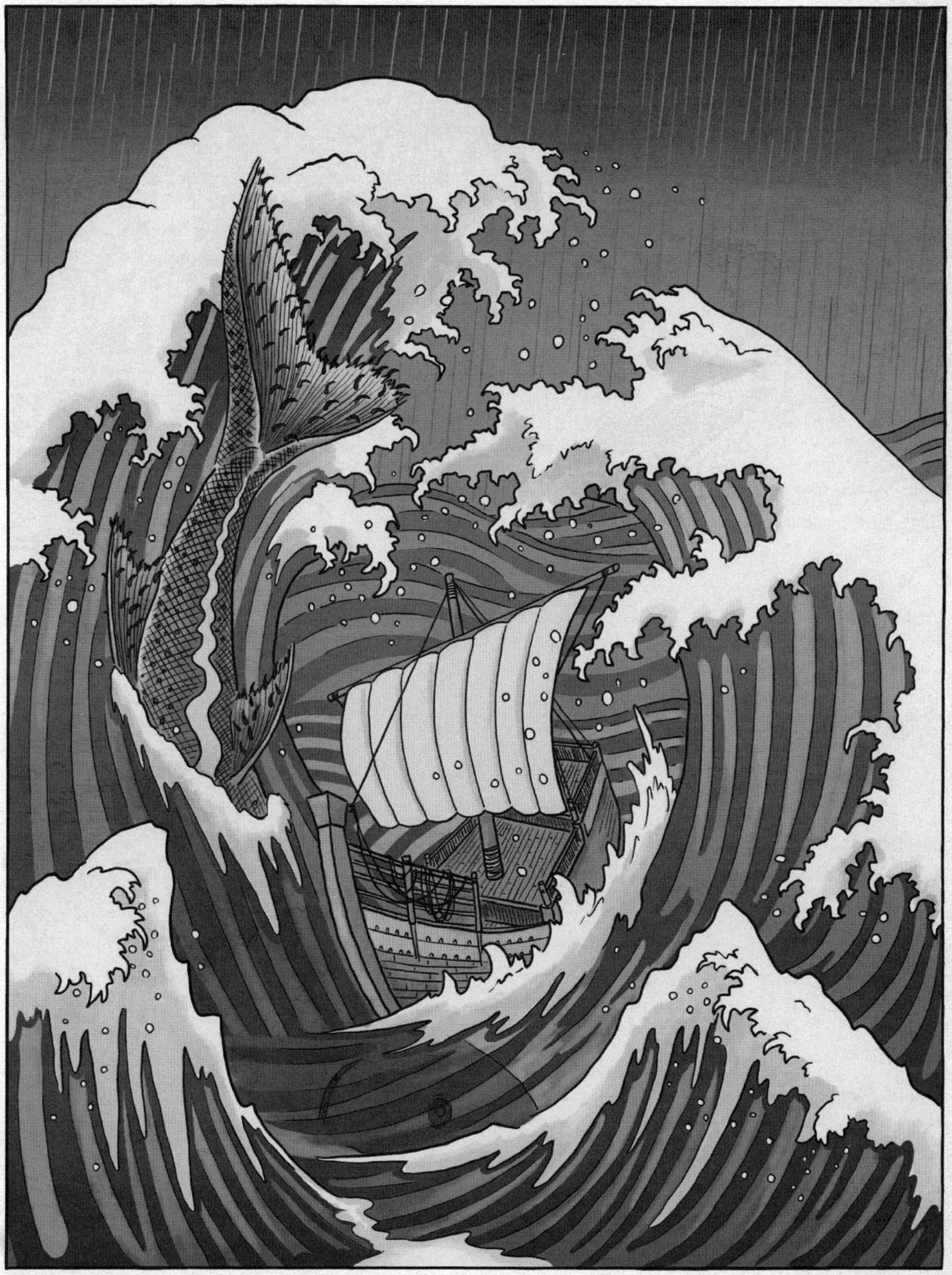

KOROMODAKO 衣蛸

TRANSLATION: cloth octopus
HABITAT: Sea of Japan; particularly near Kyōto and Fukui Prefectures
DIET: carnivorous; feeds on both tiny plankton and large ships

APPEARANCE: Koromodako are strange and terrifying octopus-like yōkai. They live in the seas bordering Kyōto and Fukui Prefectures, particularly in the bays of Ine and Wakasa. Koromodako appear similar to ordinary small octopuses. Males only reach a size of a few centimeters long, while females can grow up to five times that length. Being so tiny, they are subject to the tides and waves, and float wherever the currents take them. Females live inside of a paper-thin shell, while males have no shell (similar to the family of octopuses called argonauts).

BEHAVIOR: When koromodako are threatened, they become dangerous. They can instantly grow to many times their original size—large enough to engulf fish, fishermen, or any other creature that might try to eat them. Stretching their arms and body out wide, they resemble an enormous piece of cloth, which is how koromodako get their name. While in this form a koromodako can engulf nearly anything in the water, even entire ships. It wraps its arms and mantle around the ship, sailors and all, and drags it down into the deep, never to be seen again. After feeding, the koromodako shrinks down to its tiny size, impossible to trace.

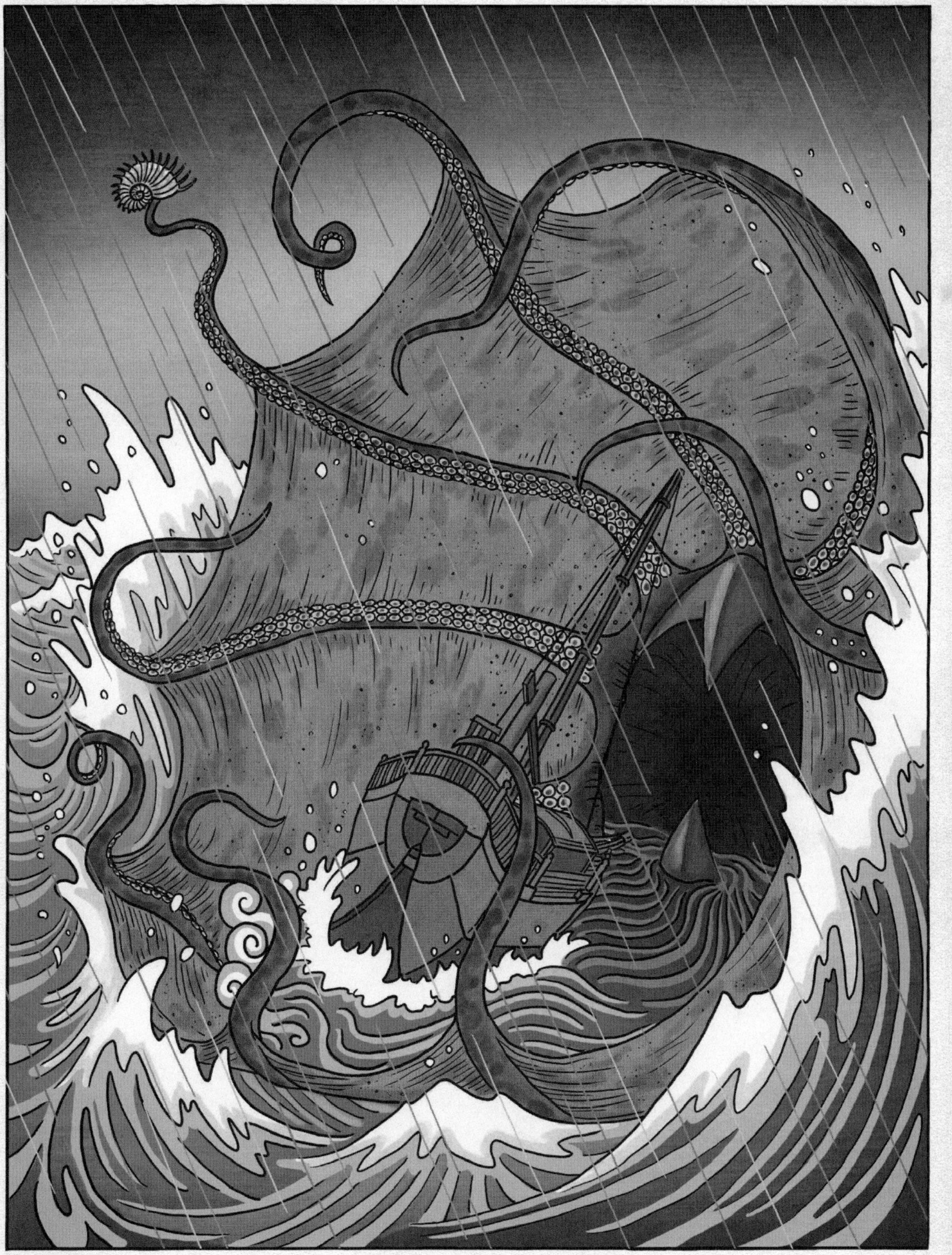

Umi bōzu 海坊主

TRANSLATION: sea monk
ALTERNATE NAMES: umi nyūdō, umi hōshi
HABITAT: seas, oceans, bays
DIET: unknown

APPEARANCE: Perhaps no other aquatic yōkai is as mysterious as the giant umi bōzu. Their true form is unknown. Umi bōzu are only ever seen from the shoulders up, but they appear to be roughly humanoid in shape, with inky black skin and a pair of large, round eyes. Eye-witnesses report a great range in size, from slightly larger than a ship to a size so unimaginable that only the creature's bulbous face is visible above the water. Its head is smooth and round like a venerable monk's, and its body is nude and as black as shadow.

INTERACTIONS: Umi bōzu appear on calm nights, when there is no sign of anything out of the ordinary. All of a sudden, with no warning, the waves and the weather whip up into a furious condition. Out from the tumult rises a titanic creature. It moves to destroy the ship, either by smashing the hull in a single blow, or taking it down bit by bit, depending on the size of both the ship and the umi bōzu.

Some rare reports make them out to be more serpentine, while others make them out to be more ghostly, like a gigantic kind of funayūrei. In the same way as the funayūrei, umi bōzu will demand a barrel from the crew. It uses this to pour huge amounts of water onto the deck, quickly sinking the boat and drowning the crew. If given a barrel with the bottom removed, the umi bōzu will scoop and scoop to no effect, and the sailors will be able to make a lucky escape.

ORIGIN: Some say that the umi bōzu are the spirits of drowned priests, cast into the sea by angry villagers (this may also be implied by their name). These priests were then transformed into ghosts due to the horrible nature of their death, making them cousins of the similarly dreaded funayūrei. Others, however, say that umi bōzu are a sea monster which lives in the deeps of the Seto Inland Sea, and that they are the progenitors of a large variety of other aquatic yōkai. Because sightings are rare and almost always fatal, it is likely that the true nature and origin of this spirit will remain a mystery for a long time.

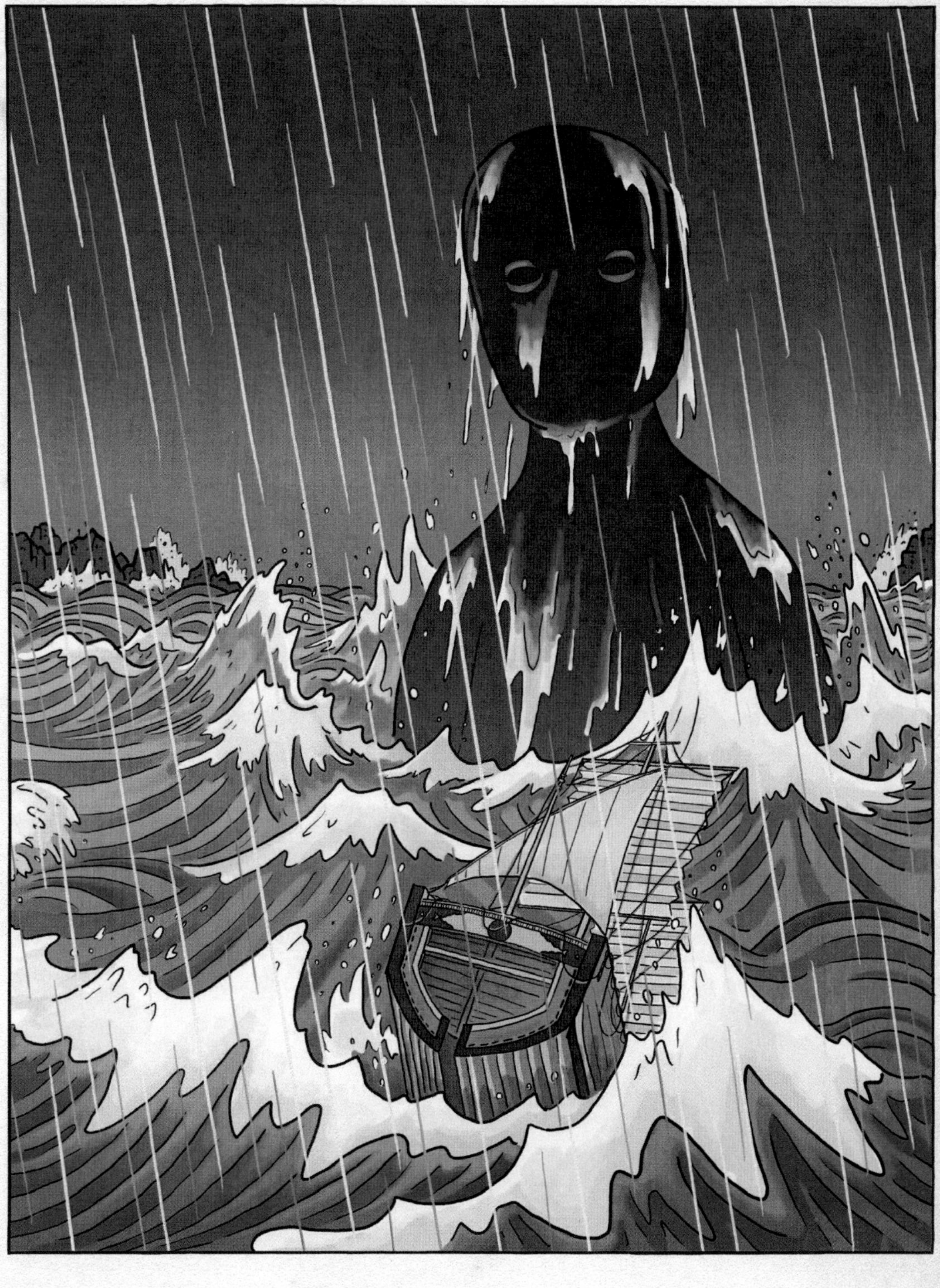

BAKEKUJIRA 化鯨

TRANSLATION: ghost whale
ALTERNATE NAMES: hone kujira ("bone whale")
HABITAT: Sea of Japan
DIET: none

APPEARANCE: Bakekujira are animated whale skeletons which sail near the surface of the sea, rising as they did in life when they needed air to breathe. They are followed by a host of eerie birds and strange fish, and appear on rainy nights near coastal whaling villages.

INTERACTIONS: In olden days, when whales were still plentiful in the Sea of Japan, a whale sighting was a blessing for the residents of the poor fishing villages. A village could reap huge amounts of wealth from the meat and oil in a single whale. Such a bounty did not come without a price, however. Many fishermen claimed that the souls of these whales lived on as bakekujira, seeking revenge against the humans who took their lives. Those who witnessed a bakekujira were infected with its horrible curse, which they brought back to their villages when they returned home. The whale's curse brought famine, plague, fires, and other kinds of disasters.

LEGENDS: One rainy night long ago, some fishers living on the Shimane peninsula witnessed an enormous white shape off the coast in the Sea of Japan. Squinting their eyes, it appeared to them to be a whale swimming offshore. Excited for the catch, they rallied the townspeople, who grabbed their spears and harpoons and took to their boats to hunt down and catch their quarry.

They soon reached the whale, but no matter how many times they hurled their weapons not one of them struck true. When they looked closer, through the dark, rain-spattered water's surface, they realized why; what they thought was a white whale was actually a humongous skeleton swimming in the sea. It lacked even a single bit of flesh on its body.

At that moment, the sea became alive with a host of strange fish that nobody had ever seen before. The sky swarmed with eerie birds which nobody could recognize and the likes of which had never been seen before. The ghost whale then turned sharply out to sea, and swiftly vanished into the current, taking all the strange fish and birds with it, never to be seen again.

The terrified villagers returned home, realizing that the skeletal whale must have been a bakekujira—a whale turned into a vengeful ghost. While the bakekujira was never seen again, other villages in Shimane felt the whale's curse. They were consumed by conflagrations and plagued by the infectious diseases that followed whale beachings.

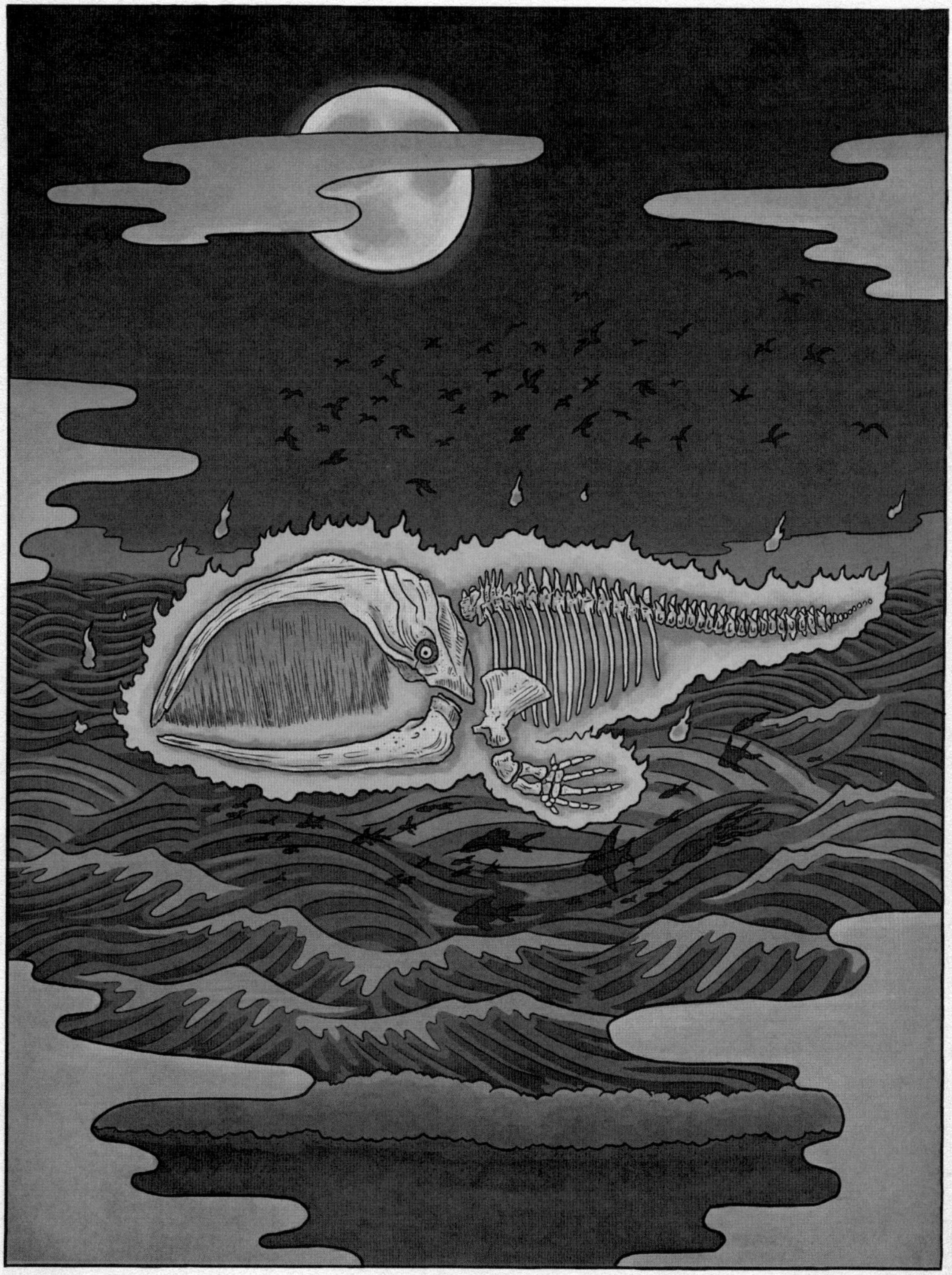

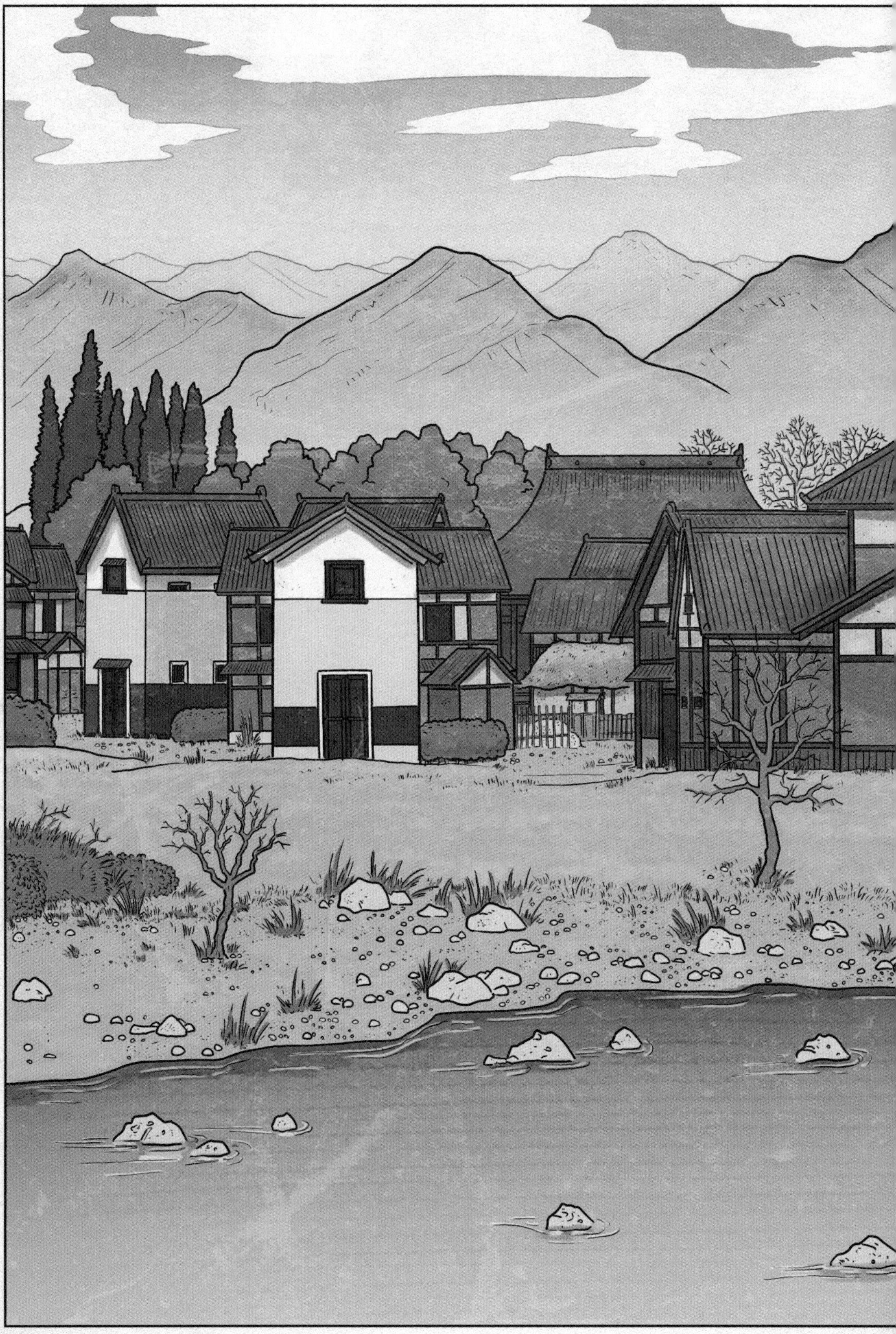

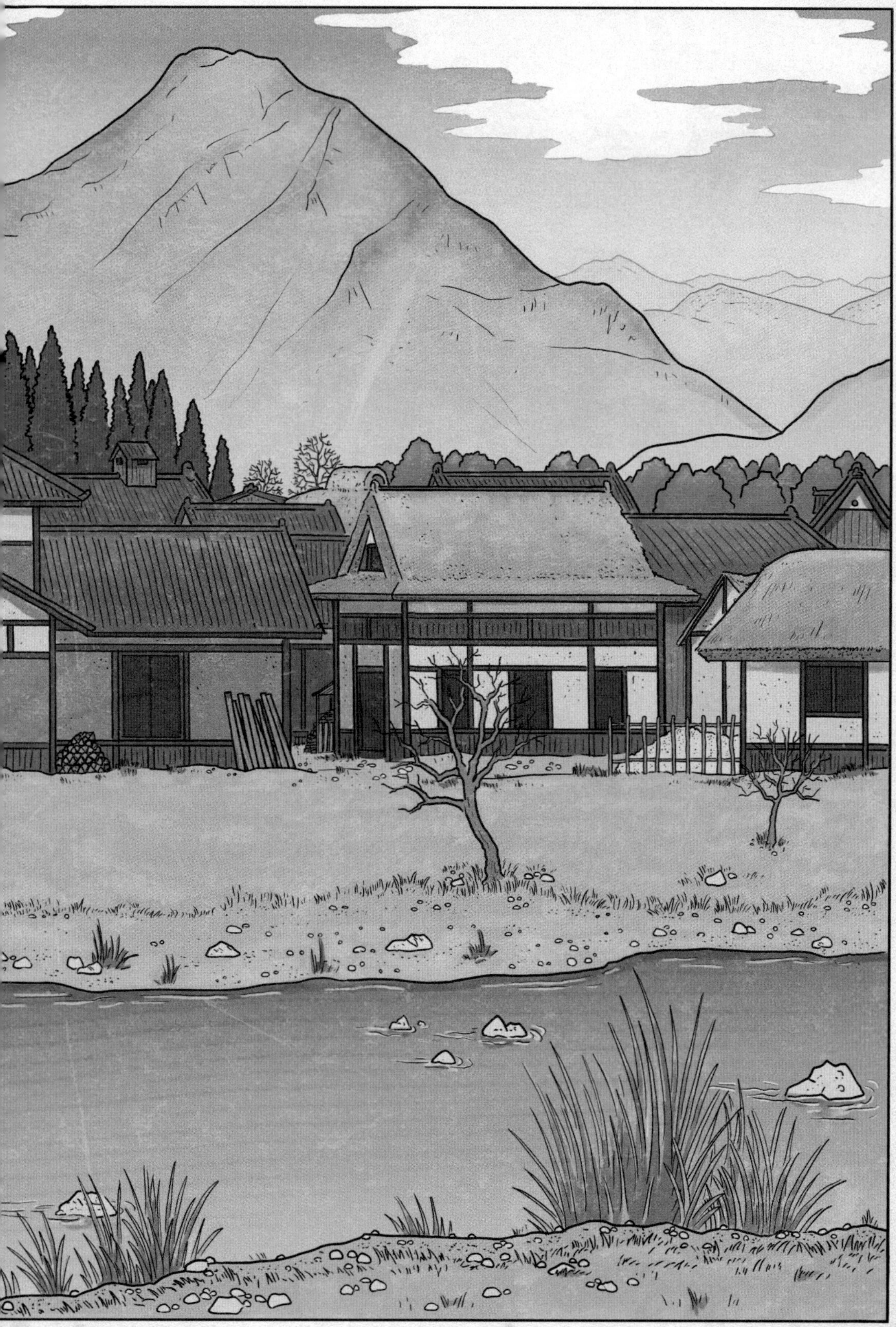

Nurarihyon 滑瓢

TRANSLATION: slippery gourd
ALTERNATE NAMES: nūrihyon
HABITAT: expensive villas, living rooms, brothels; possibly marine in origin
DIET: picky; prefers expensive and luxurious food

APPEARANCE: Nurarihyon is a mysterious and powerful yōkai encountered all across Japan. It is said appearances can be deceiving, and nurarihyon is the perfect illustration of this. Overall, he is rather benign-looking; his head is elongated and gourd-shaped; his face is wizened and wrinkled, resembling a cross between and old man and a catfish; he wears elegant clothing—often a splendid silk kimono or the rich robes of a Buddhist abbot—and carries himself in the quiet manner of a sophisticated gentleman.

BEHAVIOR: The short, comical, elderly nurarihyon is actually the most powerful and elite of all the yōkai. He travels in an ornate palanquin carried by human or yōkai servants, often visiting red light districts but occasionally stopping at mountain villas as well. Nurarihyon is known as *Kaibutsu no Oyadama*—the Supreme Commander of All Monsters. Every yōkai listens to his words and pays him respect, treating him as the elder and leader in all yōkai meetings. Along with otoroshi and nozuchi, nurarihyon leads the procession known as the night parade of one hundred demons through the streets of Japan on dark, rainy nights. He fits the role of supreme commander every bit as much when he interacts with humans as well.

INTERACTIONS: Nurarihyon shows up on evenings when a household is extremely busy. He arrives at homes unexpectedly in his splendid palanquin and slips into the house, unnoticed by anyone. He acts in all respects as if he were the master of the house, helping himself to the family's luxuries such as fine teas and tobacco. His power is so great that even the real owners of the house can do nothing to stop him. In fact, even after they finally notice his presence, the owners believe the nurarihyon to actually be the rightful master of the house. Eventually he leaves just as he came, quietly and politely slipping out of the house and into his palanquin, as the owners of the house obsequiously bow and wave him farewell. Only after he has left does anyone become suspicious of the mysterious old man who just visited.

ORIGIN: As to nurarihyon's origins there is only speculation. The oldest records of his existence are mere sketches and paintings. His name comes from *nurari* ("to slip away") and *hyon* (an onomatopoeia describing floating upwards) written with the kanji for gourd (due to the shape of his head). This connotes a slippery evasiveness—which he employs when posing as master of the house.

In Okayama Prefecture, some evidence links nurarihyon to umi bōzu. There, nurarihyon are globe-shaped sea creatures, about the size of a man's head, which float about in the Seto Inland Sea. When fisherman try to catch one, the sphere sinks down into the water just out of reach, and then bobs back up mockingly. It has been theorized that some of these slippery globes migrate to land, where they gradually gain influence and power, becoming the nurarihyon known throughout the rest of Japan. Whether this theory is the true origin of the Supreme Commander of All Monsters or just one more of his many mysteries has yet to be solved.

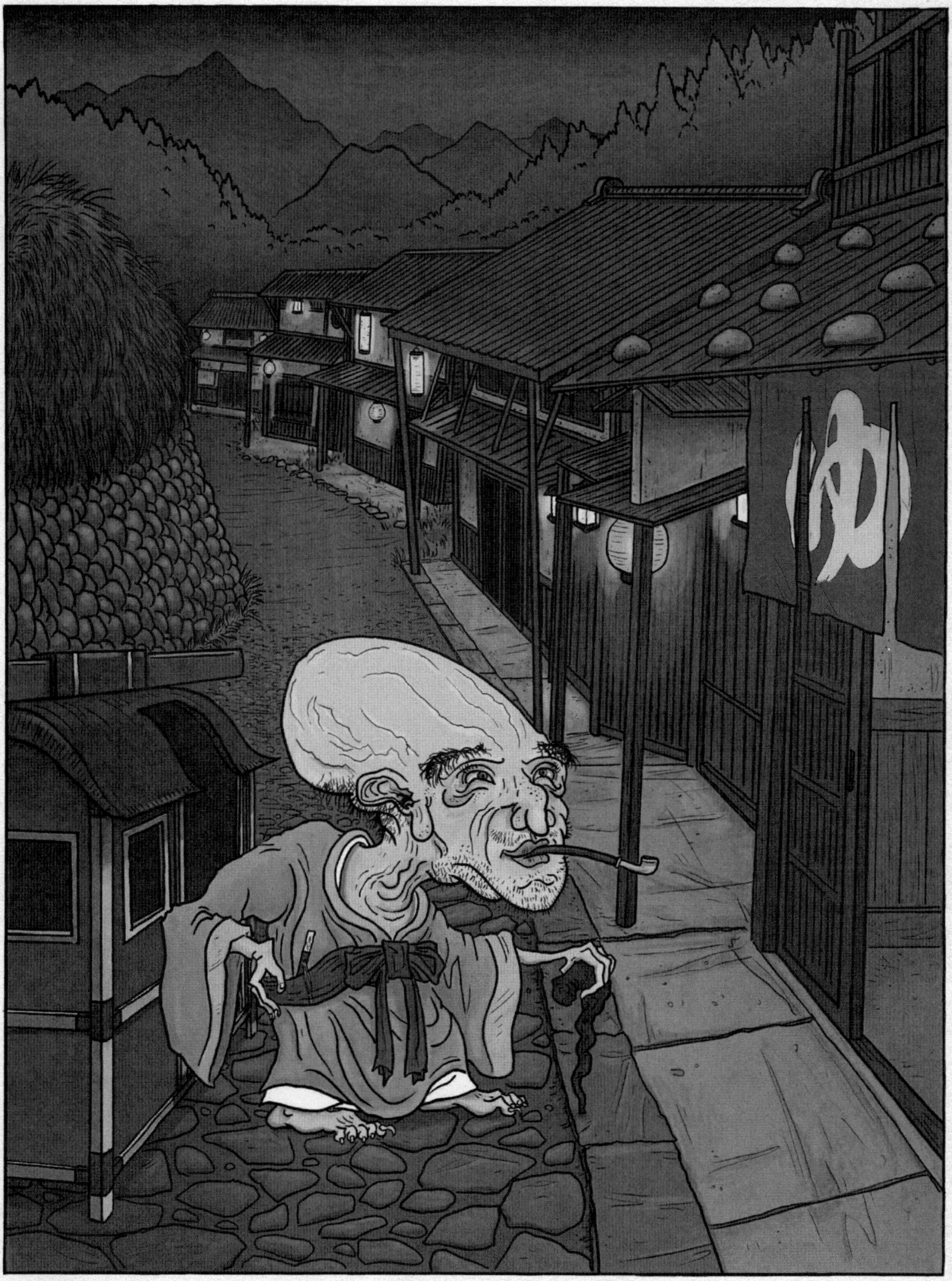
ゆ

OHAGURO BETTARI お歯黒べったり

TRANSLATION: nothing but blackened teeth
ALTERNATE NAMES: often referred to as a kind of nopperabō
HABITAT: dark streets near shrines
DIET: unknown

APPEARANCE: Late at night, a disturbing yōkai dressed in beautiful wedding clothes can be seen loitering near temples and shrines. She calls single young men over to her, and they are seldom able to resist her charms. Until of course, they get too close....

From behind, an ohaguro bettari looks like a beautiful woman wearing a kimono—often looking like a newlywed in her bridal gown. She appears at twilight outside of a temple, or inside a man's own house, disguised as his wife. At first, she conceals her head, or turns away from any viewers. Any man who comes closer to get a better look is surprised when she turns to reveal her face: an ugly, white, featureless dome slathered in thick makeup, containing nothing but a huge, gaping mouth full of blackened teeth. She follows up this initial shock with a horrible cackle, sending the man running away and screaming in terror.

ORIGIN: Ohaguro bettari are similar to a yōkai called nopperabō in appearance and demeanor. Like nopperabō they are often blamed on shape-shifting pranksters like kitsune, tanuki, or mujina looking to have a laugh at the expense of an unwitting human. It has also been suggested that they are the ghosts of ugly women who were unable to marry. Accurate eye-witness reports are hard to come by due to the embarrassment of the victims at having fallen for such an obvious gag. However as no deaths or injuries (other than to pride) have been attributed to ohaguro bettari, and because sightings are rare, a mischievous shape-shifting animal yōkai seems to be a plausible explanation.

TOOTH BLACKENING

For more than a thousand years, *ohaguro*—the custom of dyeing one's teeth black—was an aristocratic fashion. This was accomplished via a special "tea" made from vinegar and oxidized iron filings. This brew was swished around in the mouth to stain the teeth dark black. Ohaguro was begun at an early age, taking many years for the teeth to develop a deep, permanent black color. It was popular among upper-class married women and is frequently depicted in old woodblock prints.

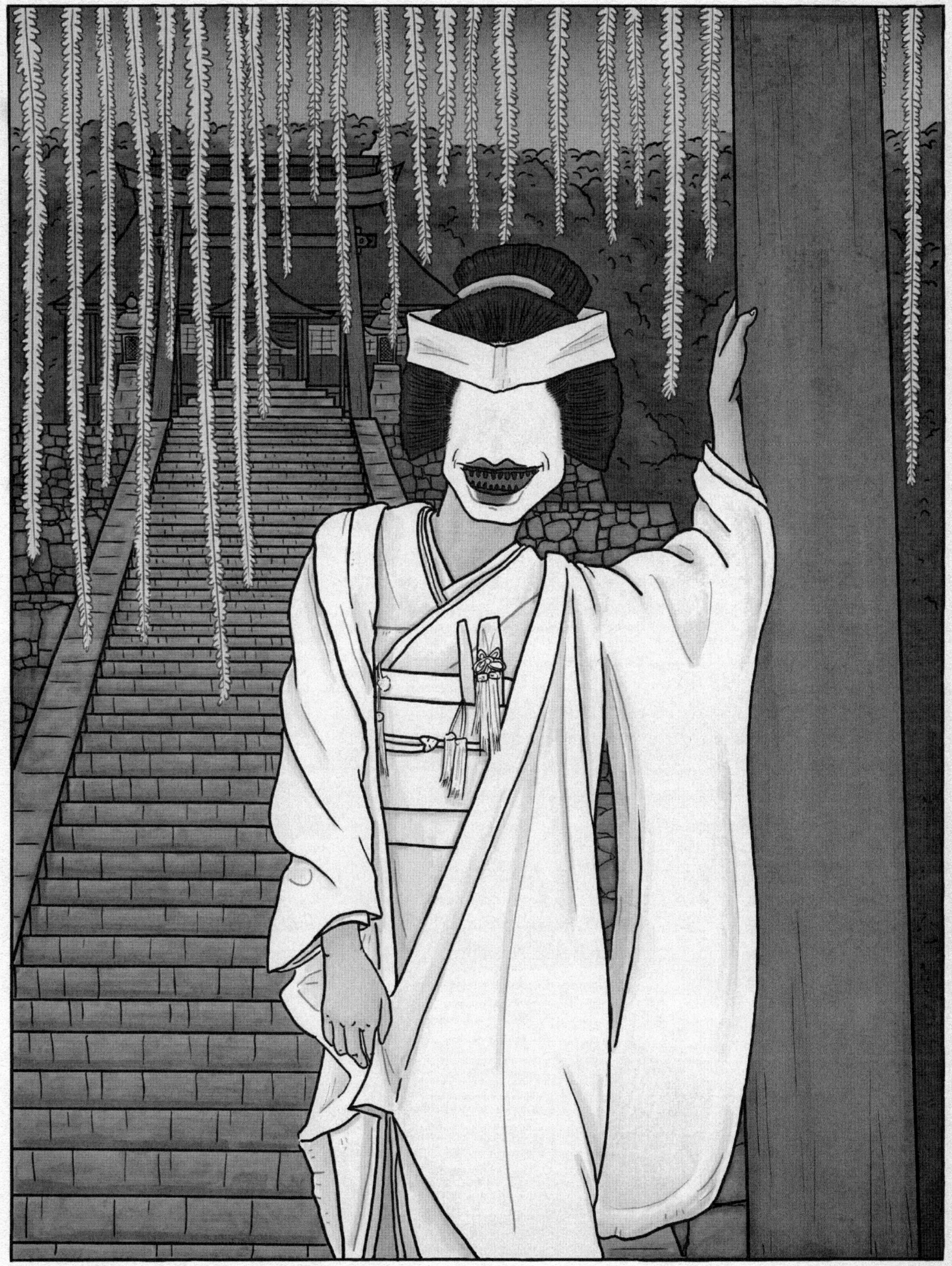

Rokurokubi 轆轤首

TRANSLATION: pulley neck
HABITAT: occurs in ordinary women; also frequently found in brothels
DIET: regular food by day, lamp oil by night

APPEARANCE: By day, rokurokubi appear to be ordinary women. By night, however, their bodies sleep while their necks stretch to incredible lengths and roam around freely. Sometimes their heads attack small animals; sometime they lick up lamp oil with their long tongues; and sometimes they just cause mischief by scaring nearby people.

ORIGIN: Unlike most yōkai which are born as monsters, rokurokubi and their close relatives nukekubi are former humans—transformed by a curse resulting from some evil or misdeed. Perhaps they sinned against the gods or nature, or perhaps they were unfaithful to their husbands. In many cases, their husbands or fathers actually committed the sin. By some cruel twist of fate the men escape punishment and the women receive the curse instead. In any case, the rokurokubi curse only affects women.

LEGENDS: A lord noticed that the oil in his lamps was vanishing at an alarming rate, and suspected one of his servant girls might be a rokurokubi. He decided to spy upon the girl. After she had fallen asleep, he crept into her room and watched over her. Soon he noticed vapors and ectoplasm forming around her chest and neck. A little while later, the servant girl rolled over in her sleep, however only her body moved! The head stayed in its place, and the neck lay stretched out between the two. The next day he fired her. She was fired from every place at which she subsequently worked. The poor girl never understood why she had such back luck with her employment. She never found out that she was a rokurokubi.

An old tale from Tōtōmi Province (Shizuoka Prefecture) tells of a monk who eloped with a young lady named Oyotsu. While traveling, Oyotsu became sick. Treating her would have used up all of their travel money, so the monk murdered Oyotsu and stole the remaining money. On his travels, he stayed at an inn owned by a man with a beautiful daughter. The wicked monk shared a bed with the innkeeper's daughter, and during the night her neck stretched and her face changed into that of Oyotsu. She angrily accused him of murdering her. The next morning the monk, regretting his evil deeds, confessed the murder of Oyotsu to the innkeeper. The monk also told the innkeeper what he had seen the night before. The innkeeper confessed that he, too, had murdered his wife for her money. He used the money to build his inn, and as a punishment his own daughter was transformed into a rokurokubi. Afterwards, the monk rejoined his temple, built a grave for Oyotsu, and prayed for her soul every day. What happened to the innkeeper's daughter is never mentioned.

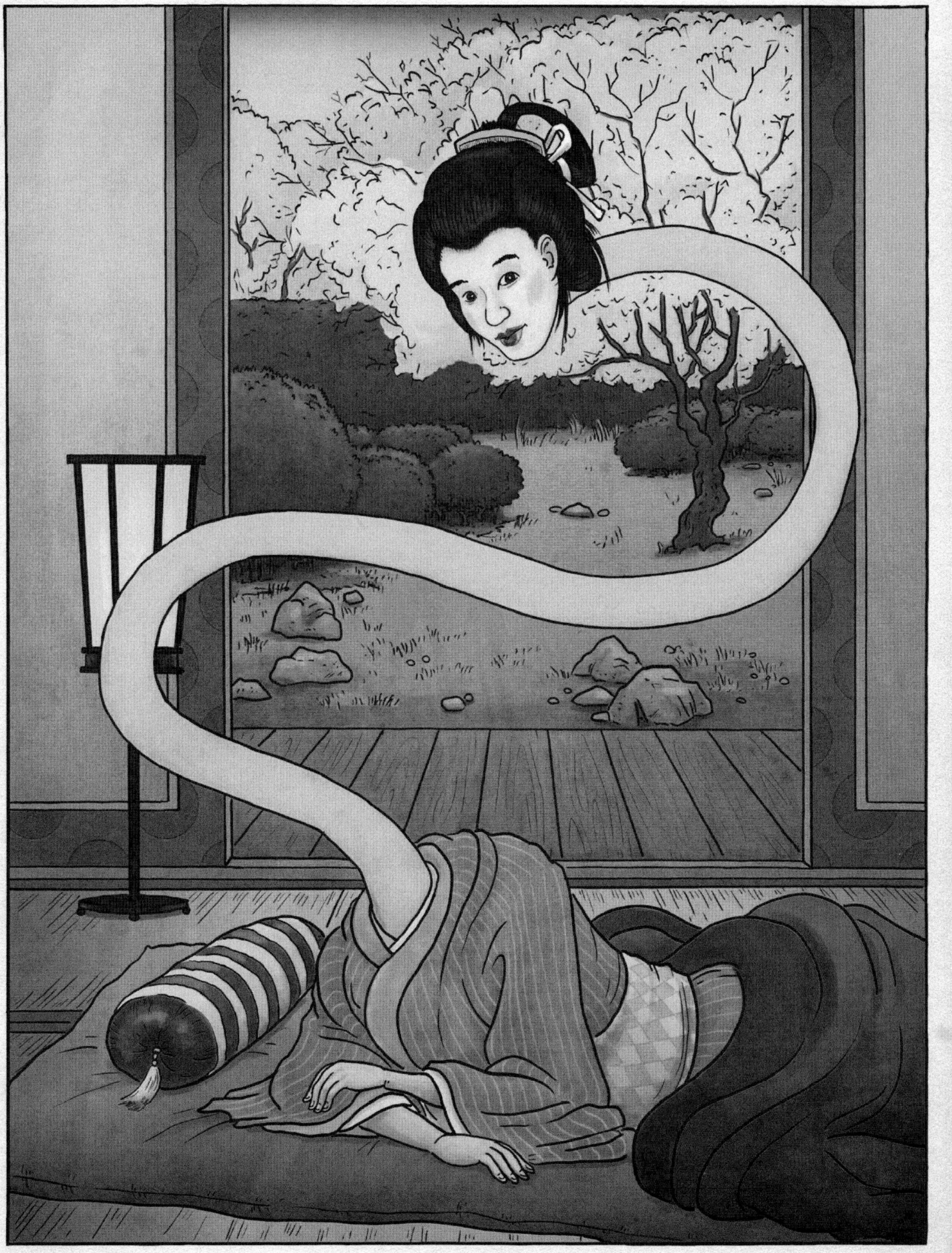

Nukekubi 抜け首

TRANSLATION: removable neck; detached head
ALTERNATE NAMES: frequently referred to as rokurokubi
HABITAT: occurs in ordinary women
DIET: regular food by day, blood by night

APPEARANCE: Nukekubi are a variant type of rokurokubi. They are similar in most respects, except that a nukekubi's head detaches itself completely from its body rather than elongating like a rokurokubi's neck. Because their heads detach, they can travel further distances than the rokurokubi.

BEHAVIOR: Nukekubi possess a thirst for blood, and are more violent than rokurokubi. Their flying head sucks the blood of victims like a vampire. Nukekubi also brutally bite humans and animals to death.

ORIGIN: Like the rokurokubi, being a nukekubi is considered a curse. Edo period scientists believed that nukekubi suffered from an infliction similar to somnambulism; only instead of walking about at night the patient's entire soul and head depart from the body. Uncured, this curse has the potential to tear a family apart, particularly due to its violent nature. Treatments for the curse of the rokurokubi and nukekubi have been long sought after—particularly because these women can often pass their curse on to their daughters who shows signs as they mature. Afflicted girls were sold off to live in brothels or human circuses, or forced to commit suicide in order to preserve their families' honor.

LEGENDS: A famous account from Echizen Province (Fukui Prefecture) tells of a young woman afflicted with the curse of the nukekubi. Her head flew about the capital city at night, chasing young men through the streets all the way back to their houses. Locked out, the head would scratch and bite their doors and gates during the night and leave deep gashes in the wood. When the young girl eventually discovered her curse, she was so ashamed that she asked her husband for a divorce. She ritually cut off all of her hair in repentance and committed suicide. She believed it was better to die than to live the rest of her life as a monster.

According to lore from Hitachi, a man married to a nukekubi heard from a peddler that the liver of a white-haired dog could remove the curse. He had such a dog, and killed it and fed its liver to his wife. Sure enough she was cured of the affliction. However, her curse was still passed on to her daughter, whose flying head took to biting white dogs to death. Other accounts claim that by removing the sleeping body to a safe place during the night, the head will not be able return, and will eventually die—however this is not a cure that most families are willing to try.

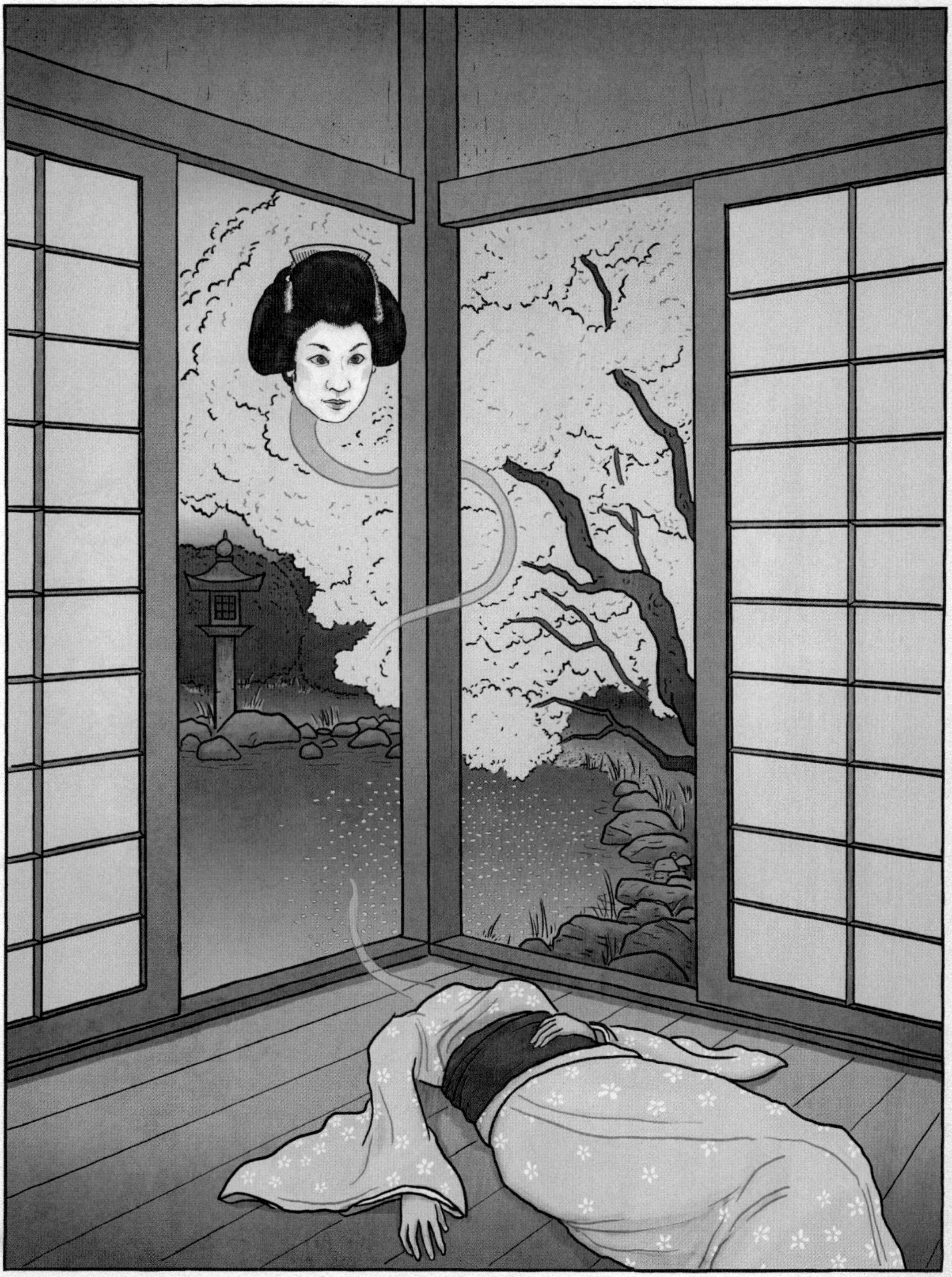

Futakuchi onna 二口女

TRANSLATION: two-mouthed woman
HABITAT: usually occurs in married women
DIET: as a normal person, only twice as much

APPEARANCE: Families who notice that their food stocks are shrinking at an alarming rate, while the women in their houses hardly eat a bite, may be the victims of a futakuchi onna. Futakuchi onna appear as regular women until their terrible secret is revealed: in the back of their skulls—buried beneath long, thick hair—is a second mouth, full of teeth and with large, fat lips. This second mouth is ravenous, and uses long strands of its hair-like tentacles to gorge itself on any food it can find.

ORIGIN: In the folk tales of Japan's eastern regions, futakuchi onna are most often thought to be shape-changed yamauba posing as young women. In the western regions they are frequently shape-changed kumo, or magical spiders. In the other tales they are the result of curses brought about by wicked deeds, similar to rokurokubi. In each story, regardless of its true nature, this yōkai is used as a punishment upon a greedy man or woman for wickedness and extreme parsimony.

LEGENDS: One story tells of how in a small rural village in Fukushima there lived a stingy miser. Because he could not bear the thought of paying for food to support a family, the miser lived entirely by himself. One day he met a woman who did not eat anything at all, and he immediately took her for his wife. The miser was thrilled with her because she never ate a thing and was still a hard worker. However, his stores of rice steadily decreased, and he could not figure why, for he never saw his wife eat.

One day, the miser pretended to leave for work. In truth he stayed behind to spy on his new wife. As the miser watched from a hidden location, his wife untied her hair, and revealed a second mouth on the back of her head, complete with ghastly lips and teeth. Her hair reached out with tentacle-like stalks and began to scoop rice balls into the second mouth, which cooed out with pleasure in a vulgar, raspy voice.

The miser was horrified and resolved to divorce his wife as soon as possible. However, she learned of his plan before he could act on it, and trapped him in a bathtub and carried him off into the mountains. The miser managed to escape. He hid in a heavily scented lily marsh where the futakuchi onna could not find him.

Another story tells of a wicked stepmother who always gave plenty of food to her own daughter, but never enough to her stepdaughter. Gradually the stepdaughter grew sicker and sicker, until she starved to death. Forty-nine days later, the wicked stepmother was afflicted with a terrible headache. The back of her head split open, and lips, teeth, and a tongue formed. This new mouth ached with debilitating pain until it was fed, and it shrieked in the voice of the dead stepdaughter. From then on the stepmother always had to feed both of her mouths, and always felt the hunger pangs of the stepdaughter she murdered.

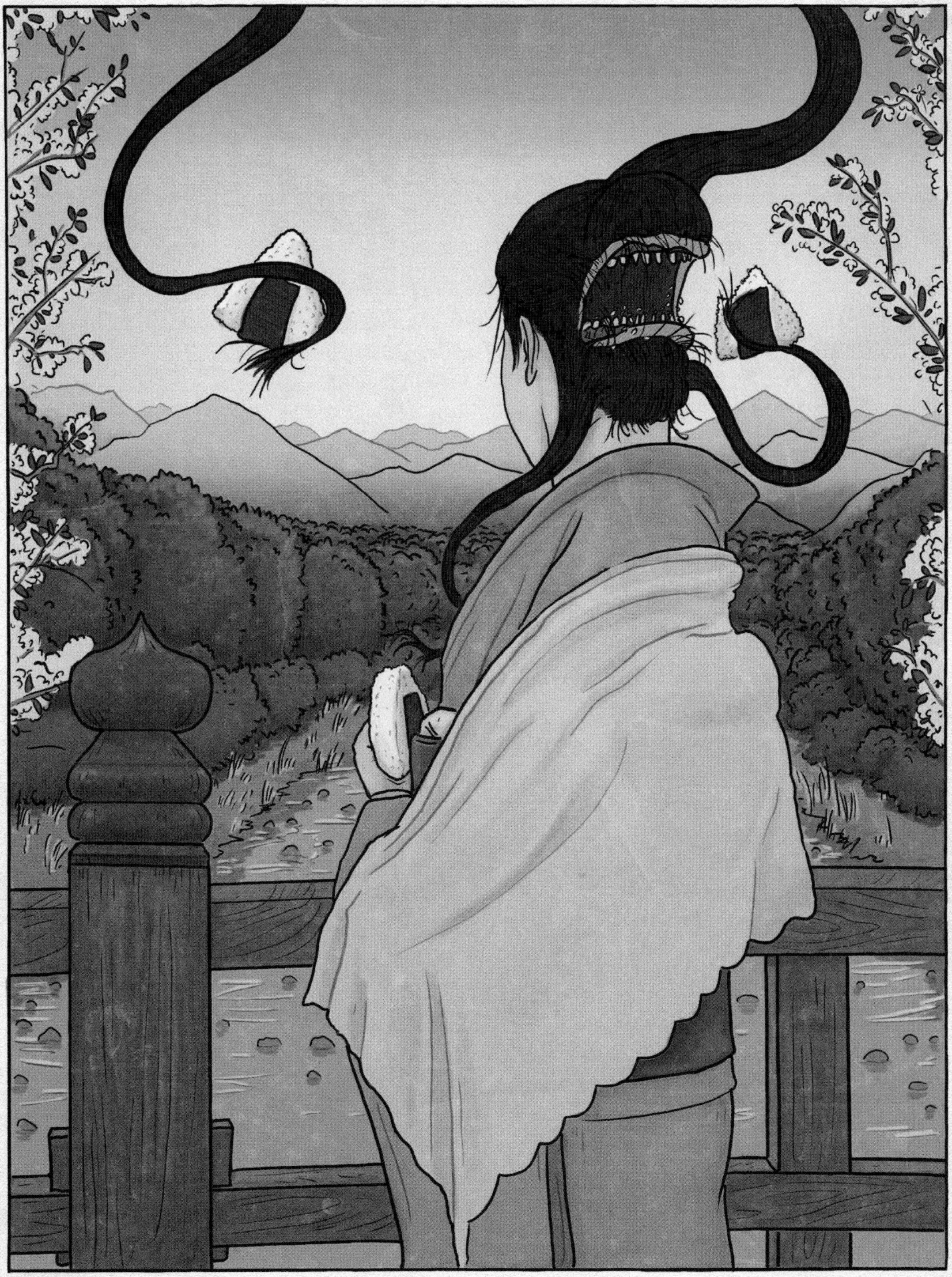

Hari onago 針女子

Translation: hook girl
Alternate names: hari onna ("hook woman")
Habitat: streets and alleys; found on Shikoku
Diet: young, virile men

Appearance: The fearsome yōkai known as hari onago appears at night on the roads of the island of Shikoku. In the dark, they are indistinguishable from ordinary young women, unusual only for their loose, disheveled hair. Upon closer inspection, the tip of each hair is fitted with a needle-like, barbed hook—although if you are close enough to notice these hooks, it is probably already too late.

Interactions: Hari onago wander the streets searching for victims—usually young, single men walking alone. When a hari onago comes across a suitable man, she smiles coyly at him. If the smile is returned, she attacks: she releases her hair, and the barbed ends lash out with blinding speed and a will of their own, sinking deep into her victim's flesh. A hari onago's strength is so great that even the strongest man can be overpowered by her hooks. Once her victim is ensnared and rendered helpless, she rips him into pieces with her hooks and devours the remains.

It is technically possible for a very fast runner to escape a hari onago, providing his home is close enough and has a sturdy door or gate. If he can get himself safely indoors before her hooks catch him, he may be able to survive until sunrise—when yōkai vanish. The scars and gouges she leaves in the wooden door frame remain as a testament to her viciousness, and as a cautionary tale to young men not to pick up strange girls.

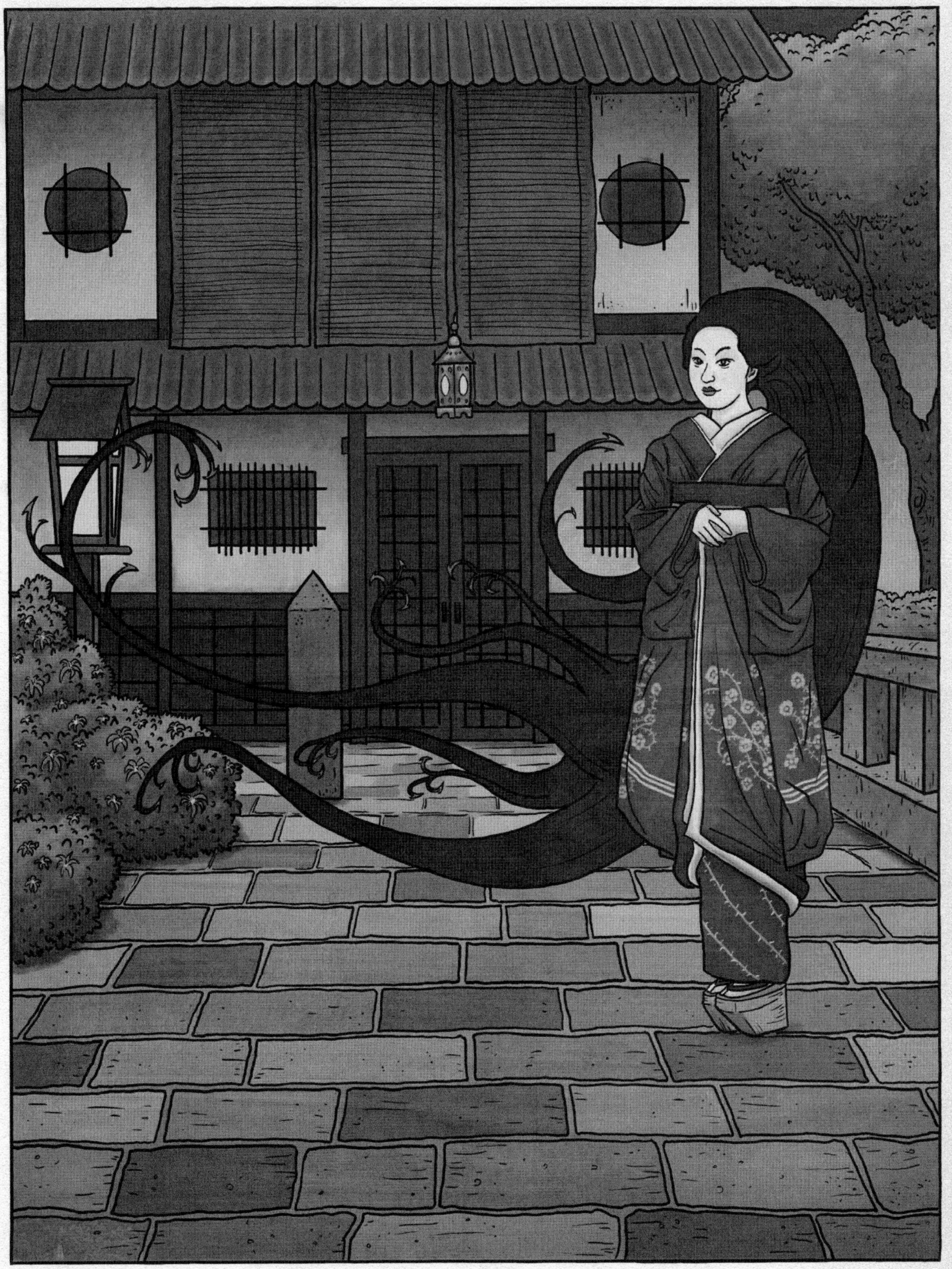

KUCHISAKE ONNA 口裂け女

TRANSLATION: slit-mouthed woman
HABITAT: dimly lit streets and alleys
DIET: none; though enjoys hard candy

APPEARANCE: The kuchisake onna is the ghost of a woman who was mutilated and has come back to wreak vengeance on the world. Her name comes from the deep, bloody gash which runs across her face, grinning from ear to ear. She appears at night to lone travelers on the road, covering her grizzly mouth with a cloth mask, a fan, or a handkerchief.

INTERACTIONS: Kuchisake onna sneaks up on her victims in the dark and asks them if they think she is beautiful: "*Watashi, kirei?*" If the victim answers yes, she pulls off her mask and reveals a red, blood-dripping, grotesque mouth. Then she asks in a grisly voice if they still think she is beautiful: "*Kore demo?*" If her victim answers no or screams in terror, she slashes him from ear to ear in an imitation of her own mutilation. If he lies and answers yes a second time, she walks away—only to follow her target home and slaughter him brutally that night.

ORIGIN: The spirits of the dead who were killed in particularly violent manners—abused wives, tortured captives, defeated enemies—often do not rest well. The kuchisake onna is thought to be one such woman. However, during the Edo period, a large number of kuchisake onna attacks were blamed on shape-changed kitsune playing pranks on young men. During the 20th century, the blame began to be placed on ghosts, serial killers, and simple mass hysteria. This resulted in an explosion of kuchisake onna sightings over Japan. Over the years, clever young people claim to have outsmarted kuchisake onna by delivering quick, confusing answers, or by throwing money or hard candy at them. This buys enough time to escape from the kuchisake onna's wrath and lose her in the darkness.

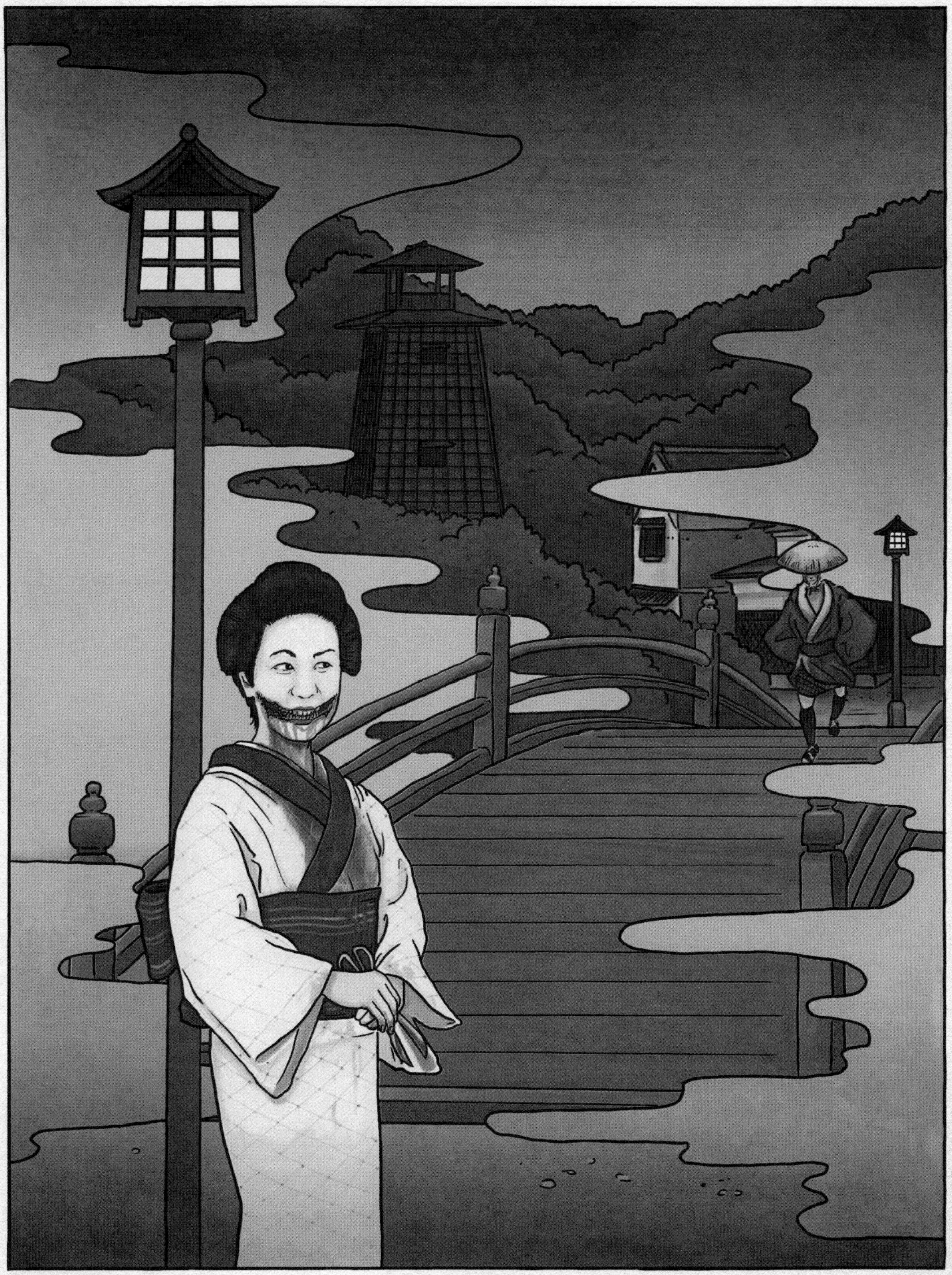

Hone onna 骨女

TRANSLATION: bone woman
HABITAT: dark streets, alleys, graveyards
DIET: none; though has a large sexual appetite

APPEARANCE: Not all who die turn into vengeful beings of grudge and jealousy. Hone onna retain an undying love that persists long after their flesh has rotted away. This allows them to continue to be with the object of their affection despite having died. These ghosts appear as they did in life—young, beautiful women in their prime. Only those unclouded by love or with strong religious faith are able to penetrate their disguise and see their true form: a rotting, fetid, skeletal corpse returned from the grave.

INTERACTIONS: At night, a hone onna rises from the grave and wanders to the house of her former lover. Her appearance shocks those who believed her to be dead. This shock quickly turns into a joy that blinds the hone onna's lover to any clues that something might be wrong. Even the hone onna herself may not know of her condition. She is driven only by love. She exists as a ghost only to continue the love she had in life. The hone onna spends the night and leaves in the morning. This unholy coupling can continue for days, or even weeks, without being noticed. However, there is a price to be paid. Each night she drains some of her lover's life force, and he grows ever sicker and weaker. Without intervention, he will eventually die, joining his lover forever in death's embrace.

In most cases, a friend or a servant of her lover will see through the hone onna's illusion and alert someone to her true identity. Though her human lover may be repulsed by her when the truth is revealed to him, the ghost may not realizes her condition and continue to visit every night. A home can be warded with prayers and magic charms against entry by ghosts, but they only work as long as the master of the house wills them to. As the hone onna's body decays further, her enchanting allure only increases. Eventually most men succumb and let her into their homes one last time, sacrificing their own lives to the ghost of the woman they loved.

LEGENDS: Perhaps the most famous hone onna is Otsuyu from *Botan Dōrō*, or *The Tale of the Peony Lantern. Botan Dōrō* was introduced to Japan in the 17th century from an old Chinese ghost story. Over the centuries, it has been adapted into puppet shows, kabuki plays, rakugo, and films, and remains an influential ghost story today.

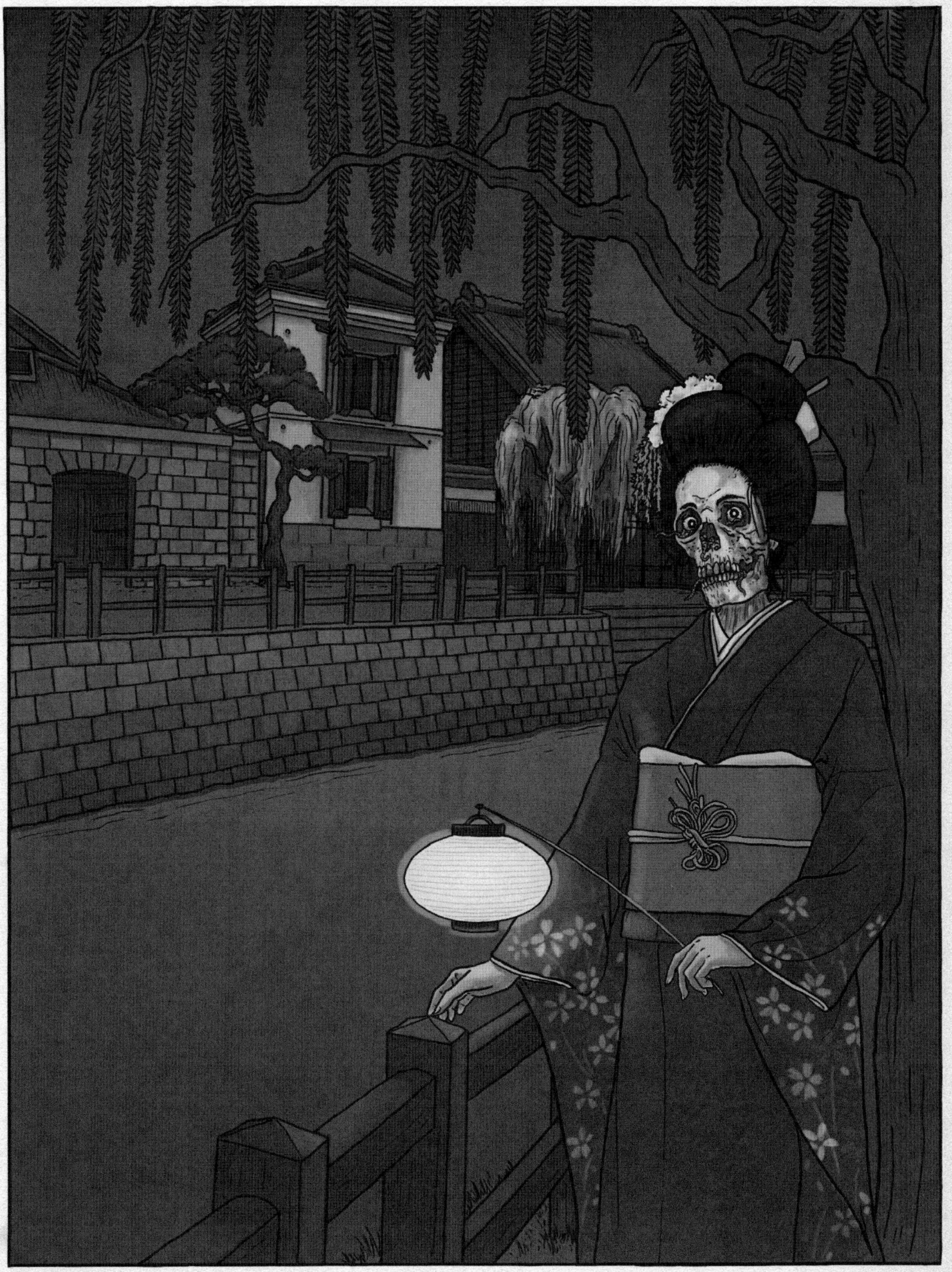

Kerakera onna 倩兮女

TRANSLATION: cackling woman
HABITAT: alleys near red light districts
DIET: none

APPEARANCE: Kerakera onna are gigantic, horrid yōkai found in red light districts. Their name comes from the cackling sound of their laughter. Kerakera onna appear as enormous, middle-aged women in colorful brothel kimonos, with thick make-up and slathered-on lipstick. They skulk around in alleyways and on empty roads, dancing, laughing, and mocking the profession that worked them to death. They are rarely seen outside of the pleasure district—the place responsible for their creation.

INTERACTIONS: When a man passes a lonely street or alley haunted by a kerakera onna, she unleashes a horrible, shrill cackle that can only be heard by him. A weak-hearted man faints right on the spot, but one who has the constitution to flee finds that no matter where he goes, or who he turns to, the cackle echoes in his ears; nobody else can hear it. Eventually these men are driven insane by the incessant laughing—repayment for the lifetime of abuse the kerakera onna went through.

ORIGIN: During the Edo period, the average lifespan of a prostitute was only 23 years. The demands and hardships of such a life were too much for most to bear. Work hours were long and difficult, pay was low, and abuse was commonplace, both from clients and employers. Very few women made it to middle age. Like most long-lived things in Japan, those who made it were said to become extremely powerful. When aged prostitutes died after serving in such a painful world for so long, their ghosts could not pass quickly and easily on to the next life. Instead, they became kerakera onna.

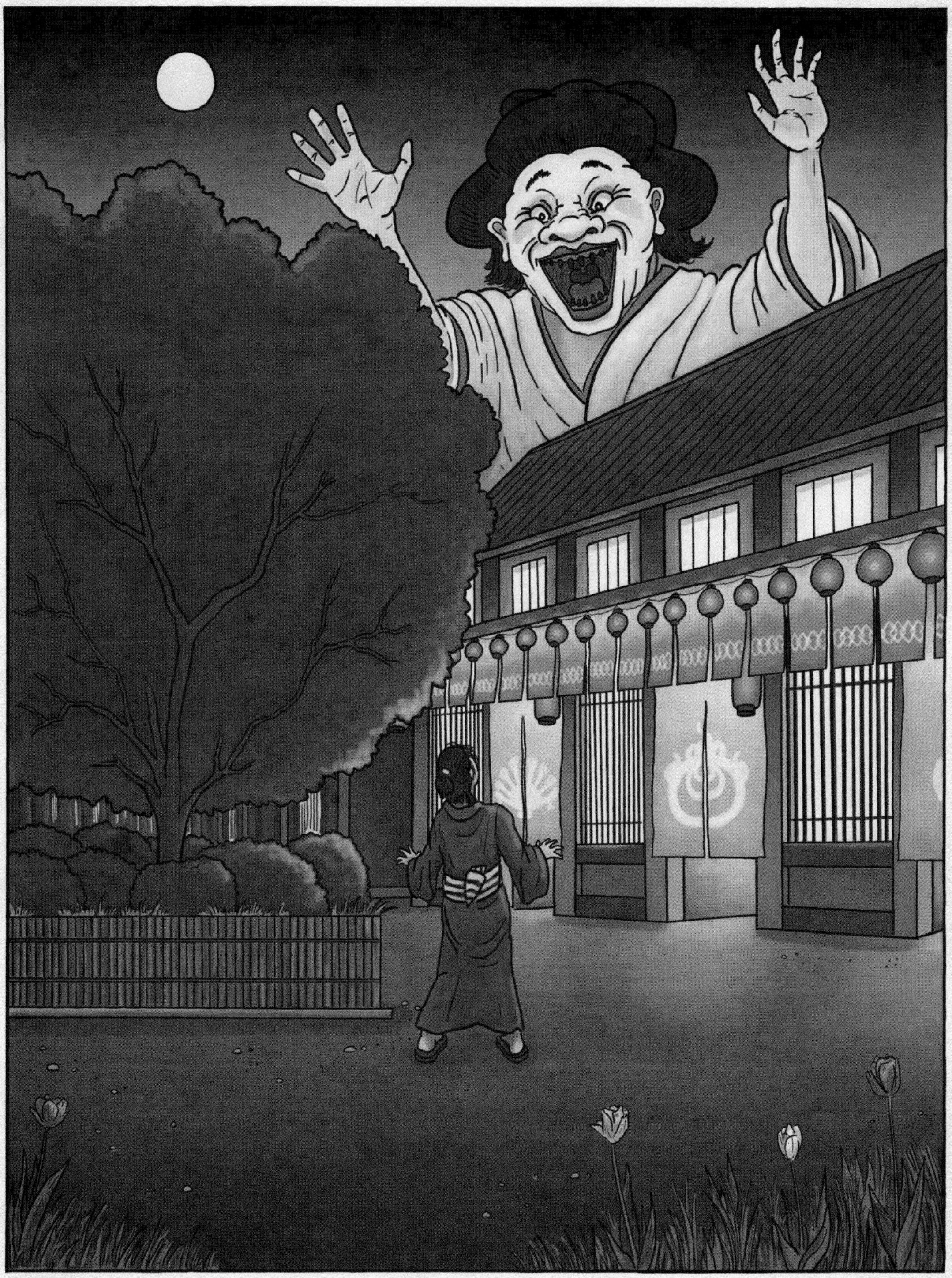

Taka onna 高女

TRANSLATION: tall woman
ALTERNATE NAMES: takajo
HABITAT: red light districts
DIET: as a normal person

APPEARANCE: Taka onna appear as ordinary, homely human women most of the time. But they have the power to elongate their bodies and grow to several meters in height. Like other brothel yōkai, they are rarely seen outside of the red light districts, but are fairly common yōkai nonetheless. Sightings of these yōkai peaked during the Edo period and continued up to the post-war period—the time when brothels and *yūkaku* ("pleasure districts") were at their height in Japan.

BEHAVIOR: Taka onna are frequently spotted peering into the second-story windows of brothels and homes where romantic liaisons are taking place. Their activities are generally limited to peeping into windows. Though they rarely attack humans physically, taka onna do enjoy scaring and harassing both men and women who frequent the pleasure districts, jealous of the physical pleasure they were never able to know in life.

ORIGIN: Taka onna were originally ordinary women who were too unattractive to marry (or to find work in the red light districts which they haunt). Through jealousy, they became twisted and corrupted, and transformed into ugly, malicious monsters that prey on others' sexual energy.

LEGENDS: Taka onna encounters were often the subject of bawdy anecdotes, as they generally revolve around trips to the pleasure districts. In one account, though, a woodcutter describes how he discovered that his own wife was a taka onna. His child mysteriously disappeared one day, and over a short period his servants also began to disappear one by one. Unable to figure out what was happening, the woodcutter began to suspect his wife. One night while pretending to sleep in bed, he witnessed his wife jump into a well. She then elongated her body and climbed back out. The woodcutter fled into the mountains, and never returned to his home.

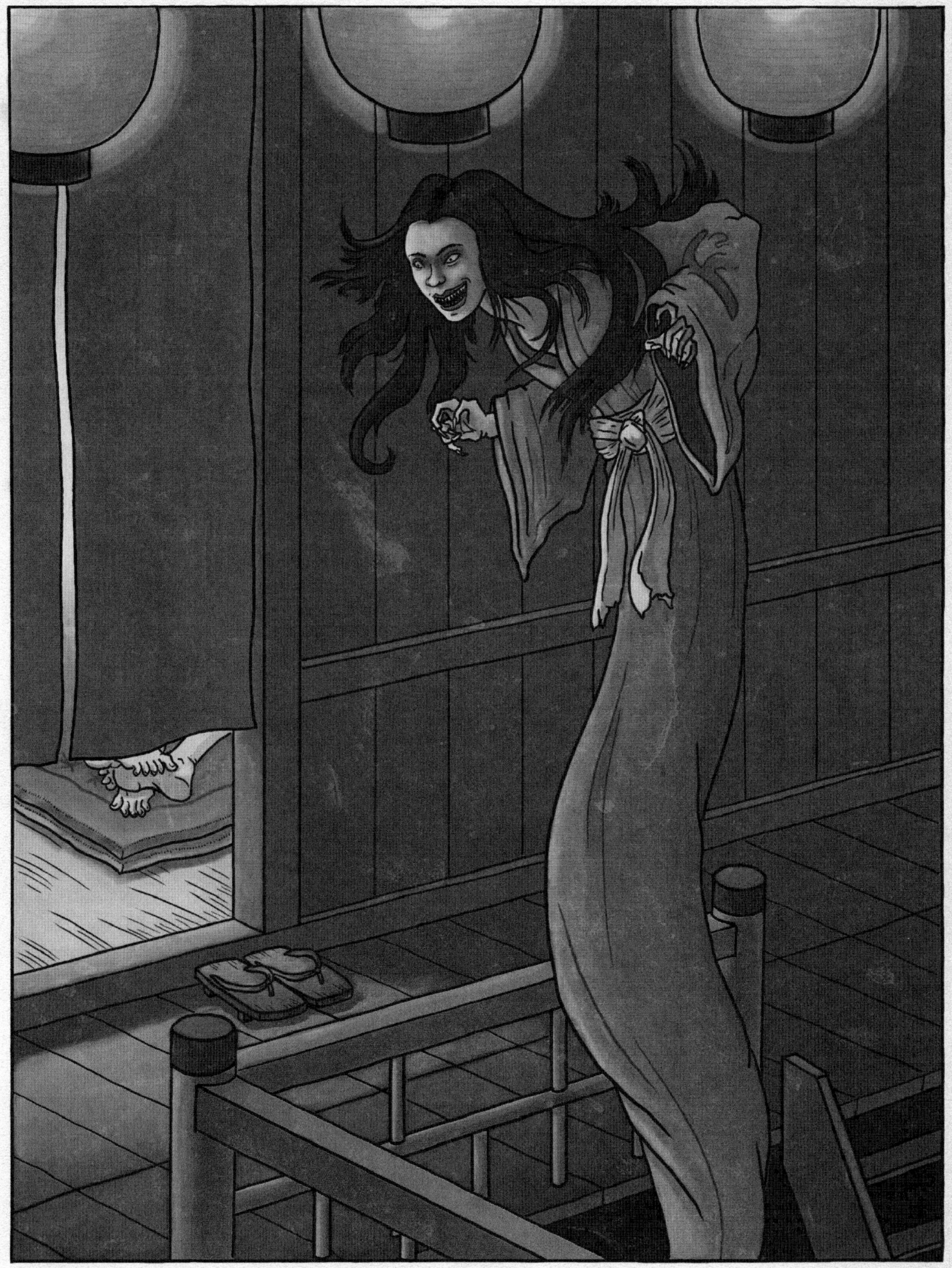

Ame onna 雨女

TRANSLATION: rain woman
Alternative Names: ame onba
HABITAT: dark streets and alleys; formerly clouds and holy mountains
DIET: unknown; possibly rain, or children

APPEARANCE: Ame onna are a class of yōkai that appear on rainy days and nights. They summon rain wherever they go, and are blamed for kidnapping and spiriting away children. They appear as depraved, haggish women, soaked with rainwater. They lick the rain off of their hands and arms like wild animals.

BEHAVIOR: Ame onna are related to minor rain deities. Unlike the gods, however, ame onna are not benevolent. Though the rains they bring might save a village in drought or bring fortune to farmers, they have a more sinister purpose—under the cover of the rain, ame onna wander the villages looking for newborn girls. If they should find a child born that night, they snatch it and carry it off into the darkness, spiriting it away to another world.

Mothers who have their babies snatched away sometimes transform into ame onna themselves, out of grief and despair. Having lost their minds, these transformed women roam the streets at night with large sacks hoping to replace what was stolen. They sneak into houses where crying children can be heard, and steal them away from their homes into the night.

ORIGIN: Ame onna go back to the ancient folk religions of Japan and China. The rains were said to be brought by benevolent gods and goddesses who lived as clouds by morning and as rain by night, forever traveling between heaven and earth. Legend has it that some of these rain-bringing goddesses became corrupted and devolved into evil yōkai. They abandoned their divinity to live among mortals and prey upon them.

RAIN WOMEN AND MEN

These days, it's not uncommon to hear somebody called ame onna or ame otoko (for men) in daily conversation. This term refers to unlucky people who seem to bring rain with them wherever they go, ruining outdoor events and generally spoiling good moods. But this colloquialism is not related to yōkai. The opposite terms, hare onna and hare otoko, refer to those people for whom the sun always seems to shine whenever they go to outdoor events.

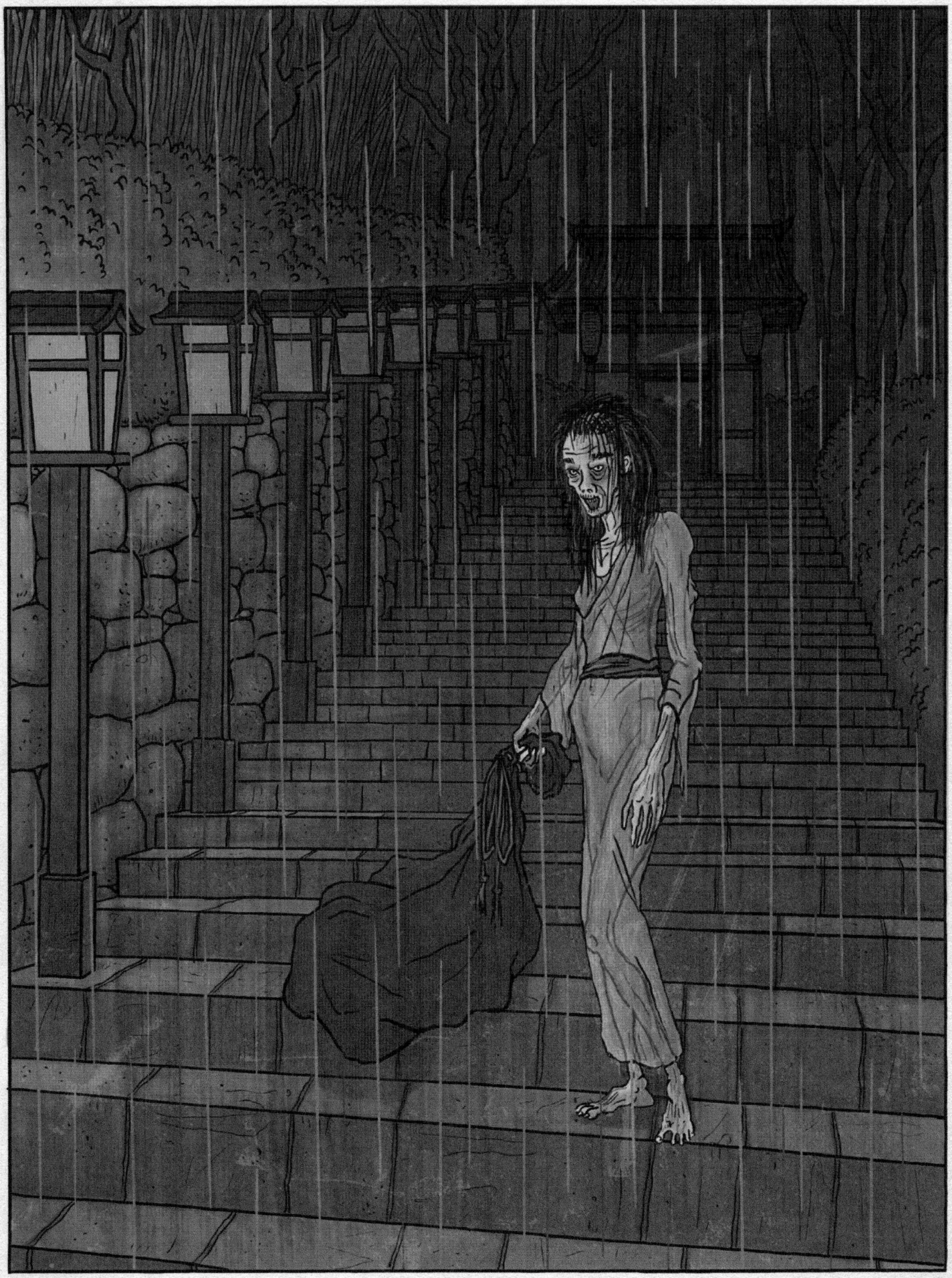

BETOBETOSAN べとべとさん

TRANSLATION: onomatopoeic; from the sound of footsteps
ALTERNATE NAMES: bishagatsuku
HABITAT: alleys and narrow, sloped roads; only appears at night
DIET: fear

APPEARANCE: Betobetosan are formless specters, and are recognizable only by their telltale sound—the *"beto beto"* clacking of wooden clogs.

INTERACTIONS: People who walk the streets alone at night might encounter these harmless, but nonetheless disturbing, yōkai. They synchronize their pace with walkers and follow them as long as they can, getting closer and closer with every step. For the victims, this can be traumatic. The haunting sound of footsteps follows them wherever they go, but when they turn around, there is nothing there.

Though betobetosan can be disconcerting, they are not dangerous. Once you realize you are being followed by a betobetosan, simply step to the side of the road and say "After you, betobetosan." That is enough to escape from this yōkai. The footsteps will carry on ahead and soon vanish from earshot, allowing you to continue in peace.

In northern Fukui Prefecture, a betobetosan which appears during cold winter sleet storms is known as bishagatsuku. Its name comes from the *"bisha bisha"* sound its phantom feet make in the slush-filled streets.

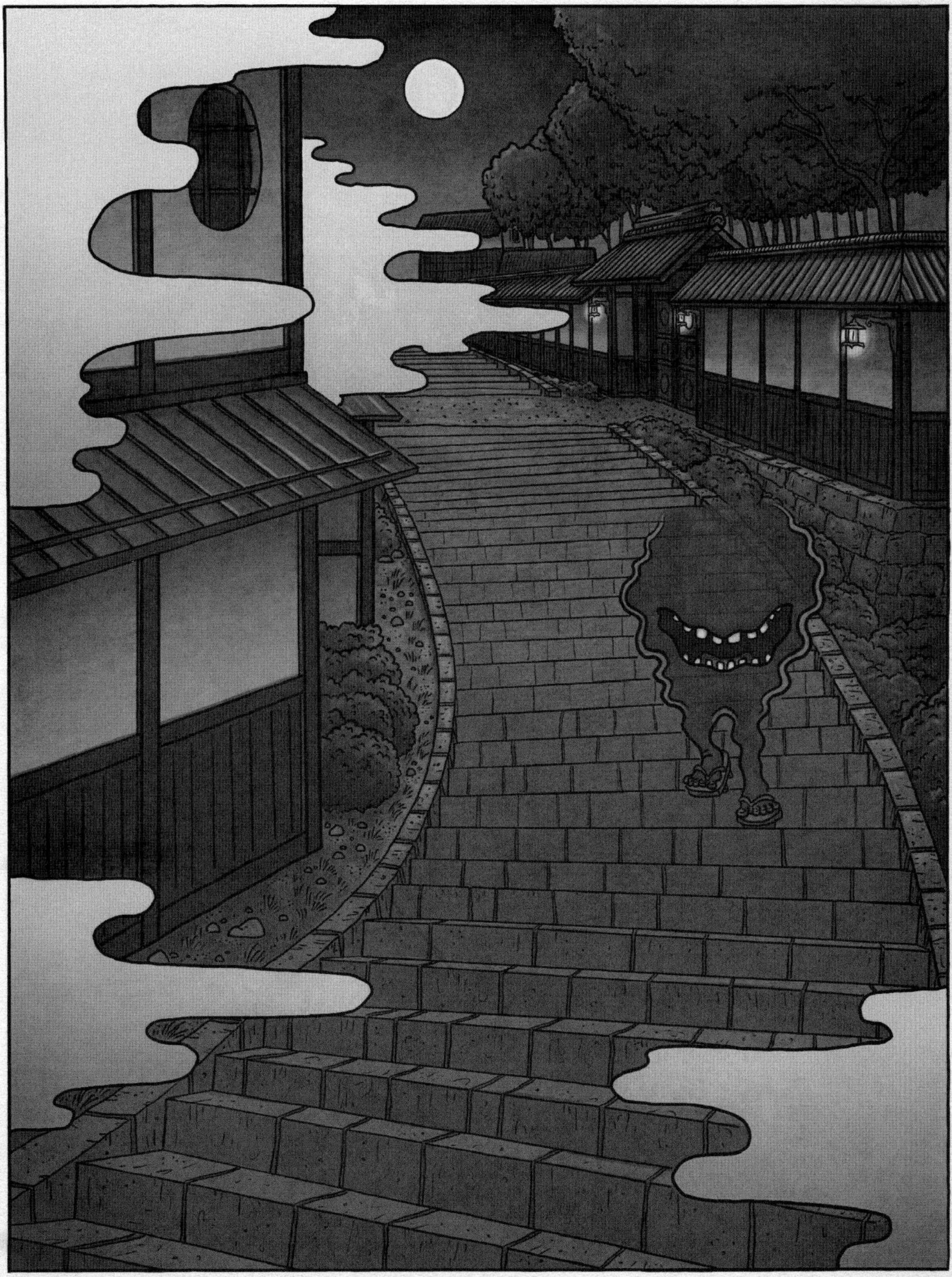

DOROTABŌ 泥田坊

TRANSLATION: muddy rice field monk
HABITAT: unused, overgrown fields
DIET: none; survives on vengeance alone

APPEARANCE: Dorotabō are the transformed ghosts of old men who toiled hard on their rice fields, only to see them lie in waste by neglectful owners after their death. They appear as one-eyed, three-fingered humanoid figures rising out of the mud at night. It is said that the five fingers of the human hand represent three vices and two virtues: anger, greed, ignorance, wisdom, and compassion. The ghostly dorotabō appears with only the three fingers representing the vices. It is a spirit of vengeance and rage—angry at the ignorance and greed that now shame its life's work.

BEHAVIOR: Dorotabō roam the overgrown fields, calling out in a mournful voice, "Give me back my rice field!" They haunt their fields after nightfall, disturbing the new inhabitants of their lands and preventing their sleep. Dorotabō continue haunting until the wasteful owners changes their ways or give up and flee, selling the field to someone who will take proper care of it.

ORIGIN: Most of Japan's land is bound up in inhospitable mountain ranges where farming is impossible. The usable land is extremely valuable. Families can save for a lifetime just to buy a small plot of precious farmland, and hope to leave it to their offspring after they die. Of course, children do not always follow their parents' wishes—a prodigal son who forsakes his father's hard-earned fields in favor of vices like gambling and drinking will find a dorotabō waiting back home.

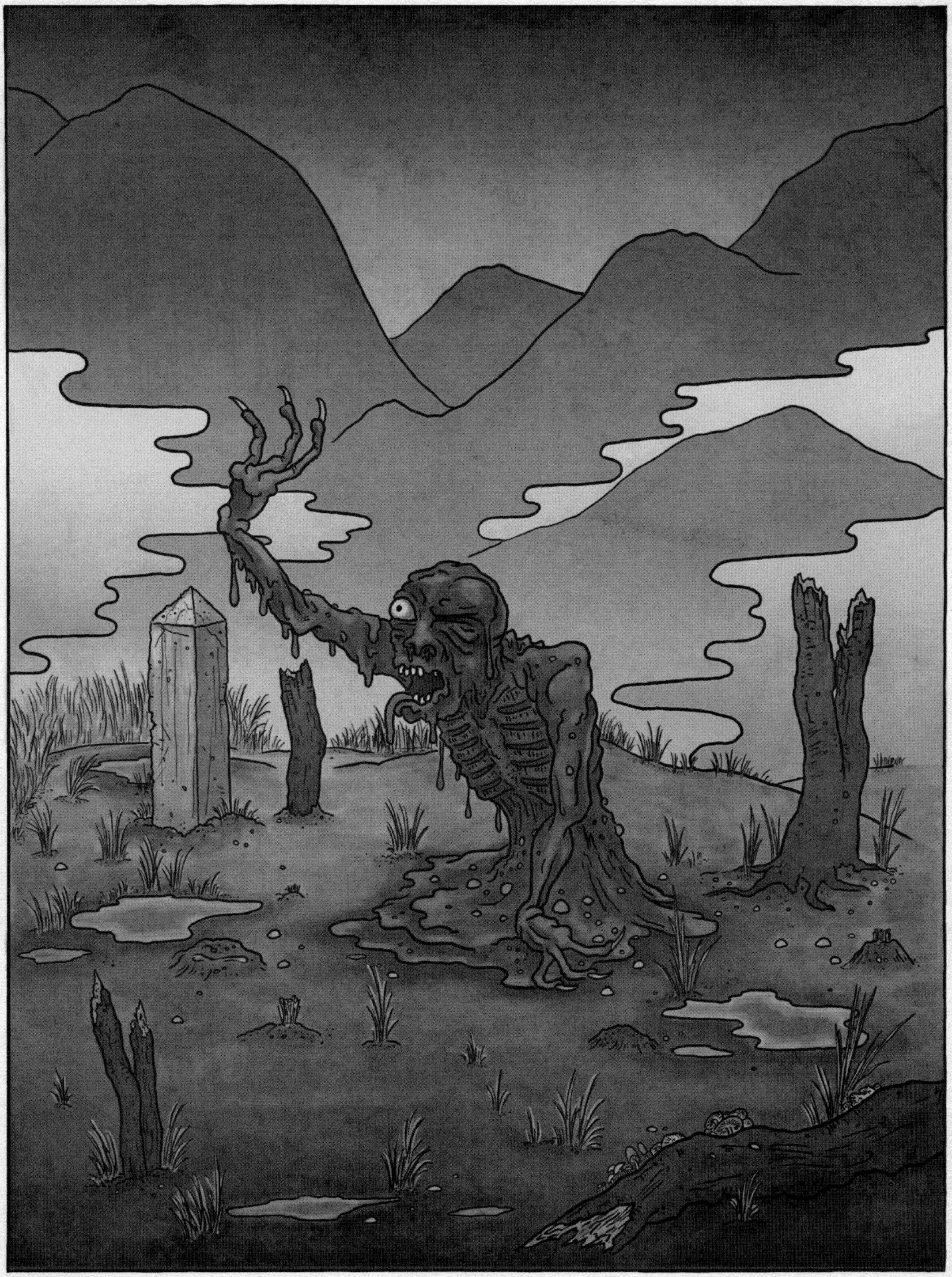

AKA SHITA 赤舌

TRANSLATION: red tongue
ALTERNATE NAMES: aka kuchi ("red mouth")
HABITAT: rice fields and farming villages; commonly found in Tsugaru
DIET: farmers

APPEARANCE: Aka shita is a mysterious spirit which takes the form of a dark cloud with sharp claws, and a hairy, bestial face. Its most prominent feature and namesake is the long, bright red tongue that lolls from its mouth. Only the shape of its hairy, monstrous face and long, bestial claws are known. The rest of its body is perpetually hidden inside of the dark, black clouds in which it lives.

BEHAVIOR: The aka shita appears during the summer months, when rain and water are at their highest demand to ensure a successful growing season. They are agents of retribution, primarily known as punishers in water disputes. Because plenty of water is essential for keeping rice paddies flooded, Japan's farmlands are interlaced with an intricate series of interconnected aqueducts and canals meant to deliver water to all of the farmers equally. In times of drought, however, a wicked farmer may open up the sluice gates and drain his neighbor's water into his own field. Such a serious crime can cost a family its livelihood, and water bandits face the violent wrath of their neighbors. Some clever water thieves are never caught, and may think they've gotten away with their crime. But then the aka shita appears, and drains the water from the water thieves' fields and snatches them up with its long, red tongue.

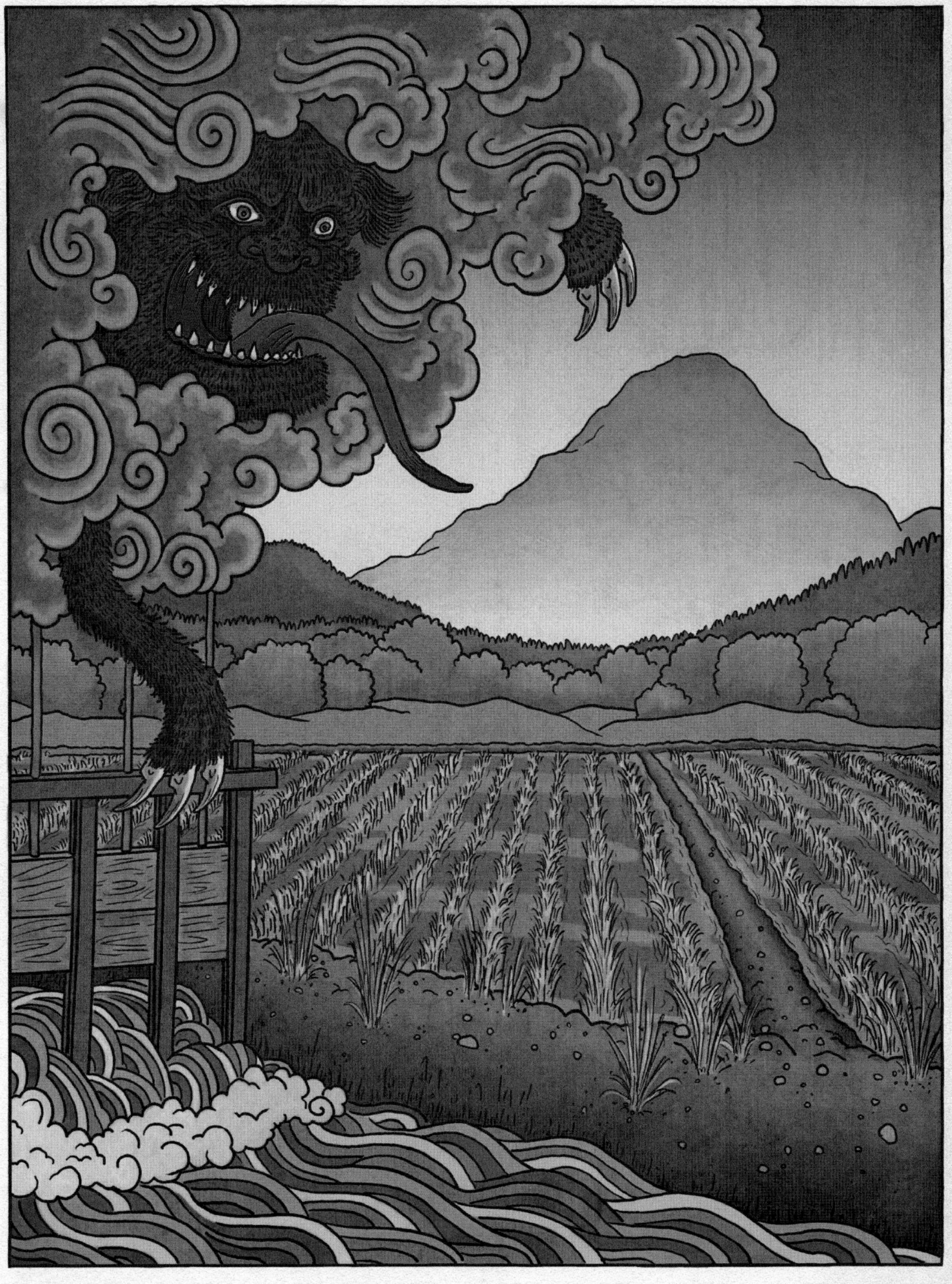

Otoroshi おとろし

TRANSLATION: a regional corruption of osoroshii, meaning "scary"
Alternative names: odoroshi, odoroodoro, keippai
HABITAT: shrines, temples, and homes; found above gates and doors
DIET: small animals and wicked people

APPEARANCE: Otoroshi are known by many regional names, most of them being wordplays denoting this monster's fearsome appearance and wild, course mane that covers its body. Otoroshi appear as hairy, hunched, four-legged beasts with fierce claws and tusks. They have blue or orange skin.

BEHAVIOR: Though its existence has been known of for centuries, little is known about this rare and mysterious creature. Otoroshi are masters of disguise and are rarely seen except for when they want to be. They are most commonly spotted in high places like roofs. Other favorite places are the torii archways at shrines and the gates above temples that separate the physical world from the realm of the gods.

INTERACTIONS: Otoroshi act as a kind of guardian of these holy places. They eat the wild animals found in shrines and temples—particularly pigeons, sparrows, and other birds. Otoroshi attack humans only rarely: when they spot a wicked or imprudent person near a holy place—or when one tries to enter through the gateway they are guarding. Otoroshi attack by pouncing on their victims from above, tearing them to shreds, and devouring their remains.

ORIGIN: While its name implies ferocity and its appearance is quite grotesque, it is only known to be dangerous to the wicked. The name otoroshi, while not a word itself, appears to be derived from variations in regional dialects. It is generally accepted to be a corruption of *osoroshii*, meaning "scary." Nothing is known of its origins; it is speculated to be related to a similar yōkai, the waira, due to their common habits and environment.

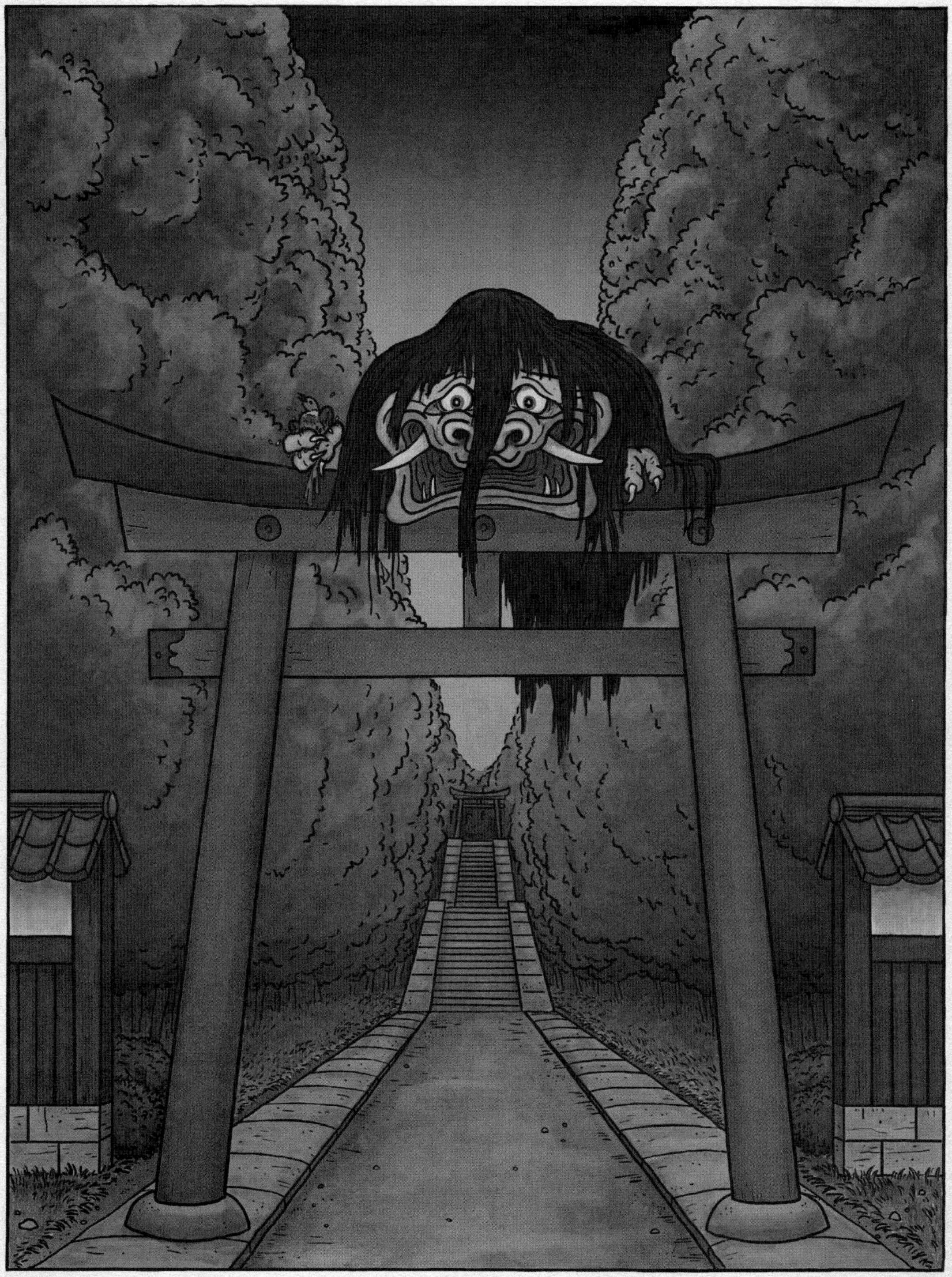

WAIRA わいら

TRANSLATION: a regional corruption of *kowai*, meaning "scary"
HABITAT: forests, mountains, shrines, and temples
DIET: small animals and wicked people

APPEARANCE: The waira is a rare and reclusive yōkai, few of which have ever been encountered. It is an ugly beast with a large body similar to that of a cow but with a single, sharp claw on each of its four long limbs. According to the accounts that exist, male waira are mottled in earthy brown colors while females are colored red.

BEHAVIOR: Waira live deep in the mountains, near heavily wooded temples and shrines. They are found near otoroshi, and are believed to guard temples and shrines from wicked people. They also use their tough claws to dig up and catch the small animals that they feed upon, such as moles, mice, and rabbits.

ORIGIN: From the colorings and environments where they are found, it is believed that waira are transformed yōkai, born from the common toad after it reaches an advanced age. It is also speculated that the waira is somehow related to the otoroshi, as they share the same habitat and are often seen together.

The waira's name, as with the otoroshi's, is a subject of some confusion. As these yōkai's names are not written using kanji, they contain few clues as to their origins. The most commonly accepted theory is that it is a corruption of a variant of the word *kowai*, meaning "scary." This further supports the speculation that the waira and the otoroshi may be somehow related.

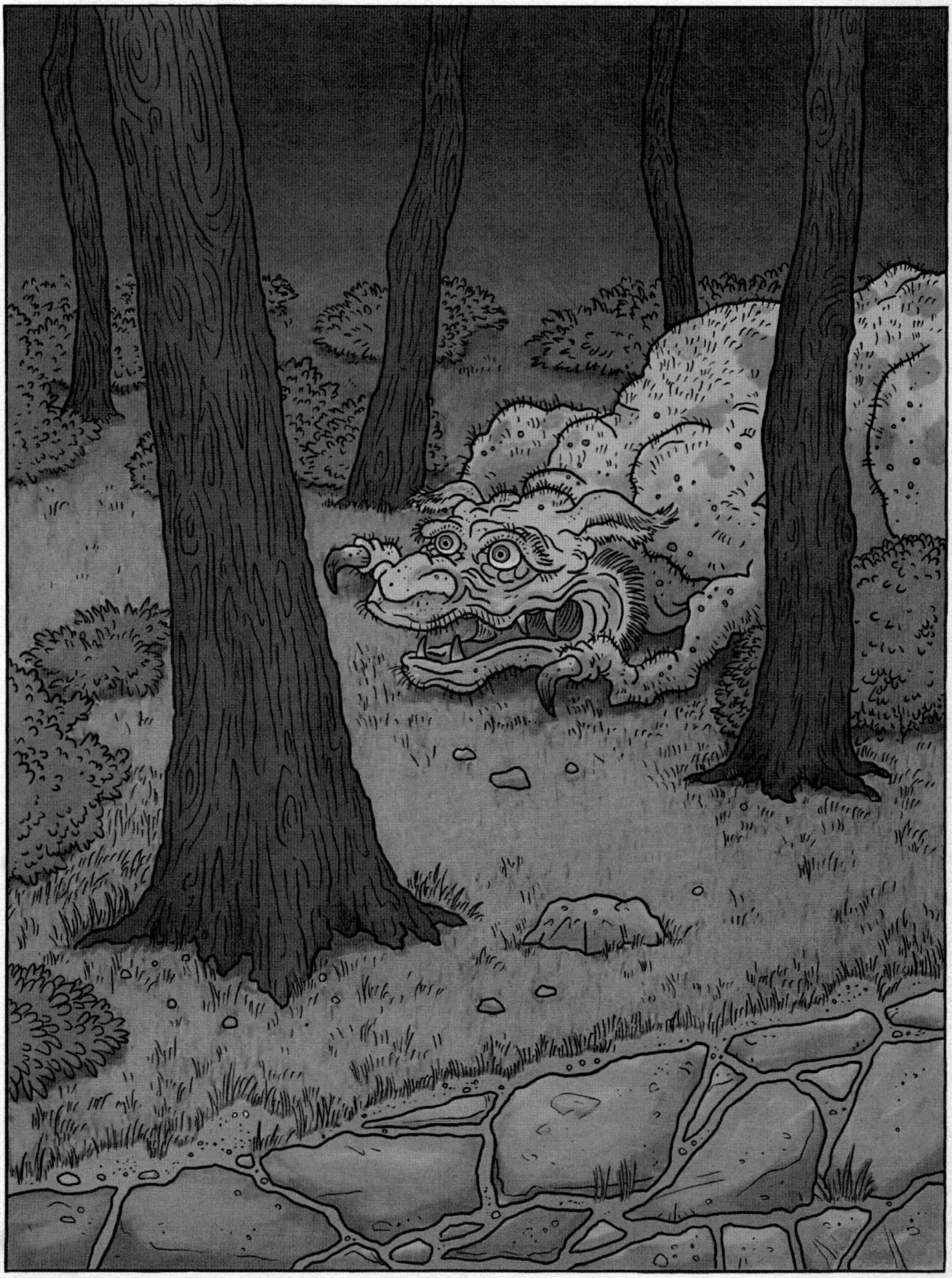

Uwan うわん

TRANSLATION: onomatopoeic; named for the sound it makes
HABITAT: empty temples, abandoned houses
DIET: lives off of the fear it causes

APPEARANCE: Another monster about which little is known, the uwan is more often heard than seen. It is named for the distinctive sound it makes, crying out from the darkness: *"Uwan!"* No written record of its physical appearance exists; the creature was thought to be formless for centuries. It wasn't until the Edo period when artist Sawaki Sūshi gave the creature its shape that uwan were considered anything more than phantom sounds.

INTERACTIONS: Uwan are occasionally encountered outside of old buildings and temples. They assault lone passersby by leaping out of the shadows and shouting *"Uwan!"* The uwan depends entirely on the surprise attack—any weak-willed victims who faint at the site of the uwan never regain consciousness. The uwan steals their essence and flees into the darkness. However, if a brave individual shouts back *"Uwan!"* then this yōkai flees and never bothers that person again.

LEGENDS: A famous uwan encounter took place in Akita Prefecture during the Edo period. A young newlywed couple had bought an old mansion and moved in together. On their first night in their new house, they were awoken by a loud voice shouting *"UWAN!"* The shocked couple searched all over and around the house, but couldn't find the source of the voice. The shouting continued for some time, erupting sporadically all night, every night. The couple was not able to sleep at all.

Some time later, the couple's neighbors began to ask why they were always so tired-looking, with blood-shot eyes and disheveled hair. The husband tried to explain about the mysterious voice, but none of his neighbors claimed to have heard the shouting. Of course, nobody in the neighborhood believed the couple. Instead, gossip quickly began to spread that the newlyweds weren't getting any sleep on account of nocturnal activity of a different kind. Embarrassed, the couple ceased asking about the strange sounds.

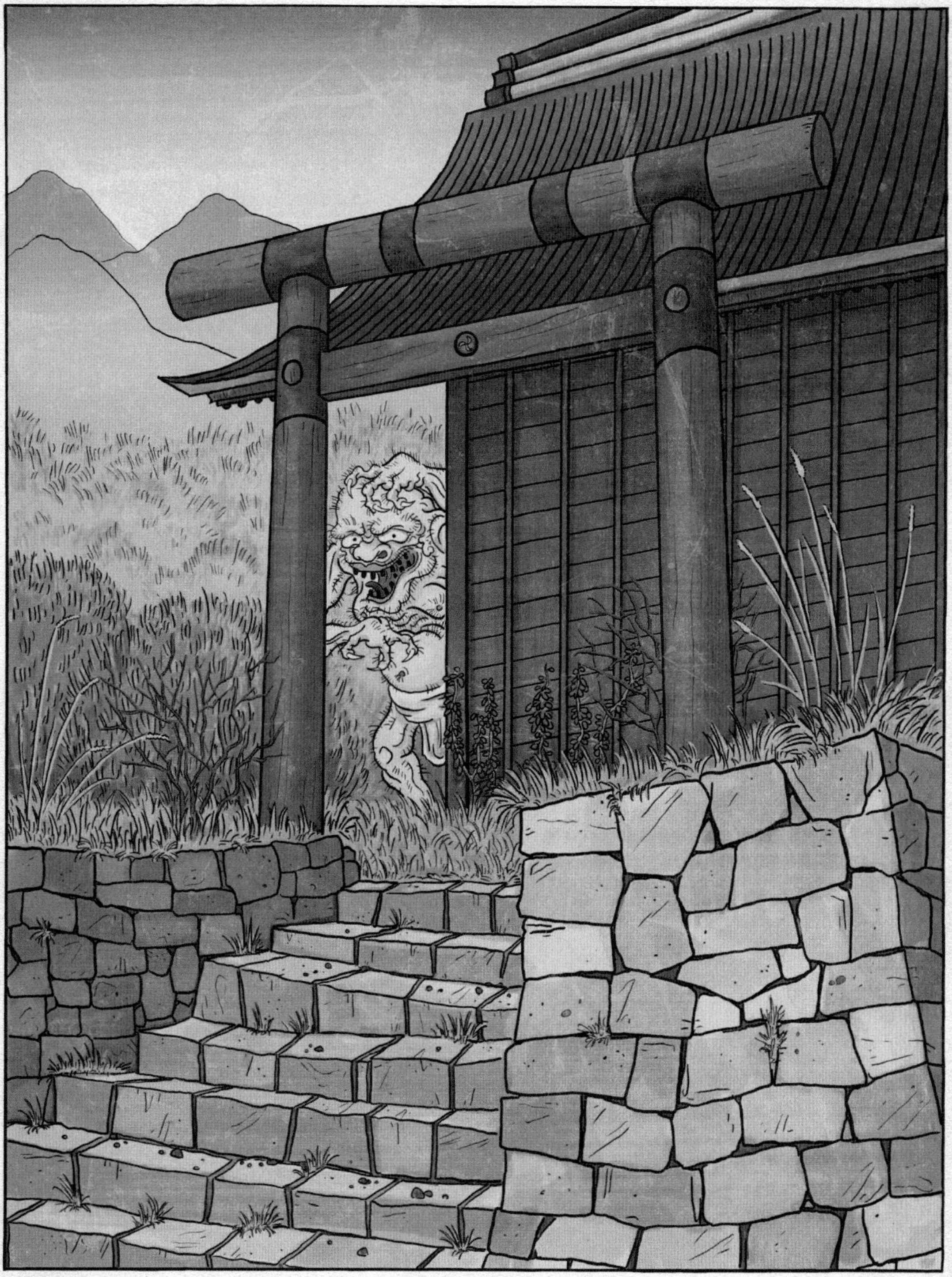

HYAKUME 百目

TRANSLATION: one hundred eyes
HABITAT: abandoned homes, temples, caves, and other shady areas
DIET: unknown

APPEARANCE: Like their name suggests, hyakume are covered from head to foot with countless blinking, yellow eyes. Underneath those eyes are fleshy, roughly man-sized bodies. With their eyes closed, they resemble pink lumps of flesh, and are nearly indistinguishable from nuppeppō (which live in a similar habitat).

BEHAVIOR: Hyakume make their homes in old temples, guarding them from would-be thieves during the night. During the day, the sky is too bright for their many sensitive eyes. They only come out at night, spending the lighter hours in dark and shadowy buildings where few humans ever go.

INTERACTIONS: Hyakume are shy and try to avoid human contact. Should a human come within a few meters of a hyakume, one of its eyes will detach from its body and fly towards the person. The eye sticks to the person's body for as long as he or she is in the area, keeping an eye out for criminal activity. Eventually the eye will return to the yōkai when they perceive there is no danger. When hyakume feel threatened, they jump out of the darkness in a menacing manner. They are not particularly violent and rely on their size and fearsome appearance to scare humans away.

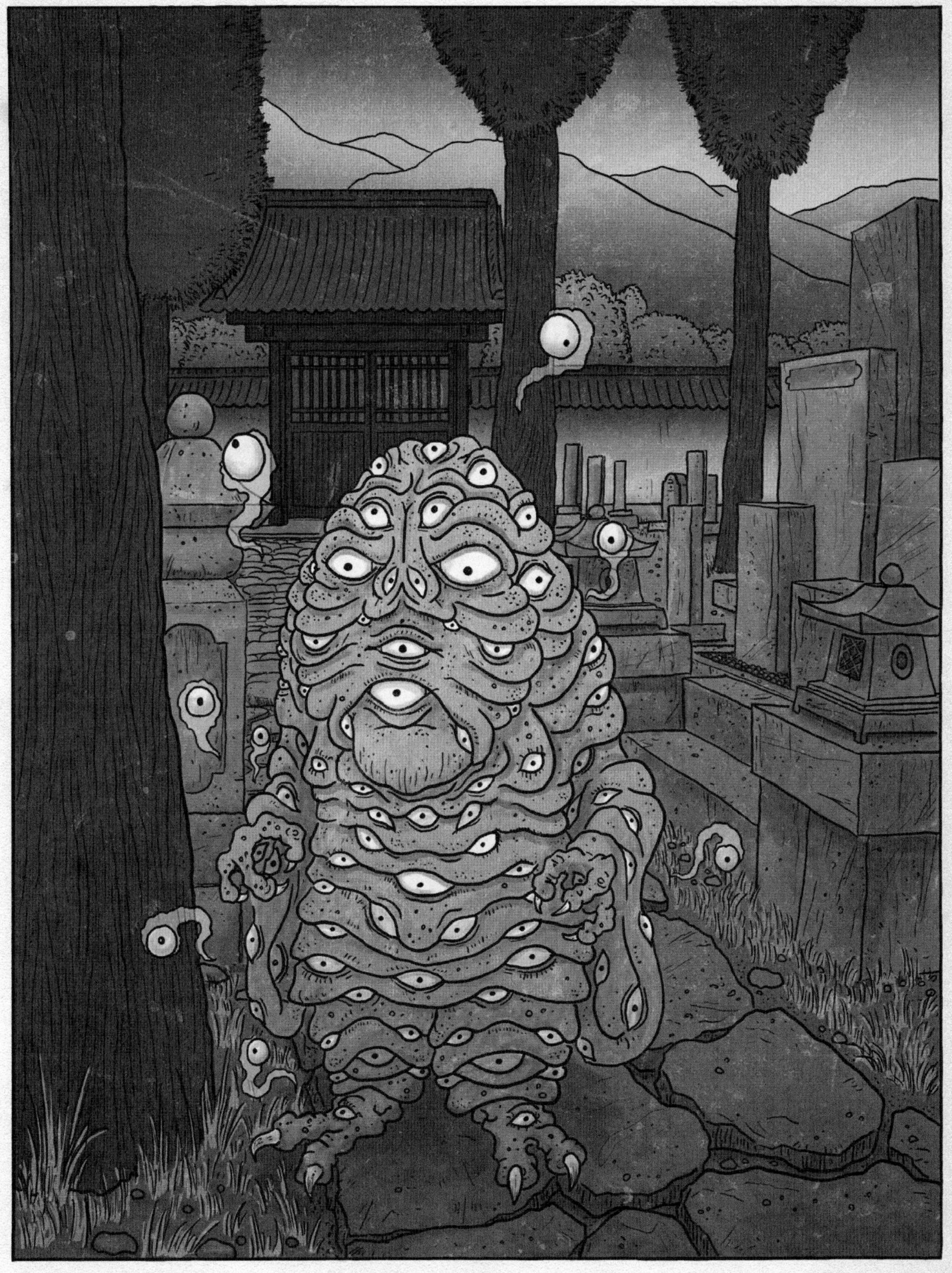

NUPPEPPŌ ぬっぺっぽう

TRANSLATION: a corruption of the slang for wearing too much makeup
ALTERNATE NAMES: nuppefuhō
HABITAT: graveyards, old temples
DIET: unknown

APPEARANCE: Nuppeppō are bizarre and creepy yōkai found in ruined temples, overgrown graveyards, and other dilapidated areas. These creatures are known for their revolting appearance and smell; they give off a strong odor of rotten meat. They look like large, flabby, roughly humanoid chunks of flesh about the size of child, with lumpy, undeveloped hands and feet, and vaguely indiscernible facial features.

BEHAVIOR: Nuppeppō appear usually only at night, and are not known to cause any particular harm or mischief—other than being disgusting. They seem to enjoy the nauseating effect their smell has on passersby. They frequently cause chaos and havoc by running around and disgusting people, and outrunning angry villagers who would try to chase them down and kill them.

INTERACTIONS: Nuppeppō are very rare yōkai. There are only a few recorded sightings, even though their grotesque form is well-known. Accounts usually describe lords sending hosts of warriors to chase the creature out of a castle or a temple, only to have it outrun the guards and escape, causing some of them to swoon and faint from its odor. Though they are passive and non-aggressive, they can move quickly and are notoriously hard to catch.

According to the records of Edo period pharmacists, its flesh imparts incredible power on those who eat it (providing they are willing and able to keep it down), and it can also be made into a powerful medicine with excellent curative properties.

ORIGIN: Nuppeppō's origins are mysterious. They are believed to be a distant relative of nopperabō. Some scholars suggest that nuppeppō may in fact be botched transformations of inexperienced shape-shifting yōkai, such as a mujina or tanuki. The origin of their name is equally mysterious. It is thought to be derived from slang for wearing too much makeup, painted so thickly that facial features become indiscernible—just as nuppeppō's features are barely discernible on their fleshy, fatty faces.

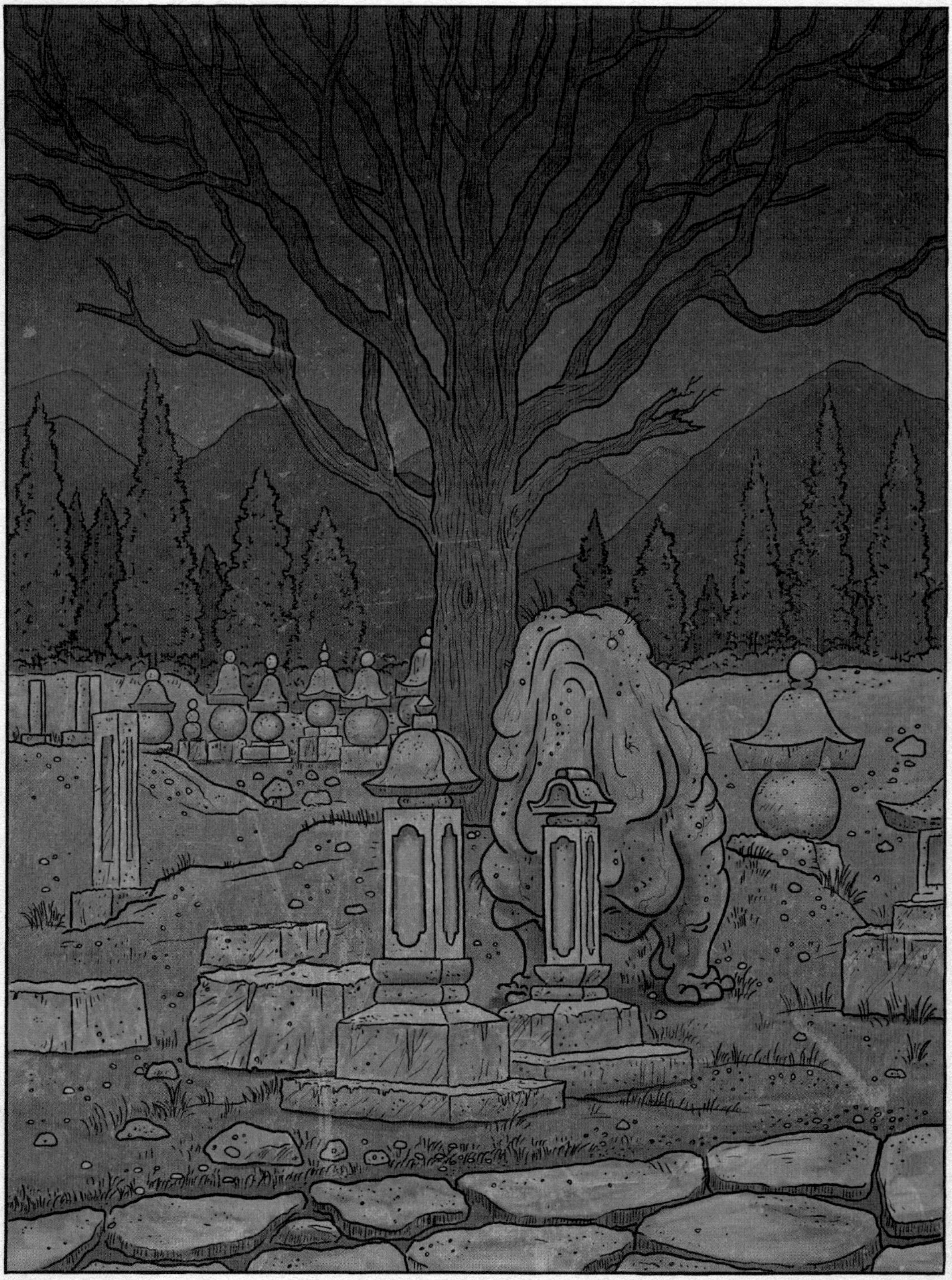

HITOTSUME KOZŌ 一つ目小僧

TRANSLATION: one-eyed priest boy
HABITAT: found all throughout Japan; often encounters on dark streets
DIET: omnivorous

APPEARANCE: Child-like and mischievous, hitotsume kozō are little one-eyed goblins that are well-known in all parts of Japan. They wear shaved heads and robes, like tiny Buddhist monks. They have long red tongues and a single, enormous eye.

BEHAVIOR: Hitotsume kozō are relatively harmless as far as yōkai go. Their most alarming trait is appearing suddenly and surprising people on dark streets. They seem to enjoy startling people; hundreds of encounters have been reported over the years, most of them very similar to each other.

INTERACTIONS: Aside from their startling play, hitotsume kozō have one serious job. In East Japan, it is said that every year on the 8th of December, hitotsume kozō travel the land, recording in ledgers the families who have been bad that year. They use this information to decide each family's fortunes for the coming year. Hitotsume kozō take their reports to the god of pestilence and bad luck, who then brings appropriate misfortune on those deserving families. However, hitotsume kozō leave their ledgers with the guardian deity of travels for safekeeping until February 8th. In a mid-January ceremony, local villagers burn down and rebuild that deity's roadside shrines in hopes that the fires will also burn the hitotsume kozō's ledgers before they come to pick them up—thus escaping disaster that year.

ORIGIN: Though similar in name to other one-eyed monsters like hitotsume nyūdō, there is little evidence suggesting a relation between the two. Many believe that hitotsume kozō's origins are connected in some way with Enryaku-ji, the head temple of the Tendai sect of Buddhism. Others believe that they were once local mountain deities who over time devolved and changed into yōkai.

LEGENDS: A man visited a friend on business. While waiting in the reception room, a young boy of about 10 appeared and began to mischievously roll and unroll the hanging scroll in the room's alcove. When the man scolded the boy for being mischievous, the boy turned around and squawked, "Be quiet!" However, the boy's face had only one eye! The man screamed and fainted, and had to be carried back to his own home. He was bed-ridden for 20 days, but made a full recovery.

In an account from Fukushima Prefecture, a young lady was walking the street at night. A little boy approached her from behind and asked "Ma'am, would you like some money." She laughed and sweetly replied yes, and turned to face the boy. He was a hitotsume kozō. Instead of bearing riches and he was grinning, staring so intensely at her with his single eye that she fainted in shock on the spot.

A similar tale from Okayama Prefecture tells of a particular street where an eerie, pale blue glow was seen one night. A man went to investigate and witnessed a ghostly one-eyed boy playing around. The man collapsed, paralyzed with fear, and was unable to move. The apparition approached the helpless man and licked him from head to toe with his long, slobbery tongue.

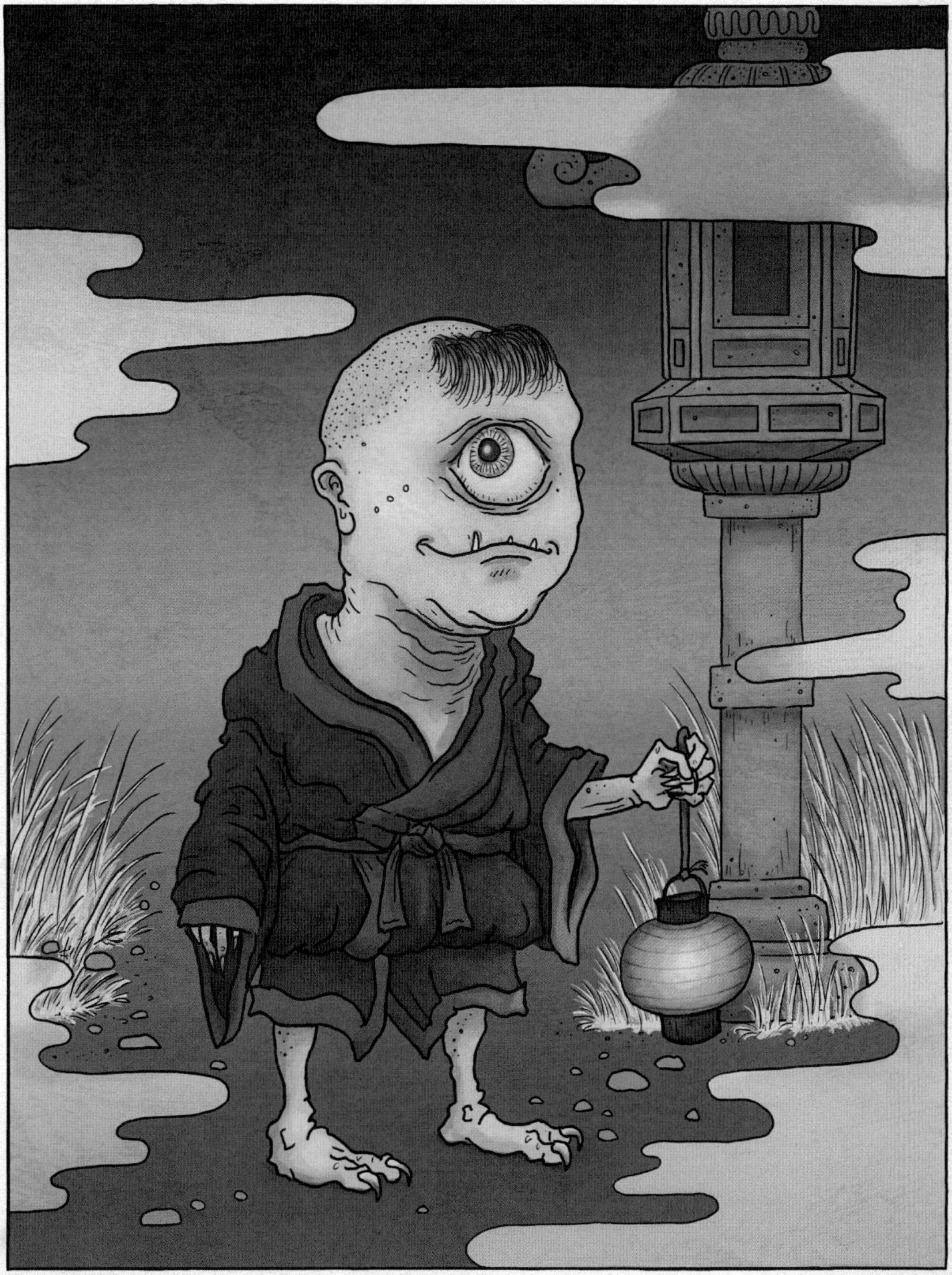

Ubume 姑獲鳥

TRANSLATION: woman in late pregnancy; often written with different characters
ALTERNATE NAMES: obo, unme, ugume, ubame tori, and many others
HABITAT: haunts the area where she gave birth
DIET: none; only exists to deliver her baby into safe hands

APPEARANCE: When a woman dies just before, during, or shortly after childbirth, anxiety for her child may prevent her spirit from passing on. This troubled attachment manifests as a ghost known as an ubume. These women appear on dark, rainy nights. Ubume can appear in many forms: a woman carrying a baby; a pregnant woman; or a blood-soaked walking corpse carrying an underdeveloped fetus. Other times they just appear as horrific, bloody, pregnant women crying out desperately into the night for help.

These variations are due to the burial traditions of different regions, as well as the circumstances of their death. In some areas, when a pregnant woman died she would be buried with the unborn fetus still inside of her. In other places, the fetus would be cut out of her and placed in her arms during burial. Women who died after delivering stillborn babies were also buried this way.

BEHAVIOR: These tragic spirits wander the areas near where they died, seeking aid from the living which they cannot provide themselves. If the mother died after childbirth but her baby survived, the newly formed ubume will try to care for the child in whatever way it can. She enters shops or homes to try to purchase food, clothes, or sweets for her still-living child. In place of money she pays with handfuls of dead leaves. These ghosts also try to lead humans to the place where their baby is hidden so that it can be taken to its living relatives, or adopted by another person.

In cases where both mother and child died, an ubume can appear carrying the bundled corpse of her infant. When a human approaches, the ghost tries to deliver the bundle into the arms of the living. If the stranger accepts, the ghost vanishes, and the bundle grows heavier and heavier until the helpful stranger is crushed under its weight.

OTHER FORMS: The name ubume is written with characters that imply a bird's name. The literal translation of these characters is "child-snatching bird" and some theories connect this spirit with another yōkai called the ubumetori. This yōkai is an evil bird which flies through the sky searching for clothing that has been left on the clothesline overnight. When it finds some, it smears its poisonous blood on the clothing. Shortly afterward, the owner of those clothes begins to develop shakes and convulsions; possibly leading to death. Ubumetori are also blamed for snatching babies and taking them away into the night sky. Whether this bird is another form of the ghostly mother or a separate spirit with a similar name is not known.

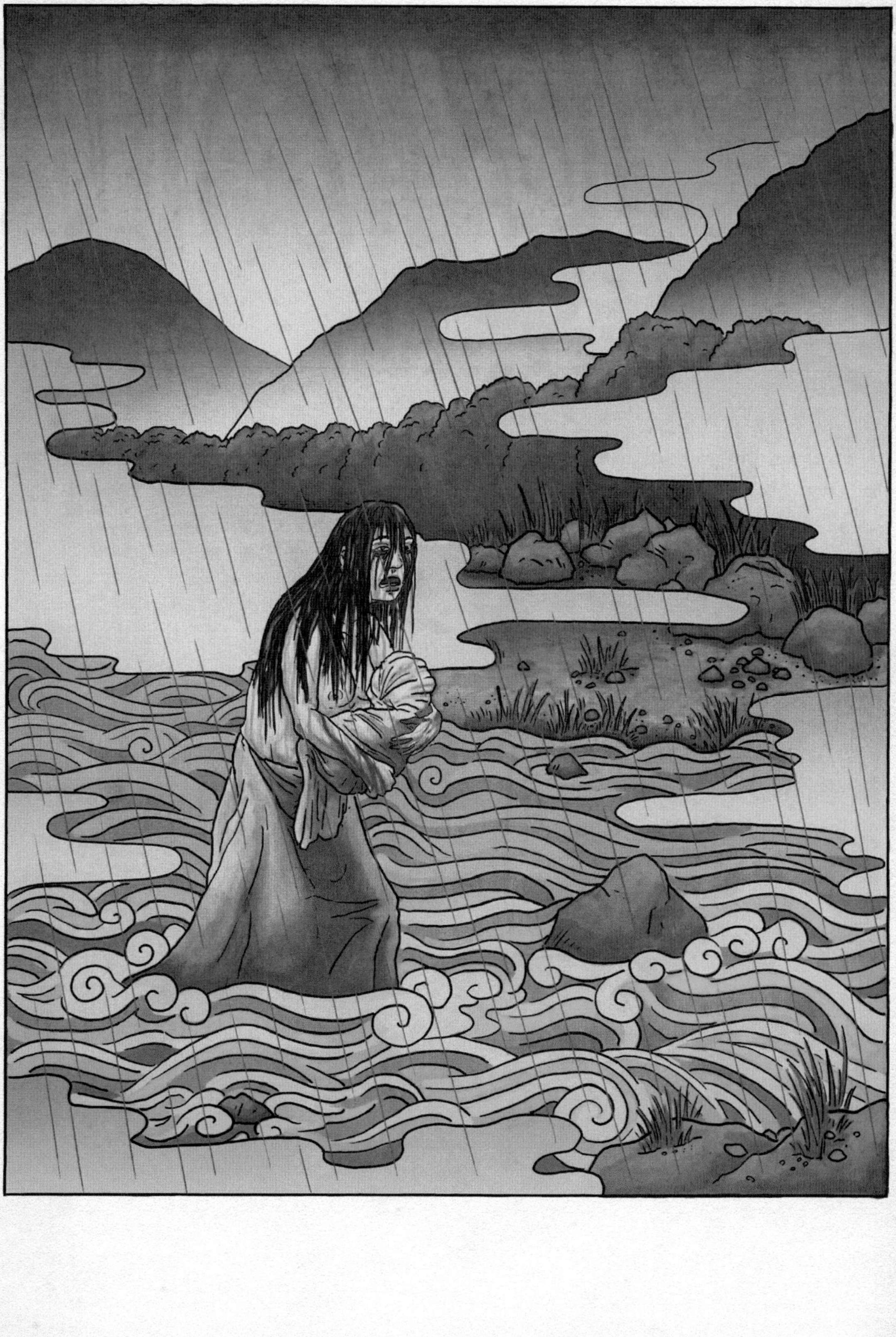

Yūrei 幽霊

Translation: faint spirit, ghost
Alternate names: obake, shiryō, bōrei; other names exist for specific variations
Habitat: any; commonly found in graveyards, houses, or near the place of death
Diet: none

Appearance: There are many different types of yūrei. In most cases, how they appear depends on the circumstances on their death. They retain the features and the clothing they wore when they died or were buried, which means they are dressed in white burial kimonos or the uniforms of fallen warriors. Occasionally, they have bloody wounds indicative of the way they died. Their hair is usually long and disheveled, often obstructing their face and adding to their disturbing appearance. Their hands hang limply from their wrists. Yūrei are translucent and only faintly visible. In most cases they are so faint that they appear to have no feet.

Interactions: Yūrei are capable of invoking powerful curses. They do not roam about, but haunt one particular place or person. In the case of a place it is often where they died or are buried. In the case of a person it is often their killer—or sometimes their loved ones. They remain stuck in this world until they can be put to rest. This might require bringing their killers to justice, or finding their lost body, or something as simple as passing on a message to a loved one. Some yūrei are reluctant to accept their own deaths and haunt their living family, bringing misfortune and unhappiness for the rest of their family members' lives.

Each haunting is as unique as the person it originated from. Only when its purpose for existing is fulfilled—or it is exorcised by a priest—can a yūrei finally rest. But the possibility that salvation exists is a glimmer of hope for those who are affected by a haunting.

Origin: According to traditional Japanese beliefs, when a person dies his soul lives on as a separate entity, passing on to a heavenly afterlife. This transition is accomplished through a number of funeral and post-funeral rites and prayers performed by their loved ones over many years. Through these rites, the soul is reunited with its ancestors and becomes a family guardian spirit. These ancestors are enshrined in the house and continue to be honored as members of the family, particularly during the summer holiday of Obon when they are said to return to the material world to be with their families.

Those who do not receive the proper funeral rites cannot pass on. They remain stuck in a purgatory that is part physical world and part ethereal. Others who die suddenly, tragically, or violently—or with grudge and malice in their hearts—are sometimes unable to pass on even with the proper prayers and rites. These lost souls transform into yūrei.

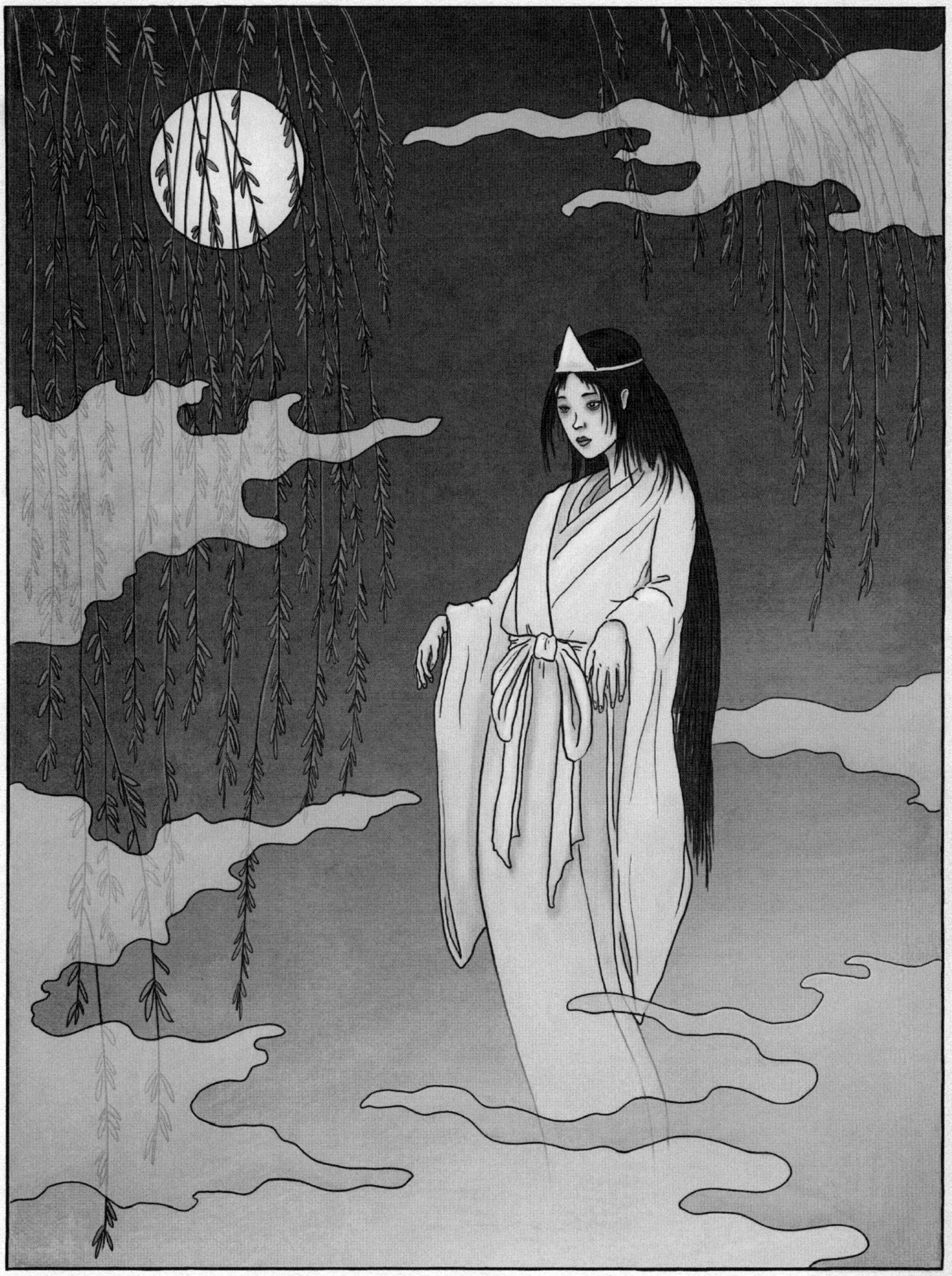

Onryō 怨霊

Translation: grudge spirit, vengeful ghost
Habitat: found all throughout Japan
Diet: none; survives solely on its wrath

Appearance: The most dreaded type of yūrei is the onryō. They are the ghosts of people who died with such strong passions—jealousy, rage, or hatred—that their soul is unable to pass on. Instead, they transform into powerful, wrathful spirits who seek vengeance on everything they encounter. Often they were victims of war, catastrophe, betrayal, murder, or suicide—and they display wounds or marks indicative of the way they died.

Interactions: Their motive is always the same—vengeance. Onryō are easily powerful enough to kill anyone. However, they prefer letting the object of their hatred live a long life of torment and suffering, watching loved ones die in their stead. Onryō inflict a terrible curse on the people or places that they haunt. This curse can be transmitted to others like a contagious disease, creating a circle of death and destruction far more devastating than any ordinary ghost. Onryō make no distinction in their targets; they just want to destroy. Moreover, an onryō's vengeance can never be satisfied. While most yūrei only haunt a person or place until they are exorcised or placated, an onryō's horrible grudge-curse continues to infect a location long after the ghost itself has been laid to rest.

Occasionally, an onryō's curse is born not out of hatred and retribution, but from an intense, passionate love that perverts into jealousy. These onryō haunt their former lovers, exacting their wrath on new romances, second marriages, new children, and eventual end up destroying the lives of the ones they loved so much in life. Whatever the origin, an onryō's undiscriminating wrath makes it one of the most feared supernatural entities in all of Japan.

Legends: Unquestionably the most well-known onryō, and one whose grudge-curse exists to this very day, is the ghost of Oiwa. A young woman who was brutally disfigured and then murdered by her wicked and greedy husband in an elaborate plot, her story is told in *Yotsuya Kaidan*, or *The Ghost Story of Yotsuya*. *Yotsuya Kaidan* has been retold many times, in books, ukiyoe, kabuki, and film. Like Shakespeare's *Macbeth*, legend has it that a curse accompanies her story, and that those who retell it suffer injuries and even death. To this day, producers, actors, and their crews continue to visit the grave of Oiwa in Tōkyō before productions or adaptations of *Yotsuya Kaidan*, praying for her soul and asking for her blessing to tell her story once again.

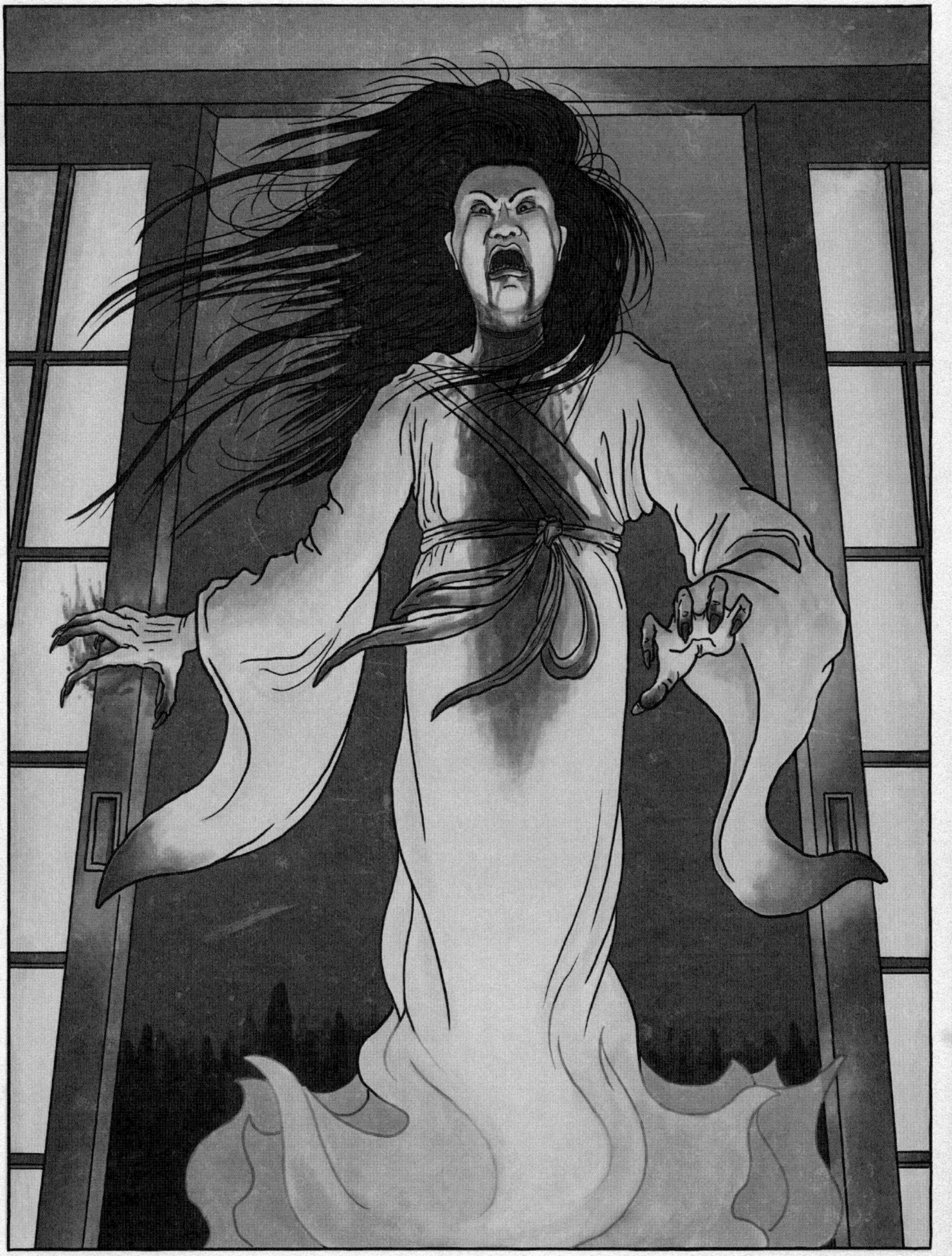

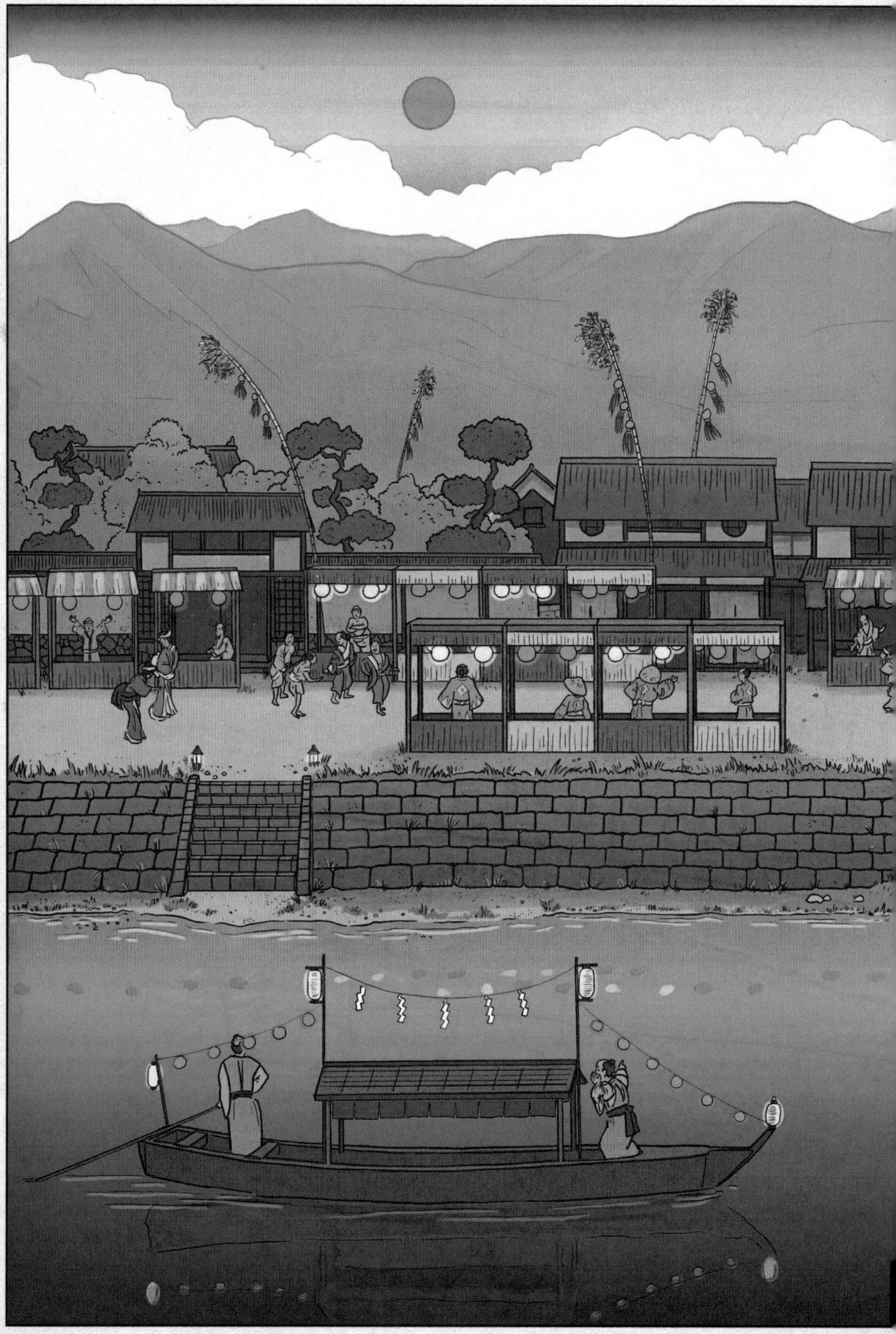

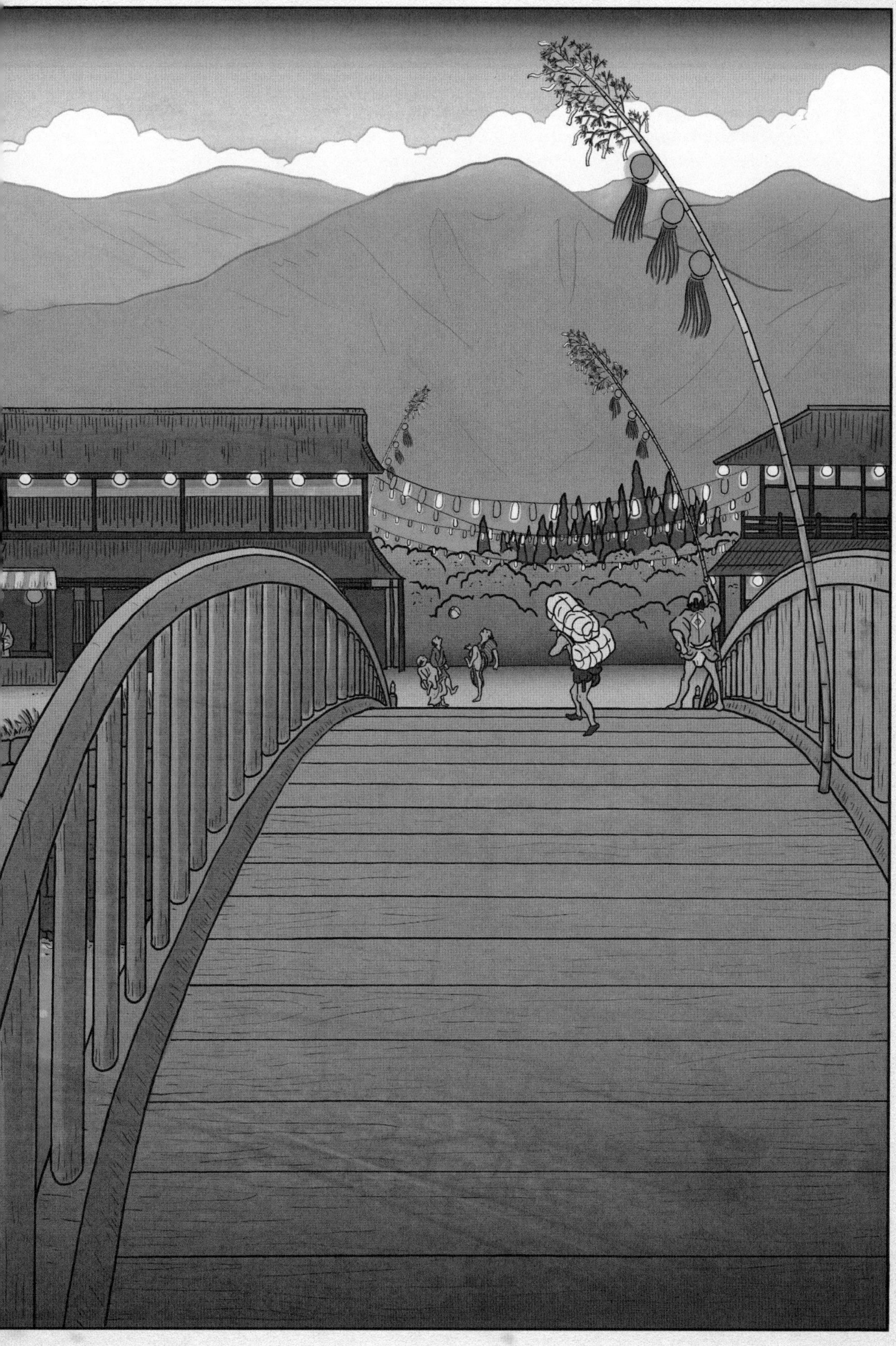

Kawauso 獺

TRANSLATION: river otter
HABITAT: rivers, wetlands, freshwater bodies
DIET: carnivorous; feeds on fish and small animals, with a fondness for sake

APPEARANCE: River otters can be found in the wilds all over Japan. They are under a meter in length, cute and furry, and well-loved for their shy, playful nature.

BEHAVIOR: As with most wild animals in Japan, kawauso develop magical powers upon reaching old age. They are particularly skilled at shape-changing and accurately copying sounds. Kawauso love alcohol, and are usually only seen in human areas trying to acquire sake. They are playful yōkai, well known for their tricks and mischief, but rarely dangerous.

INTERACTIONS: Kawauso are fond of playing pranks on humans, especially by mimicking sounds and words. They enjoy calling out human names or random words at strangers walking in the street and watching their confused reactions. They are fond of magically snuffing out lanterns in the night and leaving travelers stranded in the dark. Kawauso sometimes even transform into beautiful young women and try to seduce young men—only to run away laughing when the men take the hook.

Occasionally, kawauso commit more violent deeds. In a few instances near castles in Ishikawa, a kawauso dressed up as beautiful young woman and lured young men to the water's edge in order to catch and eat them, discarding the half-eaten bodies into the moat. But stories like this are rare.

OTHER FORMS: A kawauso's favorite disguise is the form of a young beggar child wearing a big straw hat. They use this child form to sneak into towns and try to buy alcohol from shops. The ruse often falls apart when the disguised creature is asked who it is, or where it came from. Caught off guard, the kawauso simply repeats the last word spoken to it, or makes funny nonsensical noises. This ruins its disguise and gives away its supernatural nature.

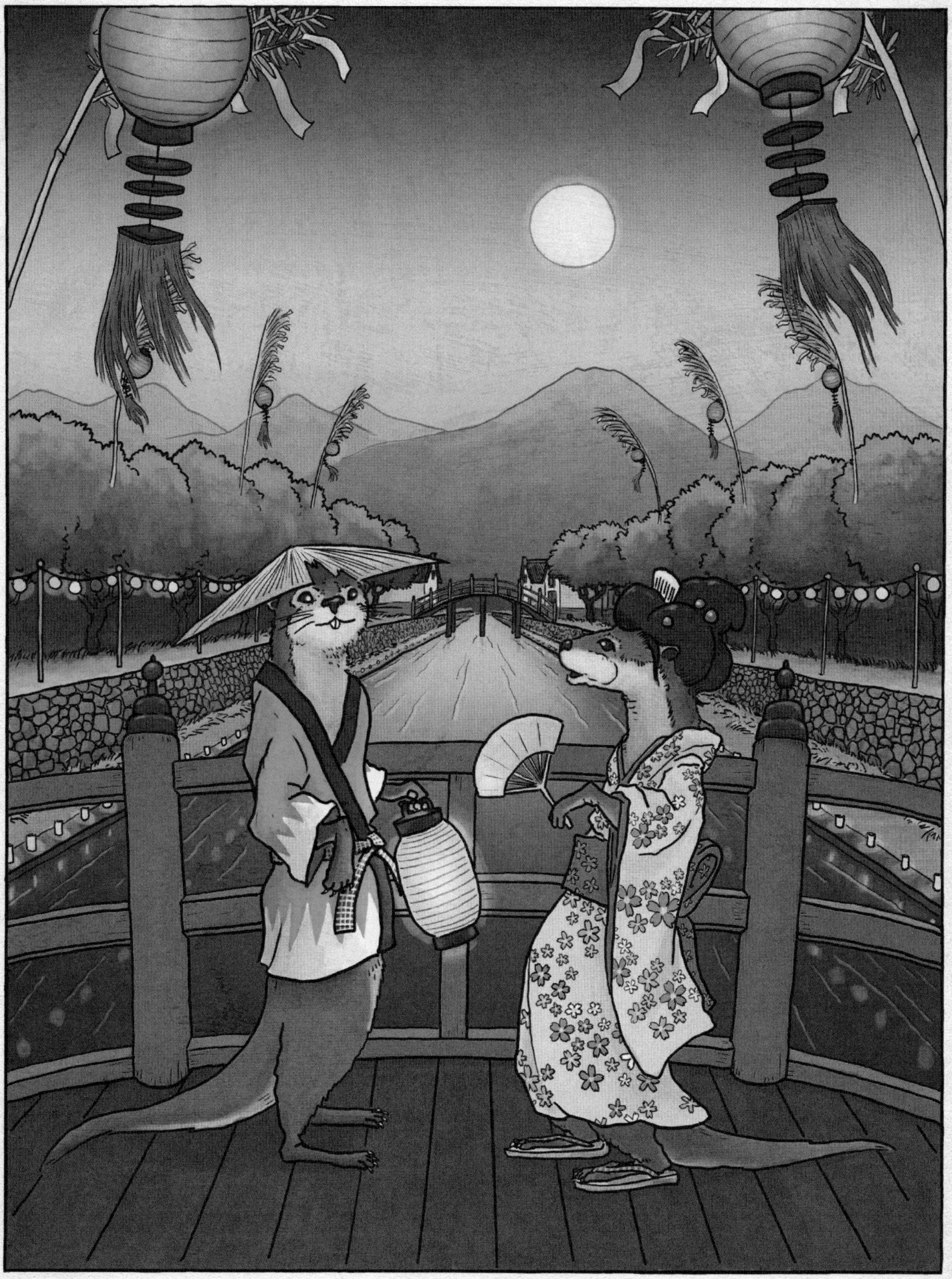

Nopperabō 野箆坊

TRANSLATION: faceless monk
ALTERNATE NAMES: often referred to as mujina
HABITAT: roads, inns, shops; blends into human society
DIET: unknown, but has no mouth and thus can't eat

APPEARANCE: Nopperabō resemble ordinary human beings in almost every way, and blend in perfectly with human society. However, the illusion is quickly shattered when met face to face—nopperabō actually have no face at all. Their heads are blank orbs with no eyes, nose, mouth, or features of any kind.

INTERACTIONS: These mysterious yōkai are encountered on quiet, empty roads late at night when nobody else is around. Like many yōkai of this kind, their main activity seems to be scaring humans. This they do remarkably well. Nopperabō usually appear in the guise of a man or a woman with his or her back turned towards the observer. When approached, the yōkai turns around and reveals its terrifying true form. To maximize the effect, they often appear with a face at first, and then wipe their face off dramatically with their hand at the most opportune time. Nopperabō revel in the terror they inflict upon their unsuspecting victims.

Nopperabō often work together in groups to scare one individual. As their victim runs away in a panic from the first nopperabō, he runs into another person who asks him what is wrong. When the victim explains what he saw, this person replies, "Oh, you mean like this?" and wipes his face away exactly like the first nopperabō. They are even known to impersonate close relatives of their victims, and sometimes a poor man will run all the way home, having run into multiple faceless monsters, only to tell his wife what he saw and have her too reply, "Oh, you mean like this? ..."

OTHER FORMS: The nopperabō is a favorite transformation of mischievous animal yōkai—kitsune, tanuki, and especially mujina. In fact, so frequently are encounters with this spirit blamed on shape-shifting badgers that the nopperabō are often mistakenly referred to as mujina.

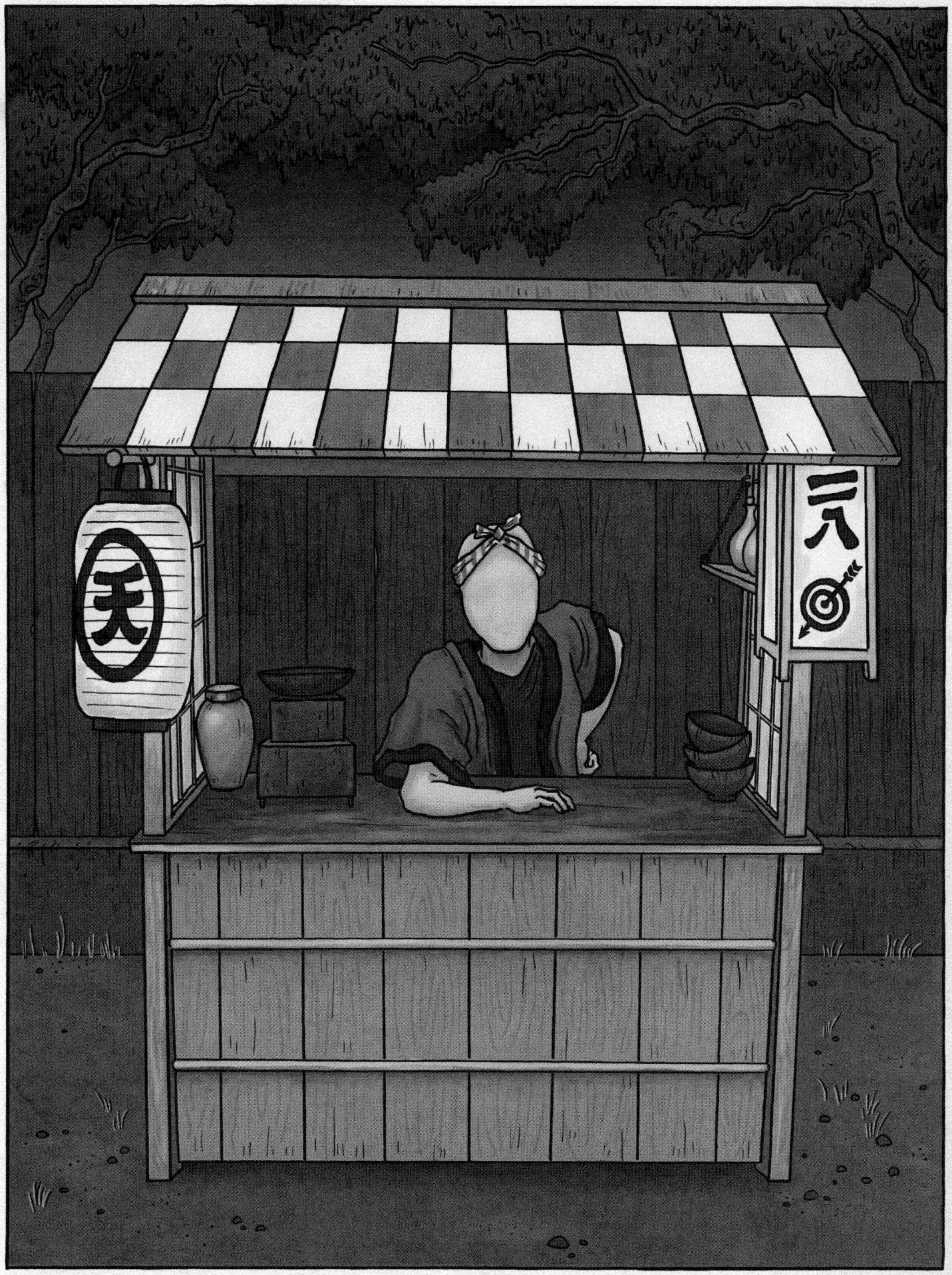
天
二八

MUJINA 貉

TRANSLATION: badger
ALTERNATE NAMES: anaguma; known as tanuki or mami in some regions
HABITAT: forests and mountains
DIET: omnivorous; feeds on small wild animals

APPEARANCE: Mujina are badgers who have developed magical powers and become yōkai. While mujina was once a common word for badger, these days *anaguma* refers to ordinary badgers while the term mujina is reserved exclusively for their yōkai form. Mujina are frequently confused with tanuki because of their similar size, appearance, and magical prowess. To further complicate matters, in some regions tanuki are called mujina, while mujina are called tanuki. In other regions the term *mami* applies to both animals.

BEHAVIOR: Mujina are less famous as yōkai than other shape-changing animals. As they live in the mountains, generally far from human society, they are not encountered as frequently as other animal yōkai. They are shy, and do not like to be seen by or interact with humans. Unlike other, more careless magical animals, the few mujina who live amongst human society take great care not to betray their true nature in any way,

INTERACTIONS: When it is dark and quiet, and there are no humans around, it is said that mujina shift into a humanoid form—usually that of a young boy wearing a tiny kimono—and sing songs in the street. If approached by a stranger, they run away into the darkness and transform back into animal form.

OTHER FORMS: The most well-known form mujina take is that of a nopperabō, a seemingly normal human form, but with no facial features whatsoever. They use this form to scare and panic humans who wander mountain or village roads at night time. Because of this, the two yōkai are often confused, and nopperabō are sometimes mistakenly referred to as mujina. However, other animal yōkai also imitate this same form, and there are non-animal nopperabō as well. Care should be taken to avoid misunderstanding.

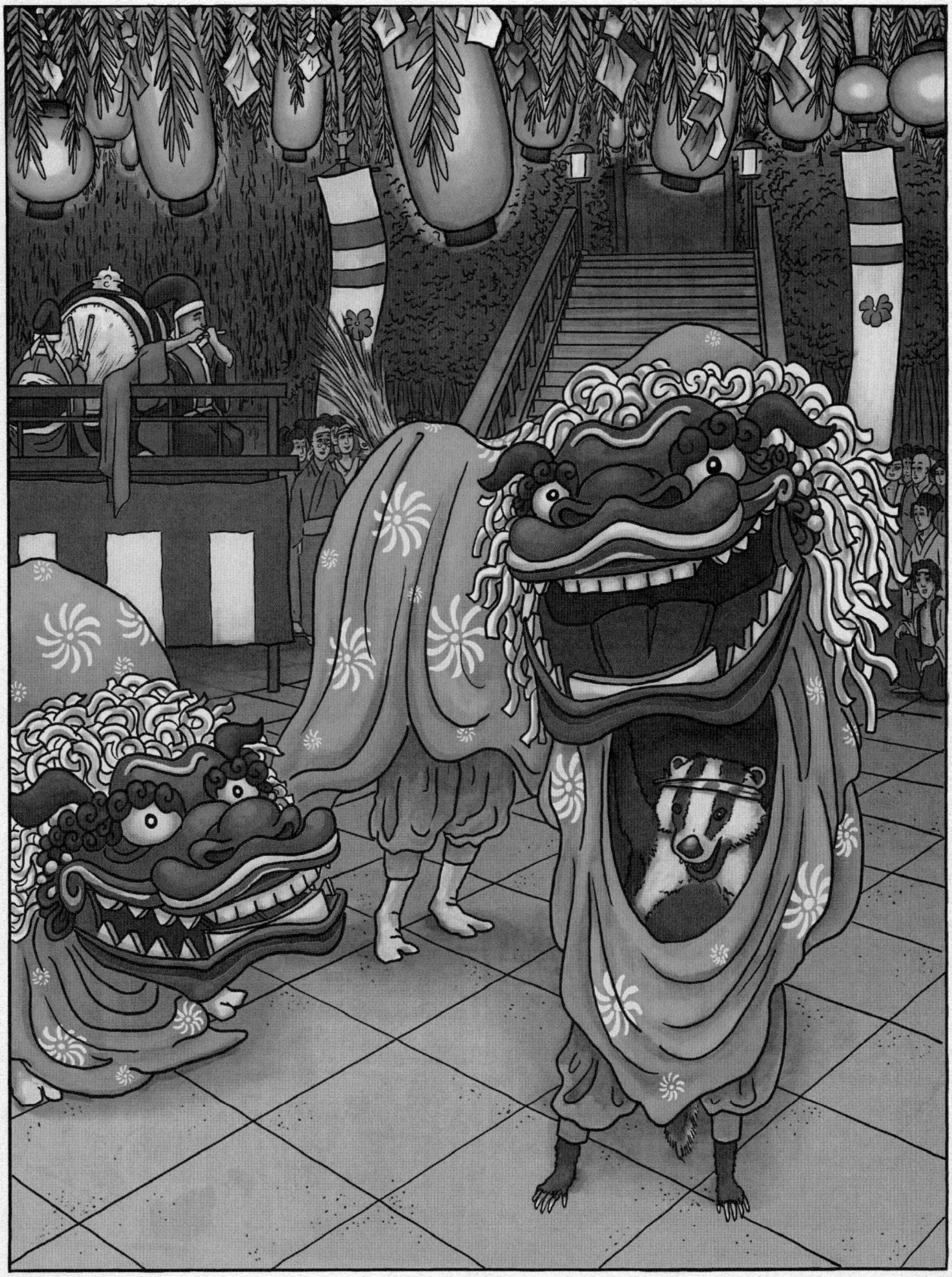

Tanuki 狸

Translation: also called tanuki in English; sometimes referred to as a raccoon dog
Alternate names: bakedanuki; referred to as mujina or mami in some areas
Habitat: mountains and forests; found throughout Japan
Diet: omnivorous; feeds on small wild animals, has a fondness for alcohol

Appearance: The tanuki rivals the kitsune for the most well-known animal yōkai. Sometimes called a raccoon dog in English, the tanuki is in fact a unique species of East Asian canine that resembles a badger or a raccoon. These shy, nocturnal animals can be found on all of the Japanese isles. Tanuki statues are popular decorations in homes and shops. They are beloved not only for their cuteness, but also for the tales of mischief and trickery associated with them.

Behavior: Tanuki possesses powerful magical abilities. They are similar to kitsune in their superb ability to change shape. Tanuki have a jovial nature, and delight in playing tricks on humans.

Aside from their powerful ability to change their shape, perhaps the most famous attribute that tanuki possess is their massive, malleable, magical testicles which they can adapt to any need. Their testicles can be used as weapons, drums, fans to keep cool, fishing nets—even umbrellas. Often, tanuki incorporate their testicles into their disguises: the tanuki becoming a shopkeeper and its testicles transforming into the shop; or perhaps a palanquin complete with servants to cart the tanuki from place to place. A famous nursery rhyme about tanuki testicles is learned by children everywhere:

Tan tan tanuki no kintama wa/Kaze mo nai no ni/Bura bura
Tan-tan-tanuki's balls/Even when there is no wind/They swing, swing

Interaction: In the ancient religions of the Japanese isles, tanuki were considered gods and rulers over all things in nature. With the introduction of Buddhism, they gradually lost their status. Like other magical animals, they took on the roles of messengers of the gods and guardians of local areas. While tanuki are not generally feared or considered malicious, they are not entirely harmless either. Like humans, each one is a unique individual. While many tanuki are jovial do-gooders who love the company of humans, some local tales tell of horrible tanuki who snatch humans to eat, or spirit them away to become servants of the gods.

Other forms: The most intelligent and magically adept tanuki have been known to adopt human names and practices, such as gambling, drinking, even administration and religious activities. Many go through their whole lives living among humans without ever being detected. In human form, tanuki have proven to be as corruptible as the humans they emulate. Some tanuki have well-earned reputations as thieves, drunkards, liars, and cheats.

Additionally, many use their shape-shifting powers to transform into stones, trees, statues, and even ordinary household items in order to play tricks on people. Some even transform into giants and horrible monsters—either to terrorize humans for pleasure, or to scare them away from places they shouldn't be.

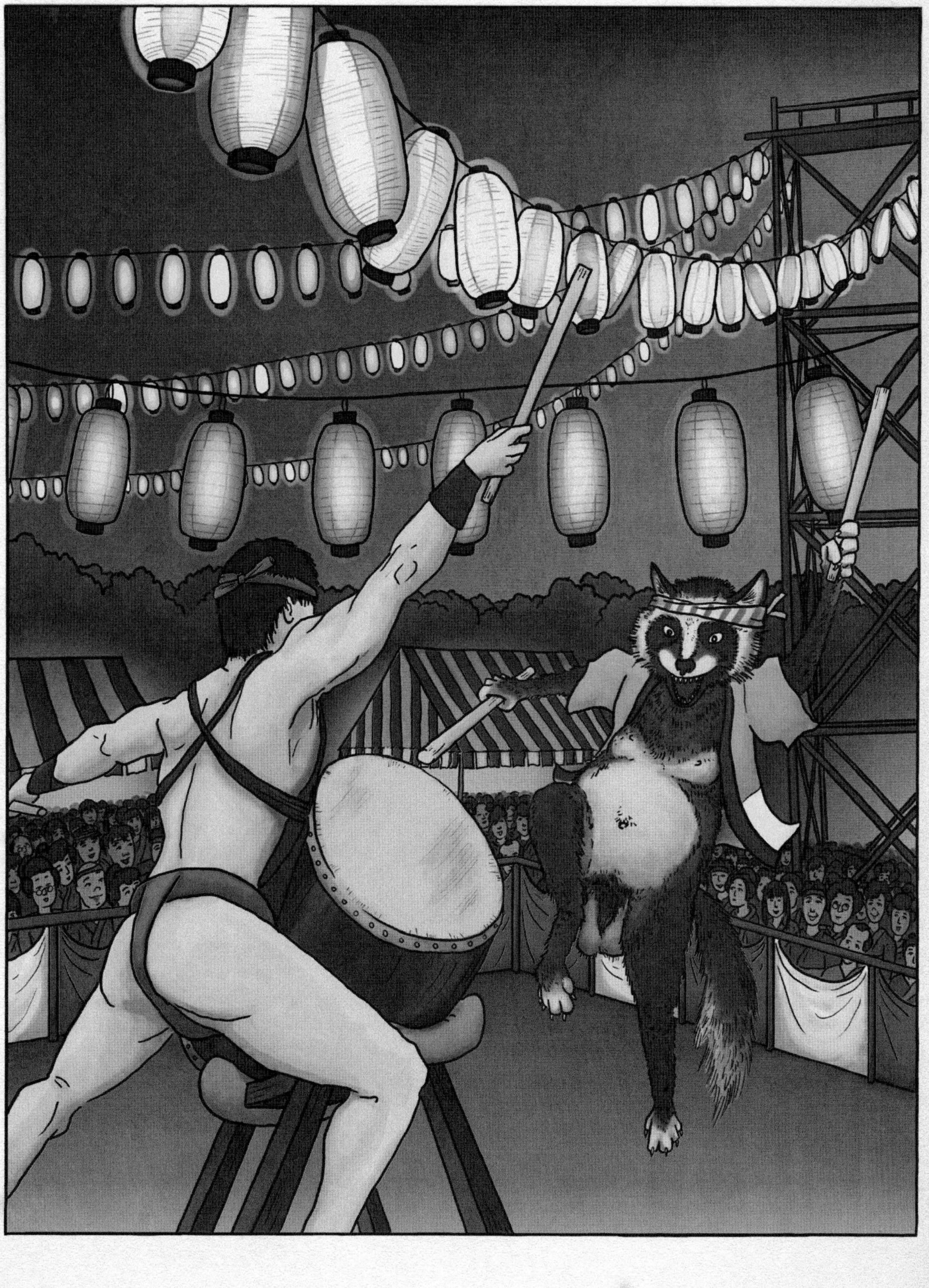

Kitsune 狐

Translation: fox
Alternate names: unique names exist in many individual instances
Habitat: found throughout Japan
Diet: omnivorous; fond of fried tofu

APPEARANCE: Foxes, or kitsune, are found all across Japan. They are identical to wild foxes found elsewhere in the world apart from their incredible magical powers. Their cute faces and small size make them particularly loved by most people.

BEHAVIOR: There are two major variations of kitsune. Holy foxes are servants of the Shinto deity Inari, and Inari's shrines are decorated with statues and images of these foxes. Legends tell of celestial foxes providing wisdom or service to good and pious humans. These holy foxes act as messengers of the gods and mediums between the celestial and human worlds. They often protect humans or places, provide good luck, and ward evil spirits away. More common are the wild foxes which delight in mischief, pranks, or evil. There are stories in which wild foxes trick or even possess humans, and cause them to behave strangely. Despite this wicked nature, even wild foxes keep their promises, remember friendships, and repay any favors done for them.

INTERACTIONS: Most tales of kitsune are about wild foxes punishing wicked priests, greedy merchants, and boastful drunkards. They vex their targets by creating phantom sounds and sights, stealing from them, or otherwise humiliating them publicly. Certain mental disorders have been attributed to possession by kitsune (known as kitsunetsuki). Mysterious illusory fires and strange lights in the sky are said to be caused by their magic, and are known as kitsunebi, or "fox fire."

OTHER FORMS: Kitsune are extremely intelligent and powerful shape-shifters. They frequently harass humans by transforming into giants or other fearsome monsters. Sometimes they do this just for pranks, and sometimes for more nefarious purposes. They are skilled enough to even transform into exact likenesses of individual people, often appearing in the guise of beautiful human women in order to trick young men. On more than one occasion, this has resulted in a marriage with an unwitting human. Some kitsune even spend most of their lives in human form, adopting human names and customs, taking human jobs, and even raising families. When startled, or drunk, or careless, a patch of their magical disguise can fail—the kitsune's true nature may be revealed by a tail, a swatch of fur, fangs, or some other vulpine feature.

NINE-TAILED FOXES

Kitsune are wise and long-lived creatures, and their magical knowledge is said to increase with age. In fact, a fox which reaches its 100th year is said to sprout a second tail; and another one every hundred years thereafter. The most powerful foxes have nine tails and brilliant white-gold fur. These nine-tailed *kyūbi no kitsune* have the power to see and hear anything happening in the world, and are said to hold infinite wisdom.

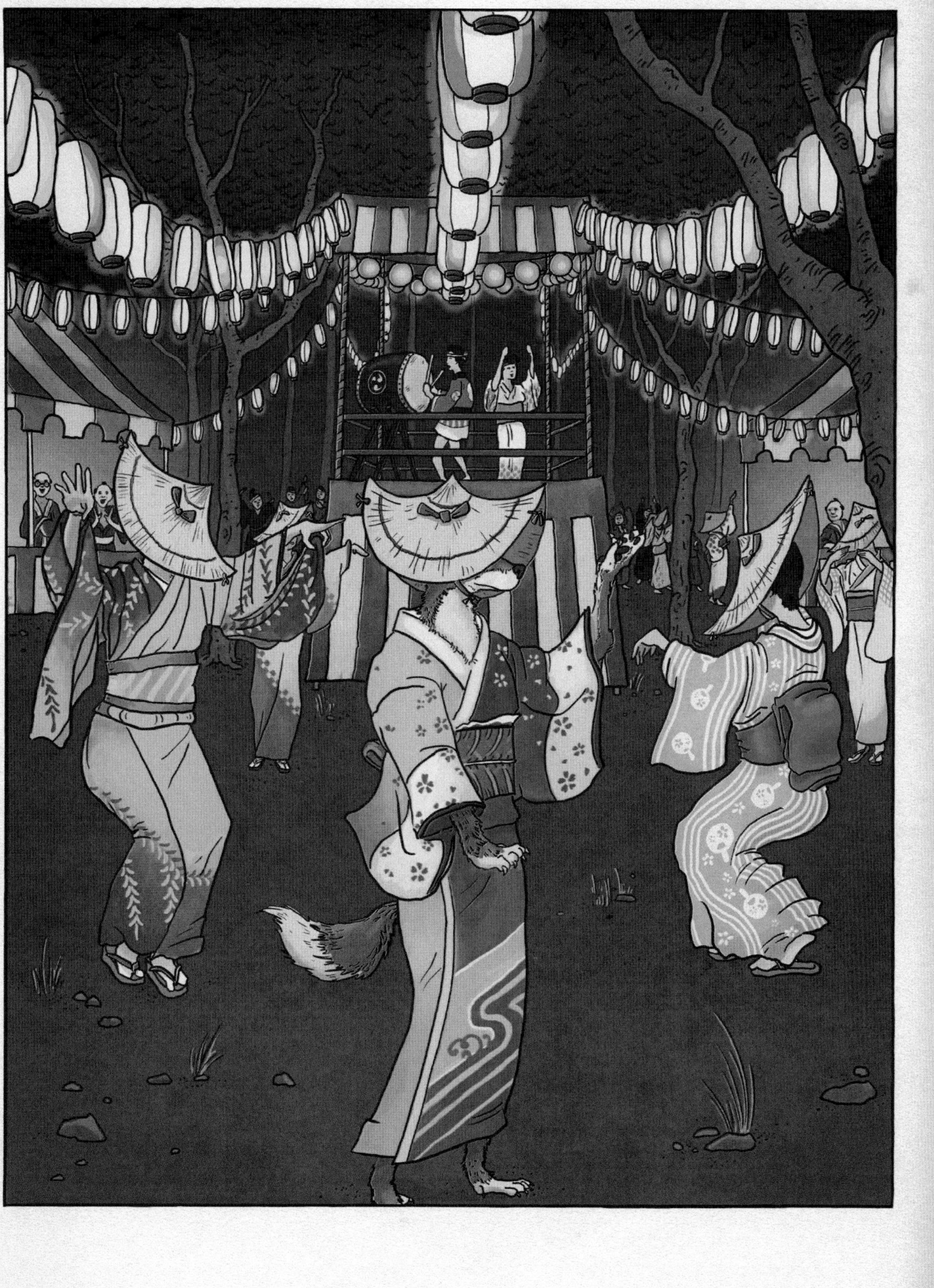

KITSUNEBI 狐火

TRANSLATION: fox fire
HABITAT: originates from kitsune and only appears when they are nearby

APPEARANCE: Kitsunebi, or foxfire, is named for the magical kitsune who are said to create it. Kitsunebi appears as a mass of floating orbs of light, usually only a few centimeters in diameter and less than a meter above the ground. The orbs are as bright as lanterns and, in most cases, appear red or orange; although they are sometimes blue-green.

BEHAVIOR: Kitsunebi appear only at night. There can be a long chain of them hundreds or thousands of meters long, as if there were lanterns carried by invisible bearers. Often the kitsune responsible for the fireballs are standing right next to the flames, invisible.

Kitsunebi are formed by foxes, which breath the ball of fire out from their mouths and use it to light their way at night. It is most often a sign that a large number of kitsune are nearby—often lighting yōkai events such as the night parade of one hundred demons, yōkai wedding ceremonies, and other processions or meetings.

INTERACTIONS: Kitsunebi are not directly dangerous to humans, however the wild foxes behind the strange lights might be harmful. Sometimes, kitsunebi are used to trick humans off of their paths at night as a malicious prank. Other times they are used to lure curious humans into the darkness towards a group of hungry yōkai. Following kitsunebi is never a good idea—they only lead people to places they should not be.

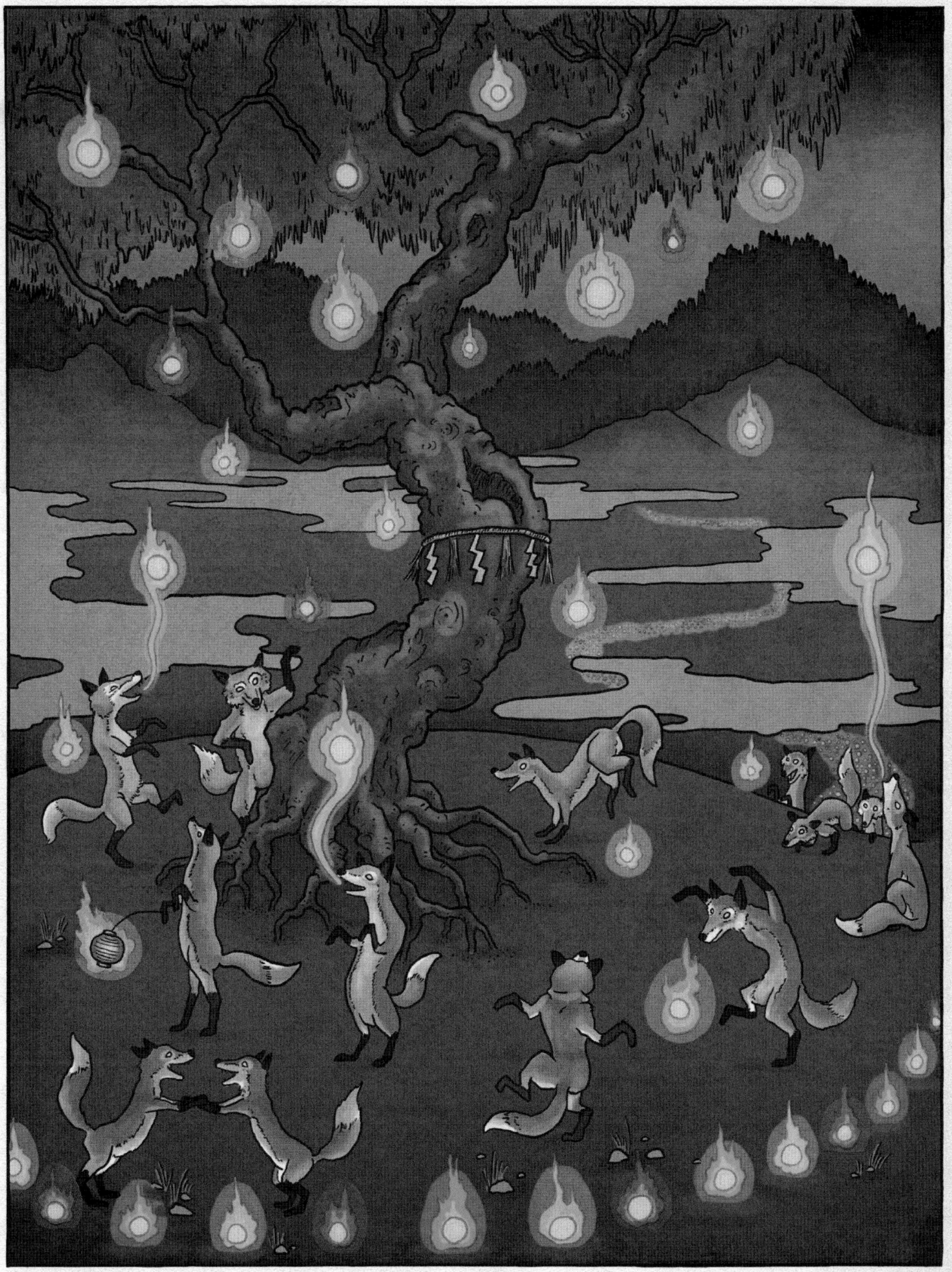

Bakeneko 化け猫

TRANSLATION: monster cat, ghost cat
HABITAT: towns and cities
DIET: carnivorous; fish, birds, small animals, and occasionally humans

APPEARANCE: Cats, feral and domestic, are all over Japan. They are in houses as pets, on farms as exterminators, or in cities and towns as strays. Like many of Japan's animals, when cats live to an old age they develop supernatural powers and transform into yōkai. Bakeneko begin their supernatural life looking almost identical to an ordinary housecat. Soon they begin to walk about at on their hind legs. As they age and their powers increase, they can grow large indeed—up to the size of a full-grown human.

BEHAVIOR: Bakeneko possess great shape-shifting abilities and disguise themselves as smaller cats or humans—sometimes even taking the shape of their own masters. Many learn to speak human languages. While in disguise, they are known to dress up as humans with towels wrapped around their heads. In this form bakeneko dance around merrily. While this sounds frivolous and even cute, bakeneko are a menace to any house they live in or near. They can eat things that are much bigger than they are, and can even consume poisonous things without difficulty. It is possible for a bakeneko to eat its own master and then assume his form, living in his place. If they do not directly kill their owners, they can bring down great curses and misfortune. They can summon ghostly fireballs and are known to accidentally start house fires, their tails acting like torches igniting any flammable materials in the house. Bakeneko also have the disturbing ability to reanimate fresh corpses and use them like puppets for their own nefarious purposes.

ORIGIN: Bakeneko can come into being as a result of a number of things, but the most common reasons are by being long-lived (over 13 years old), growing to a certain size (over 3.75 kilograms), or by licking up large quantities of lamp oil. A telltale sign that a cat may be close to becoming a bakeneko is believed to be an exceptionally long tail. The older and wiser a cat gets, the longer its tail becomes. This superstition led to the custom of bobbing cats' tails at an early age to prevent them from transforming into yōkai.

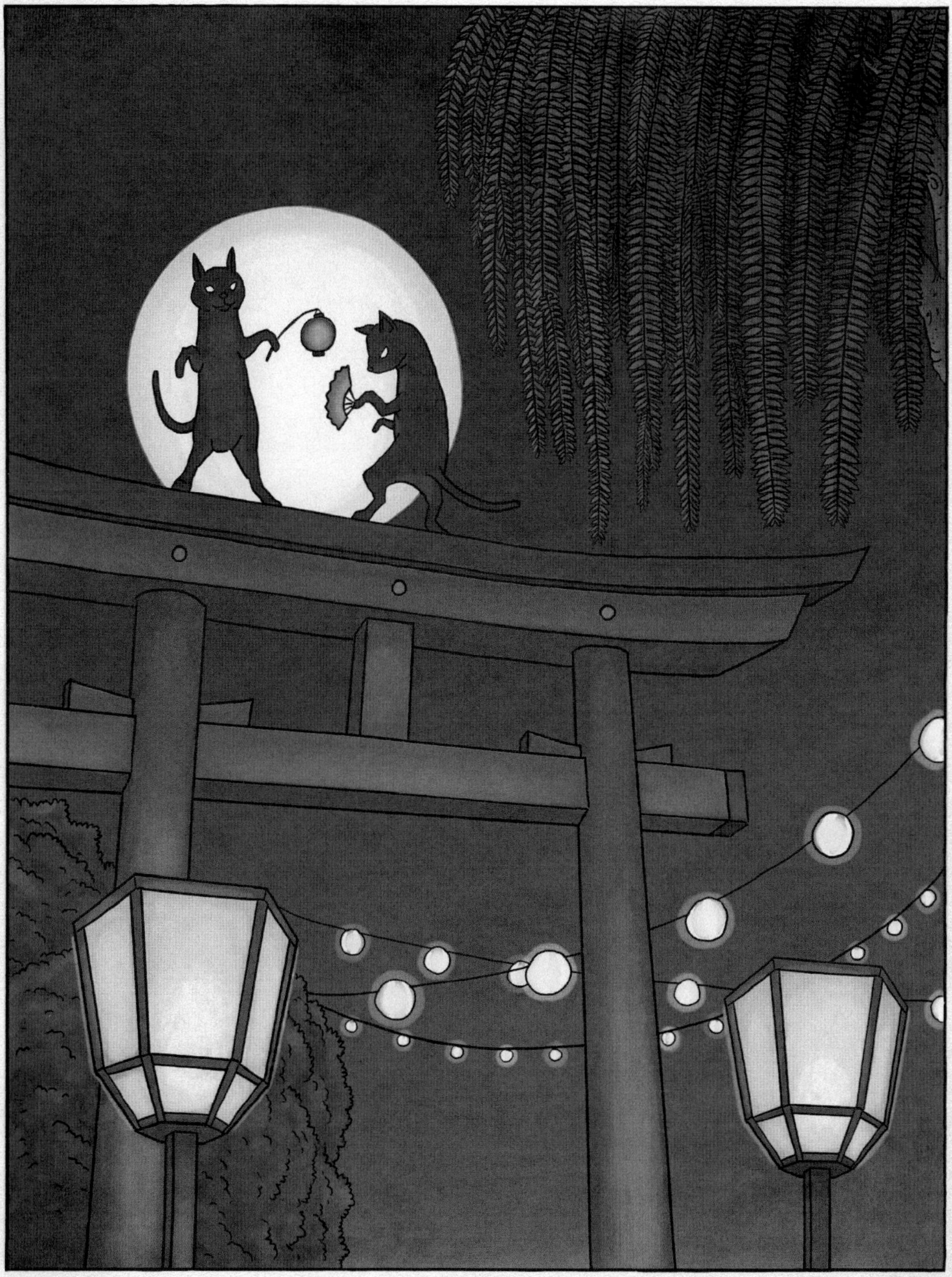

Nekomata 猫又

TRANSLATION: forked cat
HABITAT: towns and cities
DIET: carnivorous; frequently humans

APPEARANCE: One particularly monstrous breed of bakeneko is the two-tailed variety known as nekomata. Nekomata are found in cities and villages and are born in the same way as other bakeneko. However, only the oldest, largest cats with the longest tails—and thus the most intelligence—become this powerful variety. When a nekomata transforms into a yōkai, its tail splits down the center into two identical tails. These monster cats are most likely seen walking around on their hind legs and speaking human languages.

BEHAVIOR: While not all bakeneko are malicious or violent towards their masters, all nekomata are; they look upon humans with contempt. Nekomata summon fireballs and start great conflagrations, killing many people. They control corpses like puppet-masters with their necromantic powers, and they use their powerful influence to blackmail or enslave humans.

The most dangerous and powerful nekomata live deep in the mountains, where they prowl in the shape of wild cats like leopards and lions. They grow to incredible sizes, many meters long, and prey on other large animals such as wild boars, dogs, bears, and of course humans.

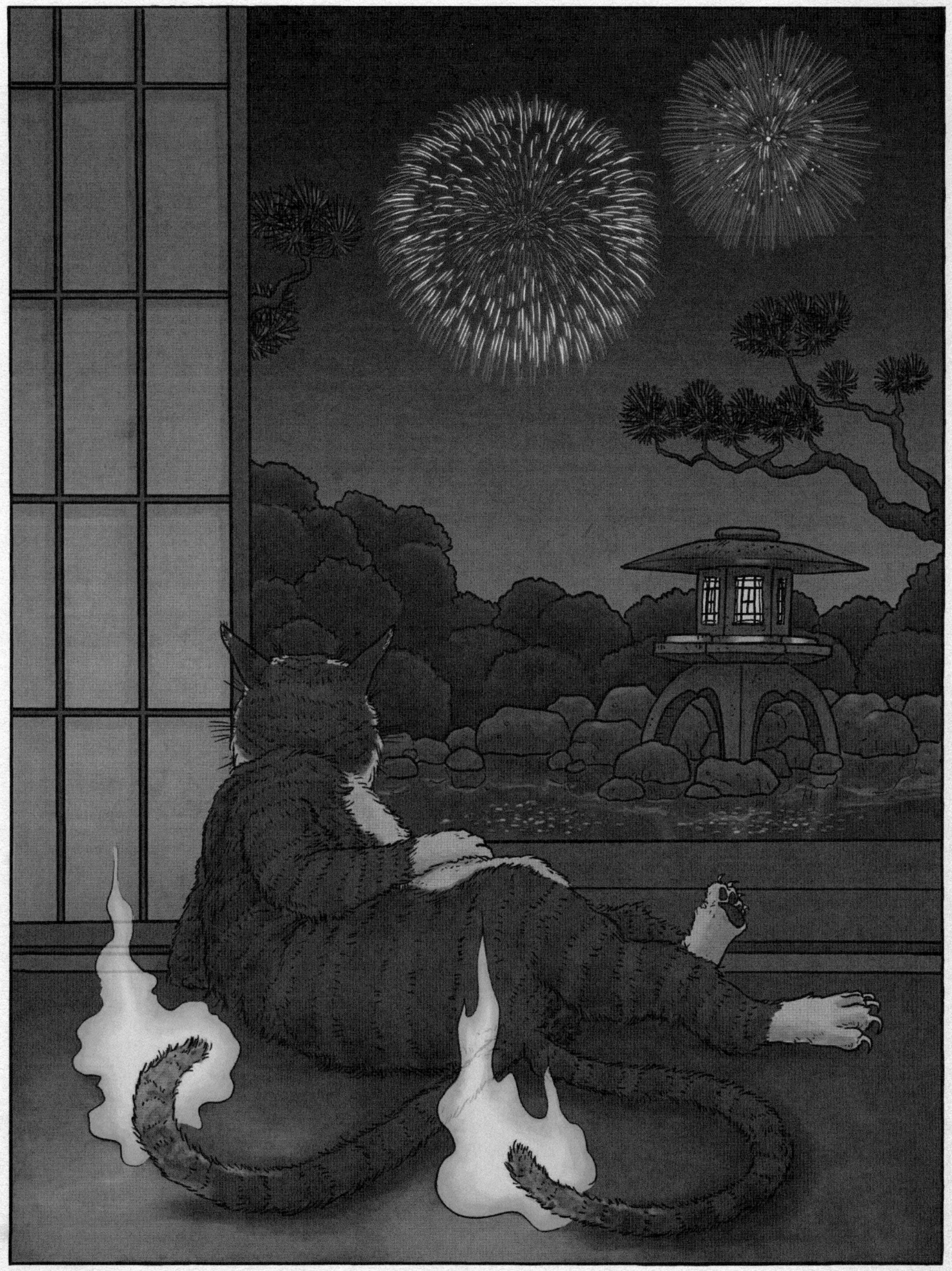

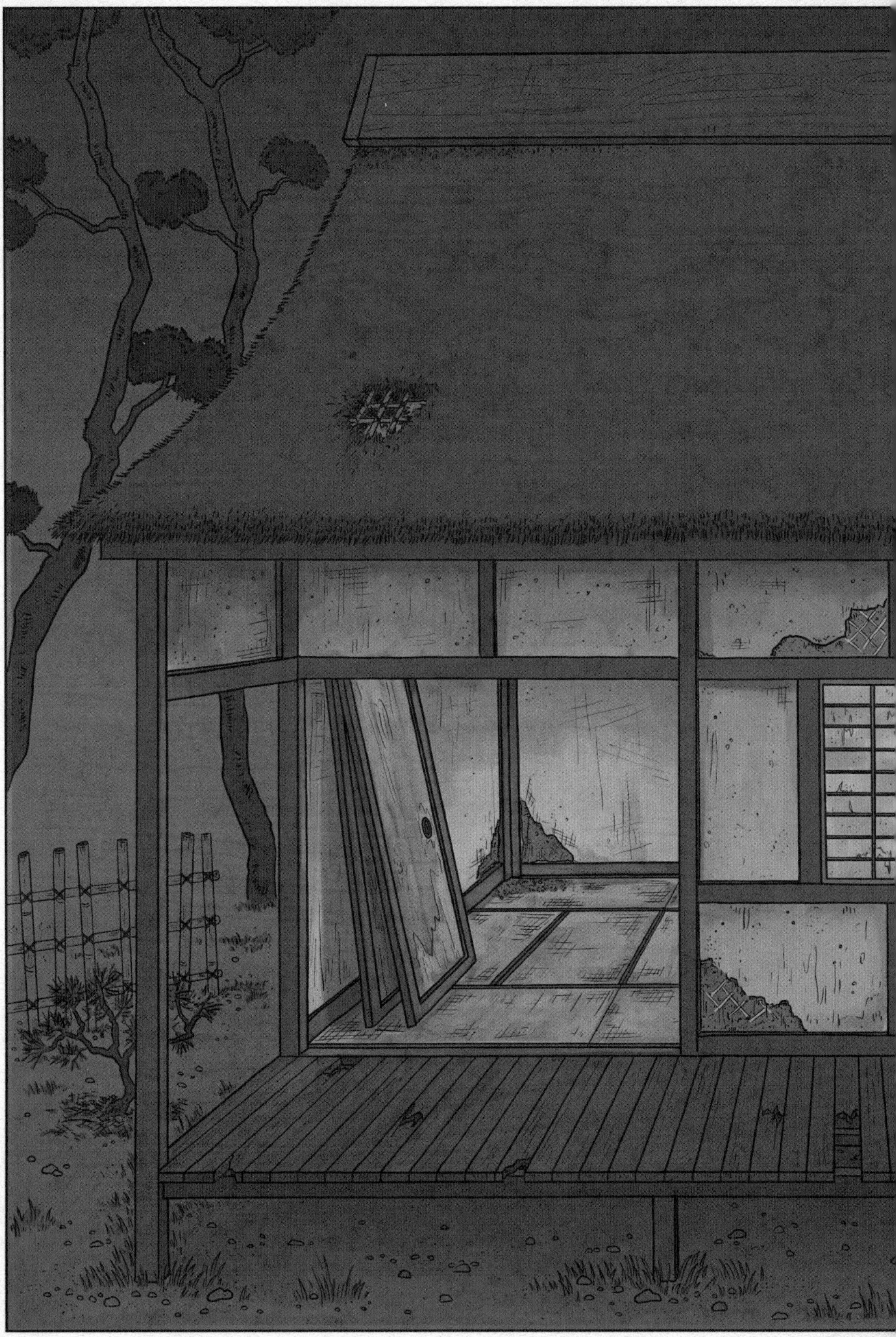

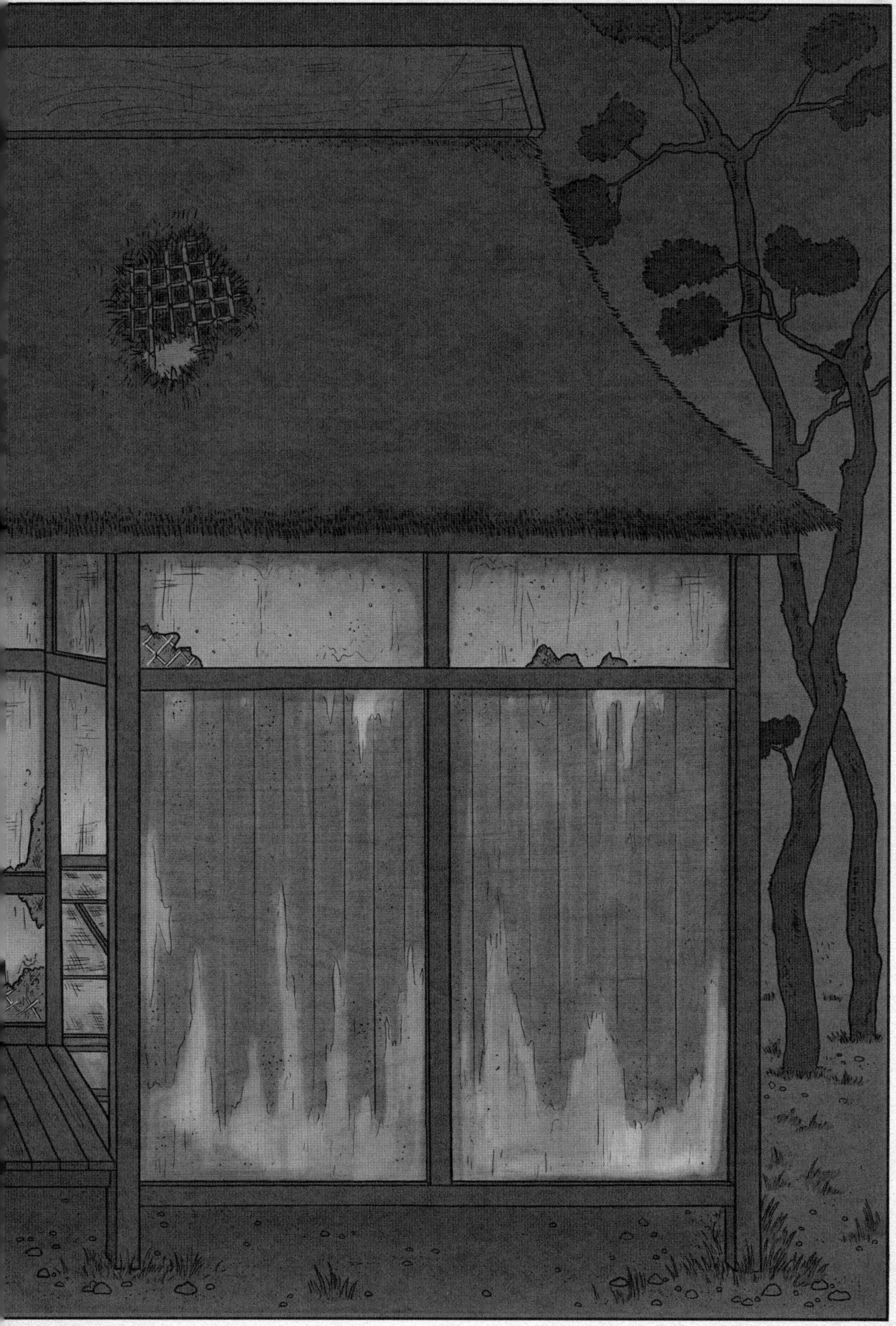

Shōkera 精螻蛄

Translation: mole cricket spirit
Habitat: rooftops, temples; only appears every sixty nights
Diet: wicked humans who try to outsmart the gods

Appearance: The shōkera is a large, dark-skinned, three-toed demon which spends most of its time lurking about on rooftops. Not much is known about this fearsome beast aside from its hunting practices. The shōkera is believed to be some kind of demon with connections to Kōshin, an esoteric Japanese folk religion with origins in Taoism.

Interactions: Shōkera only appear on special nights in the Kōshin faith which occurs every sixty nights. A shōkera spies through windows, doorways, or skylights in houses, and hunts for impious behavior. Then it pounces down in a vicious attack. Because Kōshin is no longer a widespread religion—and because victims of shōkera attacks would only be implicating themselves as wicked by admitting to seeing one—little else is known about the shōkera.

Origin: According to Kōshin, there are three spiritual worms or insects, called the sanshi, which live inside every human body. Every sixty nights, on a special night called *kōshin machi*, these worms leave the body while their host human sleeps. The sanshi travel to heaven to report on the good and bad deeds of their human. The emperor of heaven then uses this information to lengthen or shorten people's lives according to their deeds. While good people have nothing to fear from kōshin machi, the wicked might try to circumvent having their bad deeds reported by staying awake and reciting prayers all night long during these special nights so that the sanshi cannot leave the body. That's when the shōkera goes to work. It lurks about on rooftops during these nights, peers into windows, and hunts for anyone violating the laws of heaven.

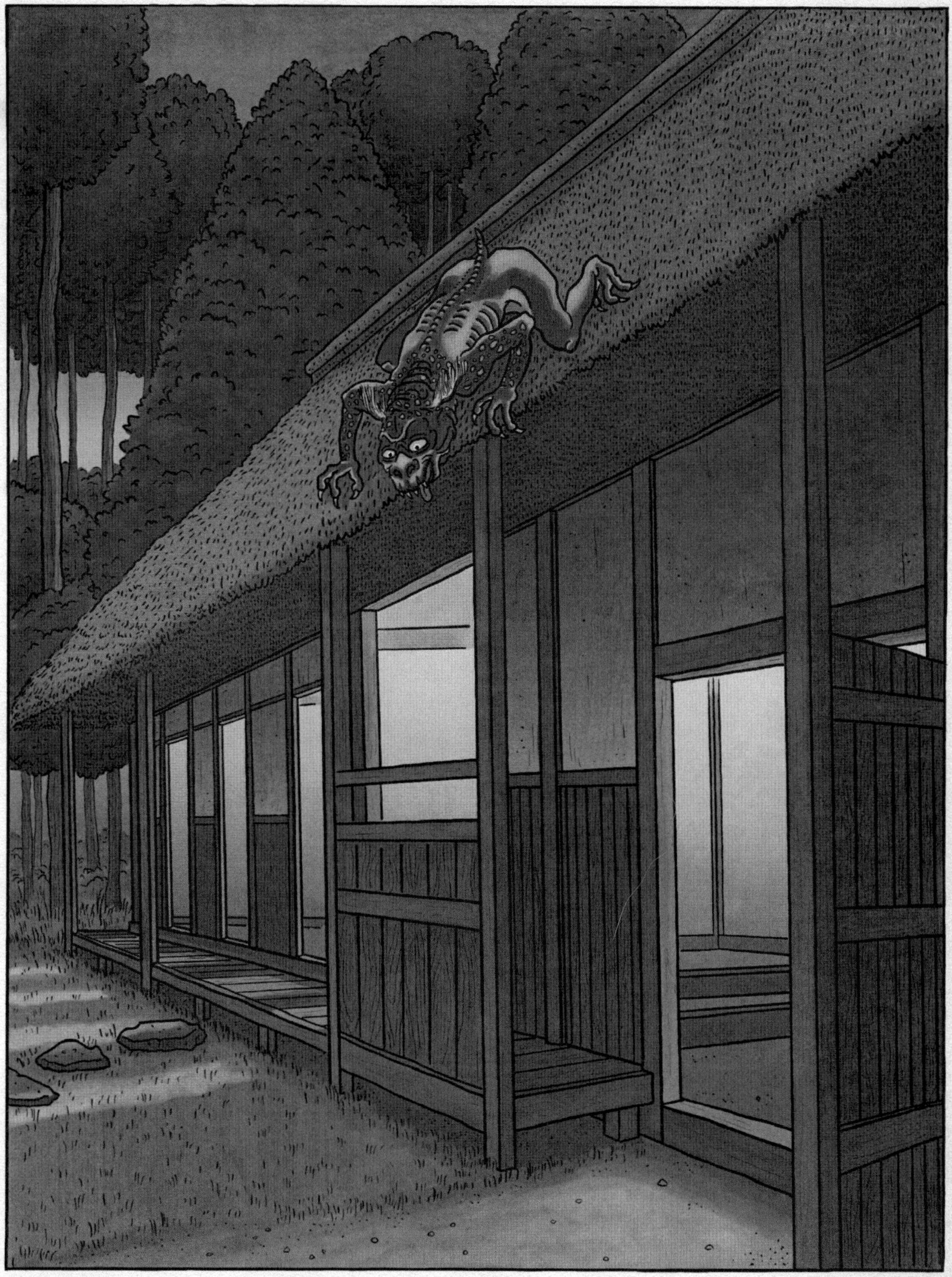

Ao nyōbō 青女房

TRANSLATION: blue lady
ALTERNATE NAMES: ao onna ("blue woman")
HABITAT: abandoned villas, mansions, and ruins
DIET: spoiled and rotten leftover food; otherwise humans

APPEARANCE: In the empty, abandoned mansions of bygone eras, there is sometimes more than spider webs and cockroaches lurking in the shadows. Often, large and dangerous yōkai take up residence in these domiciles. One of these is the ao nyōbō, an ogreish spirit of poverty and misfortune. She takes the appearance of an ancient court noblewoman. Her body is draped in the elaborate, many layered kimonos of ancient eras. Once fabulous, her gowns are now tattered and moth-ridden. She wears the white face of ancient courtiers, with high painted eyebrows and blackened teeth. Aged and wrinkled from years of waiting in musty old ruins, her beauty has long left her.

BEHAVIOR: Ao nyōbō inhabit the empty, abandoned homes of ruined families and fallen nobles. They wait in the house, constantly applying their makeup, fixing their hair, and adjusting their image. They act as if they are in anticipation for the arrival of some guest—perhaps a lover who has lost interest, or a husband who has abandoned his wife. In any case, should a trespasser visit a home inhabited by an ao nyōbō, she devours them whole. And then goes back to waiting vainly for someone who will never show.

ORIGIN: *Nyōbō* were the court ladies of old Japan. The paragons of youth, beauty, education, and refinement, nyōbō served in the palaces of high ranking families, a position they held until they themselves were married to a worthy suitor. After marriage, they idled their days in their own private residences, patiently waiting for their husbands to come home each night, or for secret lovers to show up during the day. But not all nyōbō were so successful.

The *ao* in the name ao nyōbō means the color blue. This does not refer to skin color, but implies immaturity or inexperience (just as green implies the same in English). There were some low-ranking women of the old imperial court who—no matter how hard they worked—couldn't seem to attract a husband or elevate themselves. These "blue" nyōbō were destined to grow into bitter old maids, desperate to increase their social status but never able to escape from their subordinate positions. When they died, these unsuccessful courtiers turned into yōkai.

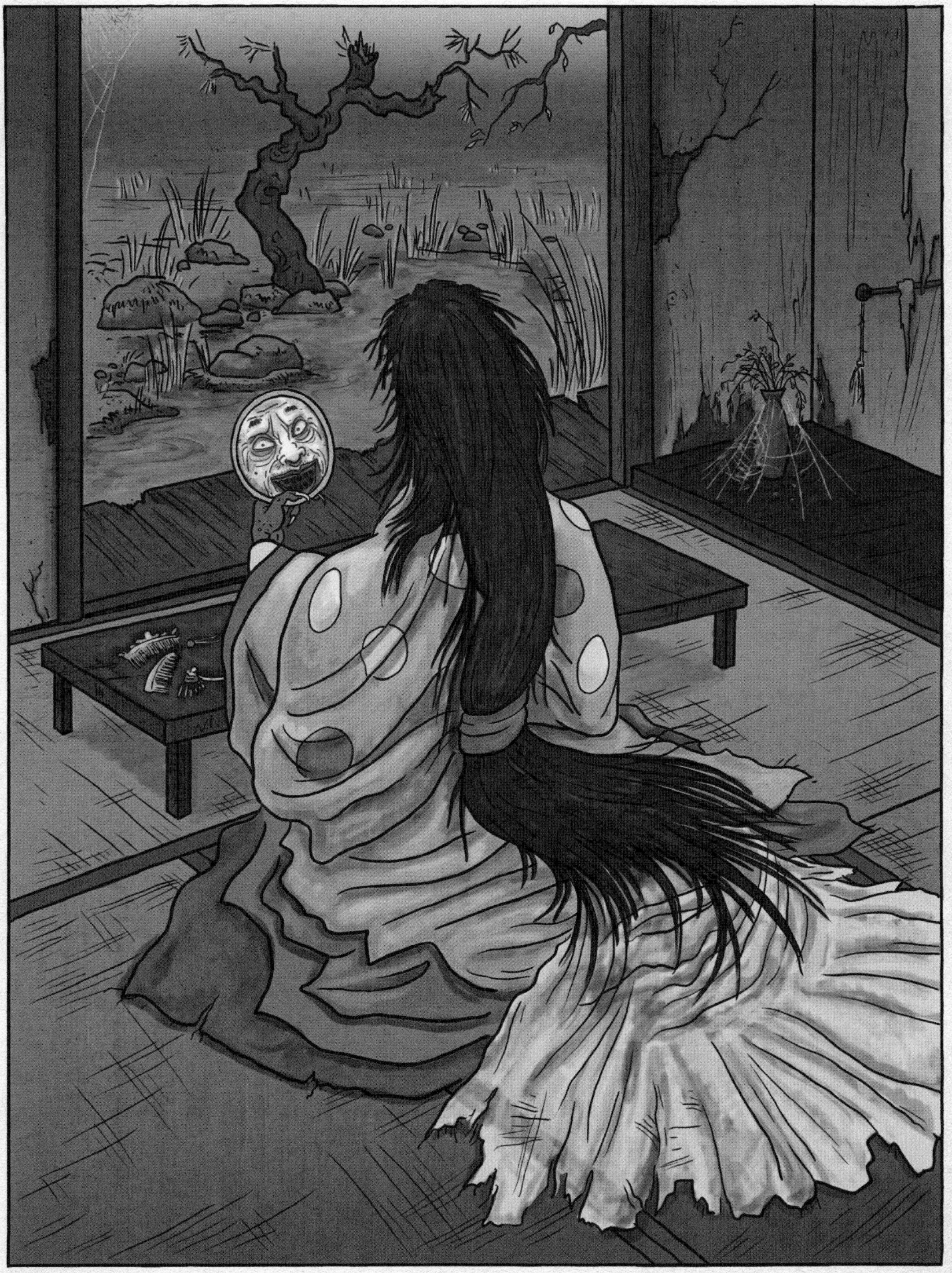

Kage onna 影女

TRANSLATION: shadow woman
HABITAT: abandoned buildings, run-down homes, haunted houses
DIET: none

APPEARANCE: Kage onna are the shadows of women projected onto windows and doors when there is no one around to cast them. They usually take the form of young ladies, though occasionally they appear as old crones with bells hanging from their necks. They appear late at night, when the moon is bright. The paper sliding doors and windows of traditional Japanese homes are particularly good at catching kage onna shadows in the moonlight.

BEHAVIOR: Kage onna make no sound, nor do they interact with the house or its inhabitants. Other than projecting an eerie atmosphere, they are not known to cause any harm. In any case, the image of a person who should not be there is enough to startle the bravest person. If the door or window is opened to see who or what created the shadow, there will be nothing waiting in the dark. However, tradition says that a house where a kage onna is seen is likely haunted—or will soon be haunted—by other yōkai as well.

ORIGIN: The moonlight frequently plays tricks on the eyes, causing people to see things in the darkness that aren't really there. The bright moon casts eerie shadows on the ground and walls that don't seem like they should fit. Most of the time, this can be attributed to an overactive mind piecing together ghost stories and wandering thoughts, or constructing some horrible figment of the imagination. Sometimes, however, a shadow is more than a shadow; sometimes it is a kage onna.

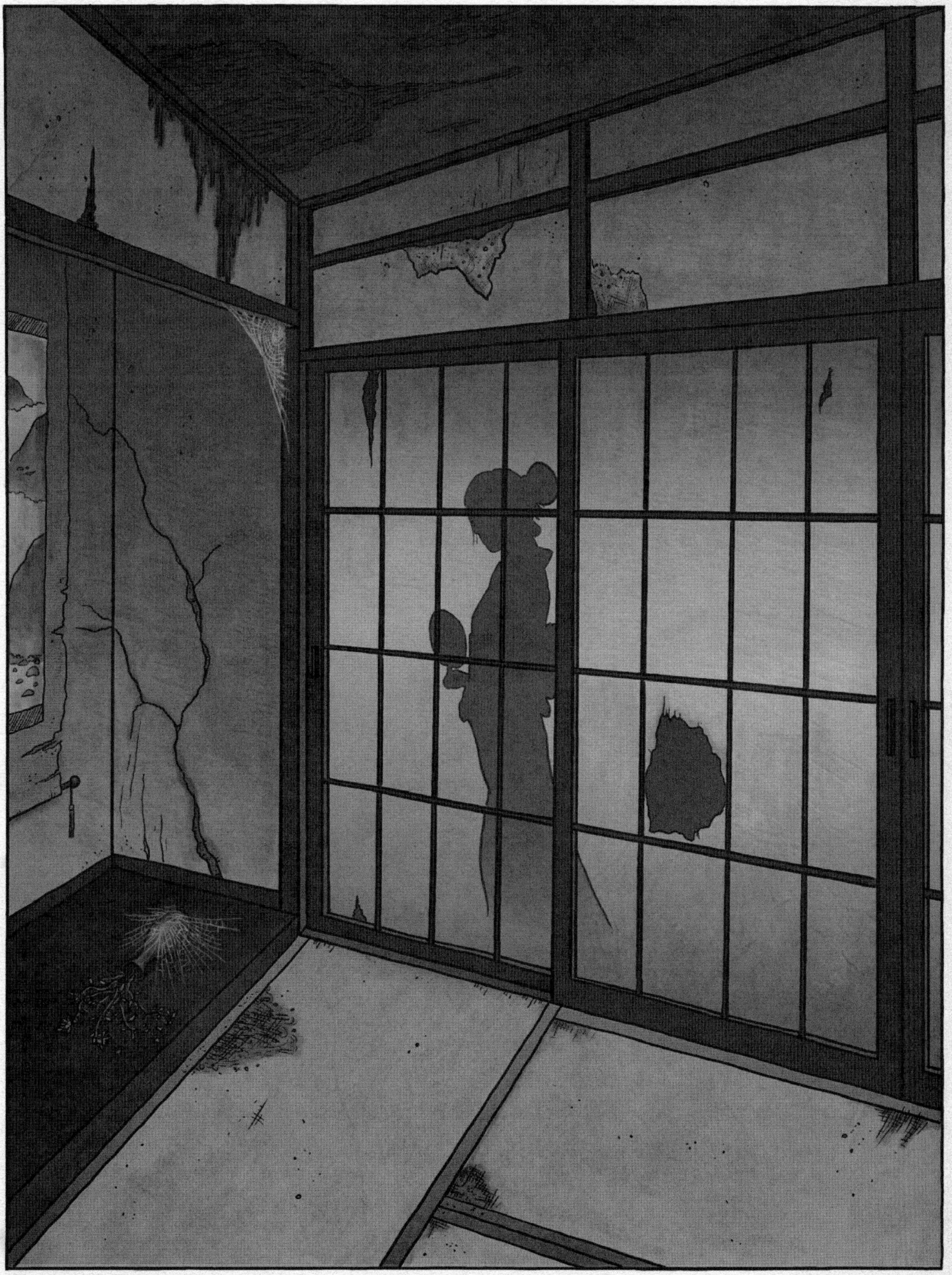

Nuribotoke 塗佛

TRANSLATION: coated buddha
HABITAT: poorly cared for family altars, run-down homes
DIET: none

APPEARANCE: Nuribotoke is a grotesque zombie-like spirit which creeps out of a butsudan, or family altar, that has been accidentally left open at night. It is a soft, flabby, corpse-like spirit with oily black skin and a pungent smell. Trailing behind is a catfish-like tail connected to its spine. The most striking and disturbing feature is this spirit's eyeballs, which dangle wildly from its eye sockets.

INTERACTIONS: Nuribotoke do not do much other than fly about, flap their tails, and terrorize the families whose butsudan they crawled out from. They dance about impishly and revel in their ability to terrorize the living. Occasionally they try to trick foolish humans by giving false prophecies. They can be kept at bay by sprinkling salt on the floor, which they will avoid crossing. Nuribotoke must return to the butsudan before sunrise, and they vanish altogether during the day. Even though they are mostly harmless, it is best to prevent their appearance altogether by shutting the butsudan at night.

ORIGIN: In most Japanese homes there is a large, ornate, wooden shrine called a butsudan. Inside are religious icons, scrolls, mantras, statues, and other holy items. It serves as the center of household spirituality, and the ancestors of a family are all enshrined in it. During the day, the butsudan stays open. During holidays and special occasions, it is treated like a member of the family and treated to offerings of food and sake. The doors to a butsudan are always closed at sunset—the butsudan is a gateway to the spirit world. Superstition warns that if the butsudan is left open certain spirits can wander freely back and forth between the land of the living and the land of the dead. Nuribotoke is one of these spirits.

COATING THE DEAD

Nuribotoke's skin is black because of lacquering, which helps explain the meaning of its name—"coated Buddha." Japan is a wet country, and corpses did not last long in the old days. Before modern preservation techniques came to the country, corpses would putrefy during the hot and humid summers. Embalming a corpse in lacquer was one method of preservation. Lacquer embalming was particularly used with the corpses of important priests. The nuribotoke's lacquered skin reflects the high status it had during its lifetime.

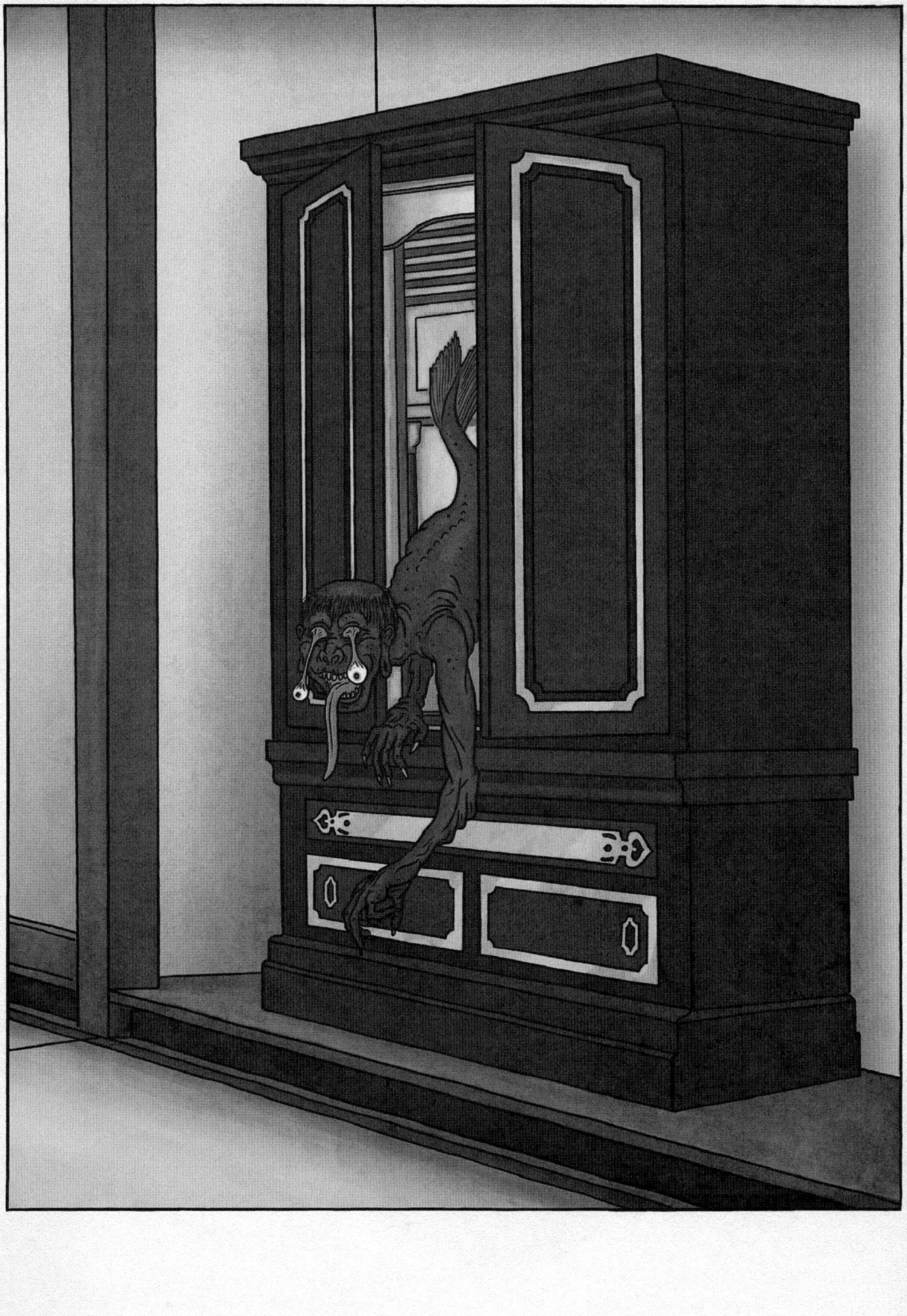

Zashiki warashi 座敷童子

Translation: zashiki child
Alternate names: many, depending in the region and variety of spirit
Habitat: zashiki (a kind of sitting room covered in tatami mats) and other rooms
Diet: none, but enjoys candies and treats left out for it

Appearance: Zashiki warashi are house spirits. They are fond of mischief, loved by all, and believed to bring great fortune and riches to those whose houses they haunt. Direct sightings of these spirits are rare. It is often difficult to make out any details other than a vague, child-like shape. When they can be seen, zashiki warashi appear as ghostly children, five or six years old and with blushing red faces. The boys are dressed in child-sized warrior costumes and the girls in patterned kimonos and with hair that is either short and bobbed or long and tied back. In rare stories they appear as wild, hairy, brutish figures. It is said that only children and the house's owners are able to see these spirits. They are usually known only by their pranks.

Behavior: Zashiki warashi love mischief. Often the first signs that one's house may be inhabited is by a trail of children's footprints going through ashes or soap powder. Other mischief includes making phantom noises. These noises sound like children's games—tops spinning all night long, paper crinkling, children's voices, or kagura—Shinto holy music. Most hauntings involve a single zashiki warashi, while some involve multiple spirits.

Interactions: Zashiki warashi are considered guardian spirits of the house, and gods of luck. It is said that a house with a zashiki warashi will prosper and grow rich, and a house that drives away such a spirit will fall into decline and ruin. In one account, a family witnessed a zashiki warashi leaving their home, and soon they all succumbed to food poisoning and died. In another well-known legend from Iwate Prefecture, a wealthy man's son shot a zashiki warashi with a bow and arrow. Soon after the family's fortunes collapsed.

In many homes, these spirits befriend the children of the house, teaching them songs, games, and nursery rhymes. They keep elderly or infertile couples company, and these couples often treat the zashiki warashi as if it were their own child. The desire to attract and keep these friendly yōkai has led to customs like setting out food in the zashiki for them, and even laying coins in the foundation when building a new house. The Japanese take great care to maintain their formal reception room so as not to drive out any guardian spirits dwelling there.

Other forms: Their common name comes from the zashiki, the formal reception room for guests in a Japanese house where these spirits most often reside. Zashiki warashi are known by many different names in other areas, such as kura bokko or "warehouse child," and makura gaeshi, or "pillow turner." Countless variations of zashiki warashi exist across Japan, with minor differences in their appearance and behavior.

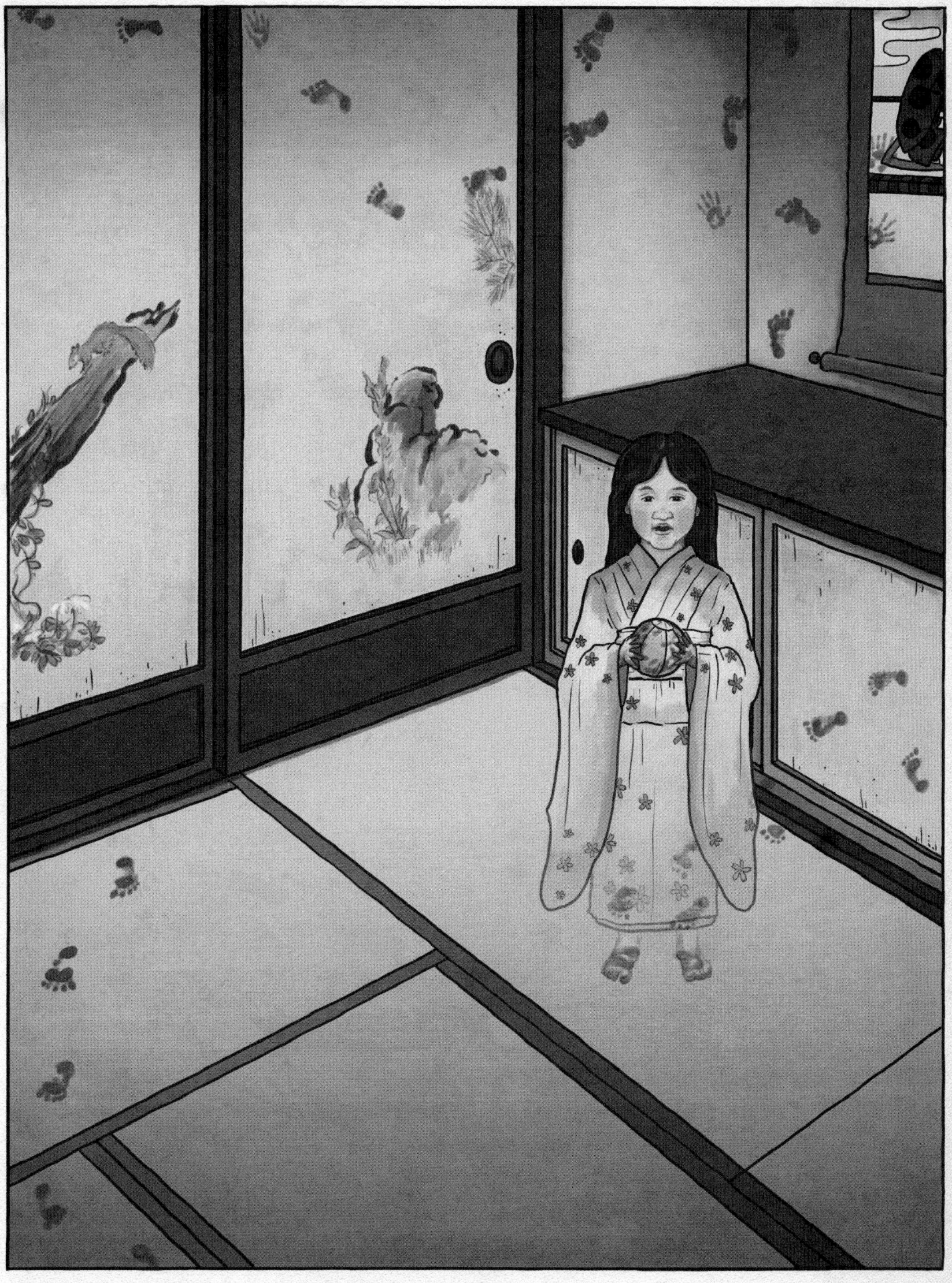

CHŌPIRAKO チョウピラコ

TRANSLATION: none
ALTERNATE NAMES: often simply referred to as zashiki warashi
HABITAT: inner parlors and living rooms
DIET: none, but enjoys candies and treats left out for it

APPEARANCE: Chōpirako are similar to ordinary zashiki warashi, only they are much more beautiful. Their skin and clothing glows with pure, radiant white light. Their features are more beautiful than human children. Chōpirako are usually found in the homes of families that had an only child who died—but who was loved and lavished with gifts before they passed away.

BEHAVIOR: Like other zashiki warashi, chōpirako bring richness and prosperity to the houses they inhabit, and promote happiness and well-being among the inhabitants. They require more maintenance to keep them happy than zashiki warashi do; but in return they bring more wealth and good luck than other kinds of house spirits.

ORIGIN: Rich families who could afford it often presented lavish funerals for deceased children, with beautiful burial gowns. The deceased child's room is turned into a shrine, full of lavish toys, books, and games that the child would have loved in life. The chōpirako resides in the this room, rather than in the zashiki, and few people are allowed to enter in order to keep it in the pristine condition this spirit requires.

A few inns in Japan advertise that they are inhabited by zashiki warashi or chōpirako in order to attract spirit hunting guests or people seeking good luck and fortune.

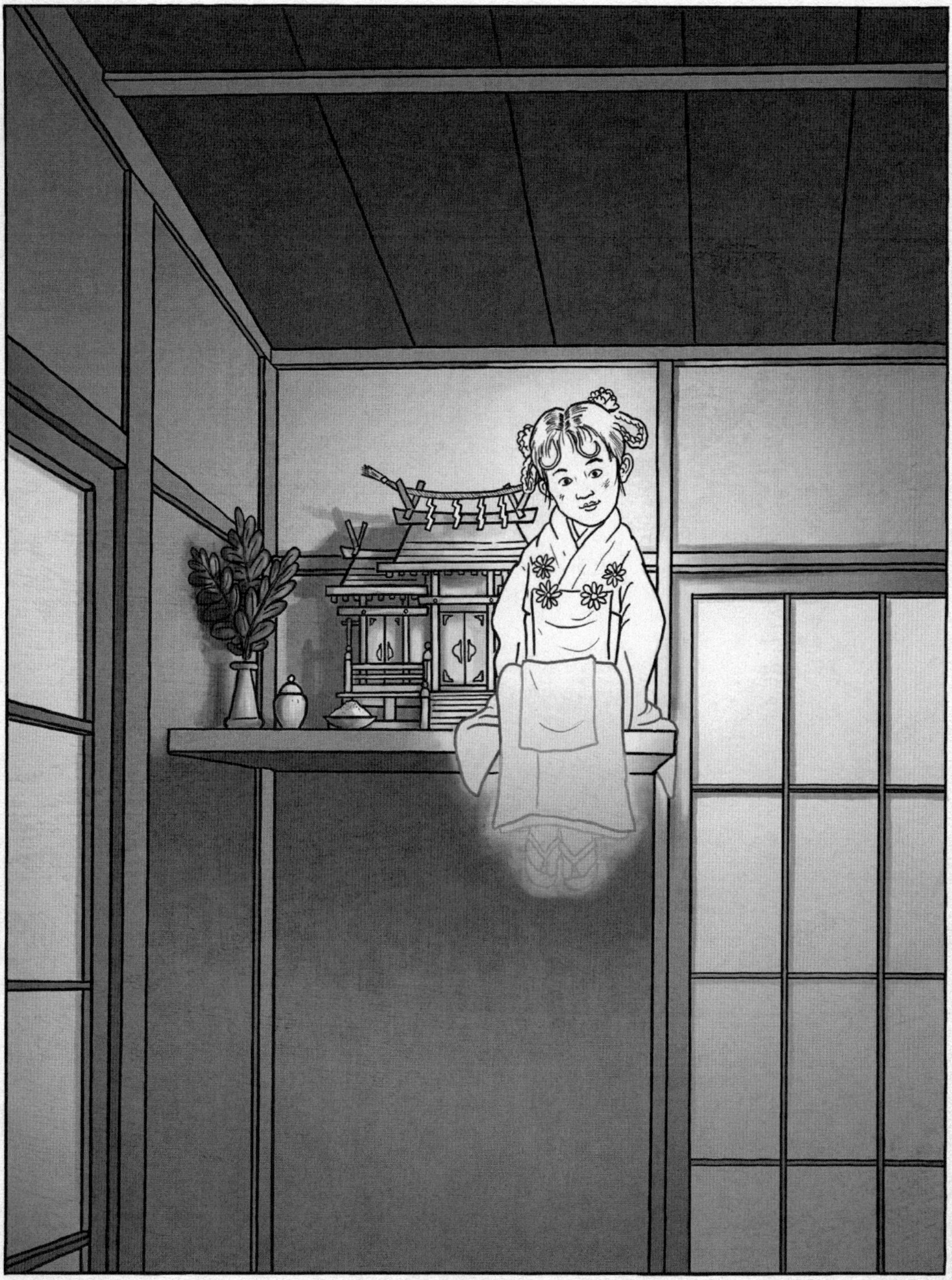

Usutsuki warashi 臼搗童子

TRANSLATION: mortar pounding child
ALTERNATE NAMES: notabariko
HABITAT: warehouses, storage sheds, under floorboards
DIET: none

APPEARANCE: One particularly unpleasant variation of the zashiki warashi is the usutsuki warashi, named for the eerie thumping noise that these low ranking house spirits make.

BEHAVIOR: Unlike their bright and cheerful cousins, usutsuki warashi crawl out from the dirt underneath the floorboards and roam about the house at night. They make creepy noises, creaking and thumping, and track dirty footprints throughout the house. Usutsuki warashi do not cause any actual harm, though they spread unease and discomfort in houses that they infect. Unlike other zashiki warashi, these troublemakers do not bring any good fortune to their homes. However, a house which drives these spirits away will still fall into ruin, just like a house that drives away the more pleasant zashiki warashi.

ORIGIN: This spirit's origin is similar to that of the yamauba. It comes from the old and terrible practice of *kuchiberashi*, or "reducing the mouths to feed" by thinning out families during times when food was scarce. Some houses with too many mouths to feed had no other choice but to sacrifice the newly born. The cost of a funeral also being too high, these children were buried underneath the house or in a storage shed. Instead of a tombstone, often an usu, a large mortar, was placed as a grave marker.

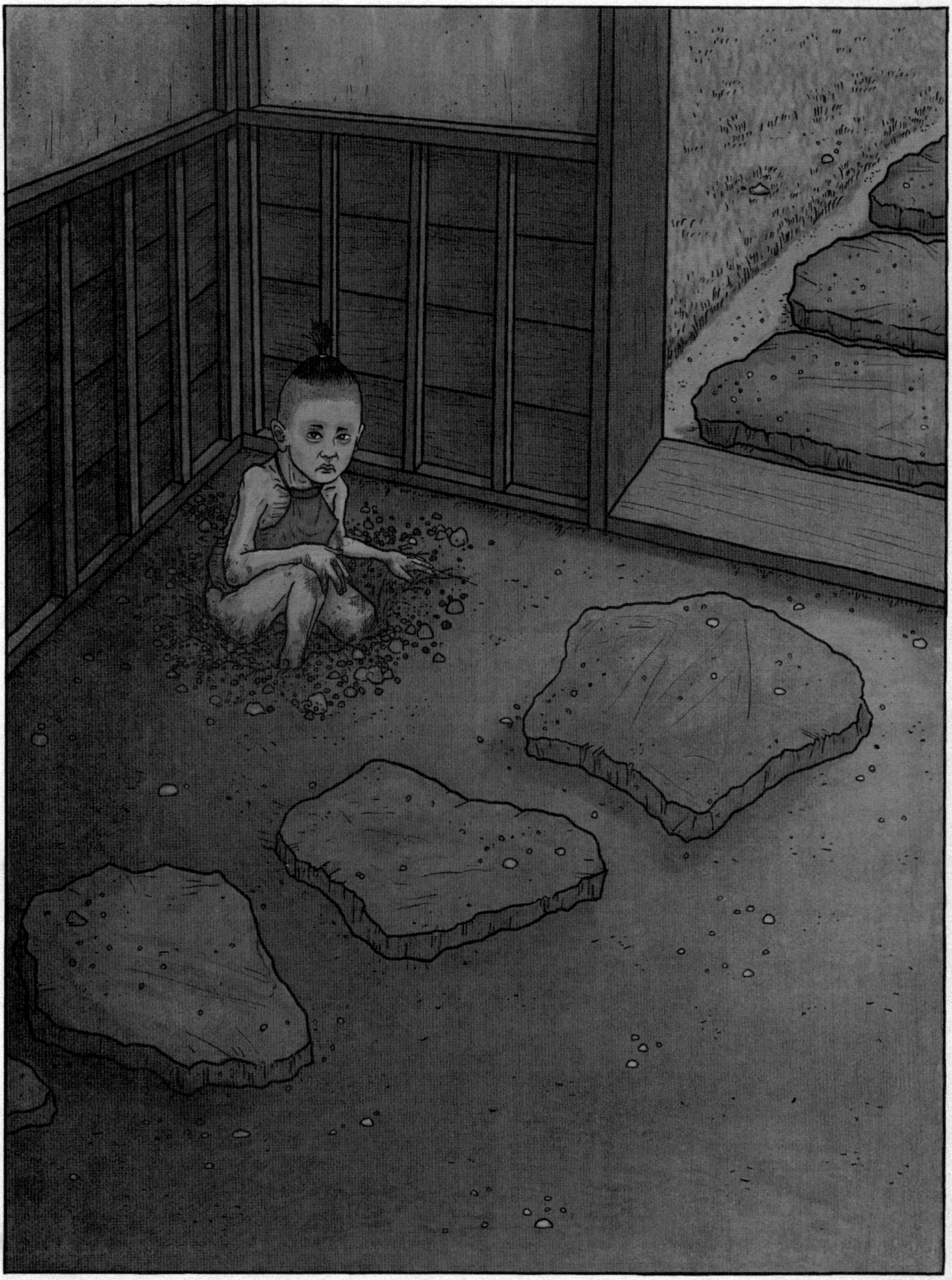

AKANAME 垢嘗

TRANSLATION: filth licker
HABITAT: dirty baths, filthy toilets, abandoned homes
DIET: slime, mold, scum, hair, human waste, etc.

APPEARANCE: Akaname are small, goblin-like yōkai which inhabit only the dirtiest homes and public baths. They are about the size of a child or a small adult, though they generally appears much smaller due to their hunching posture. Akaname have a mop of greasy, slimy hair on the tops of their heads. Their bodies are naked, and their skin is greasy like their hair. Akaname come in many colors and varieties, ranging from a dark, mottled green reminiscent of mold, to the ruddy pink of bedsores. They come in both one-eyed and two-eyed varieties, and can have anywhere from one to five fingers and toes. All akaname have an extremely long, sticky tongue. They use this to lap up the slime, grease, hair, and other filth found in bath houses and behind toilets.

BEHAVIOR: Like cockroaches, rats, lice, and other pests, akaname detest clean, well-kept homes. They only appear where the owners show a complete lack of sanitary discipline. Akaname are shy and stay clear of humans, scattering in the light like cockroaches. They spread disease, so it is a good idea to keep bathrooms and houses clean enough that akaname do not wish to settle down.

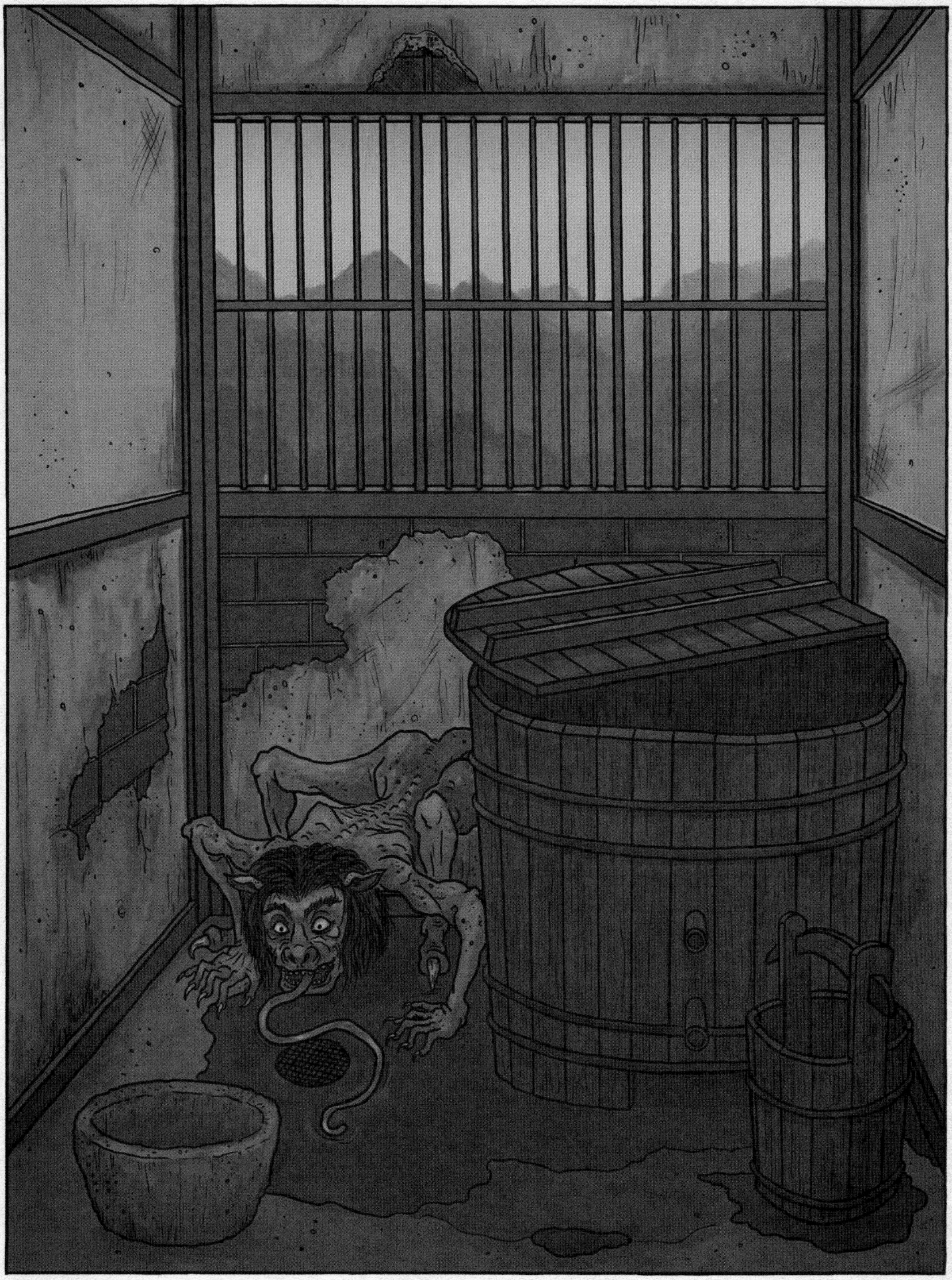

KEUKEGEN 毛羽毛現

TRANSLATION: hairy, fluffy sight; alternatively, rare and dubious thing
HABITAT: damp homes, dirty gardens, moldy closets, under floorboards
DIET: mold, dirt, and garbage

APPEARANCE: Keukegen are filthy monsters commonly found in populated areas. They are the size of a small dog and appear as a mass of long, dirty hair. Keukegen make their homes in cool, damp, dark places; they are particularly fond of living under floorboards and around run-down homes, where stuffiness, moisture, and lack of human activity create the perfect breeding place for sickness.

BEHAVIOR: Despite their apparent cuteness, Keukegen do not make good pets. They are actually a kind of minor spirit of bad luck, disease, and pestilence. They bring sickness and bad health to those whom they live near. Being shy by nature, they try to avoid human contact and are rarely seen. Those who claim to have seen them are often accused of overactive imaginations. However, their proximity is apparent when members of a household mysteriously fall sick or have a run of bad luck. Keukegen are easy to avoid, however. Just clean your house. Keukegen keep away from clean, kempt houses.

ORIGIN: Keukegen's name is a pun. It is commonly written with characters that mean "a hairy, fluffy sight." But it can also be written with different characters that mean "rare and dubious."

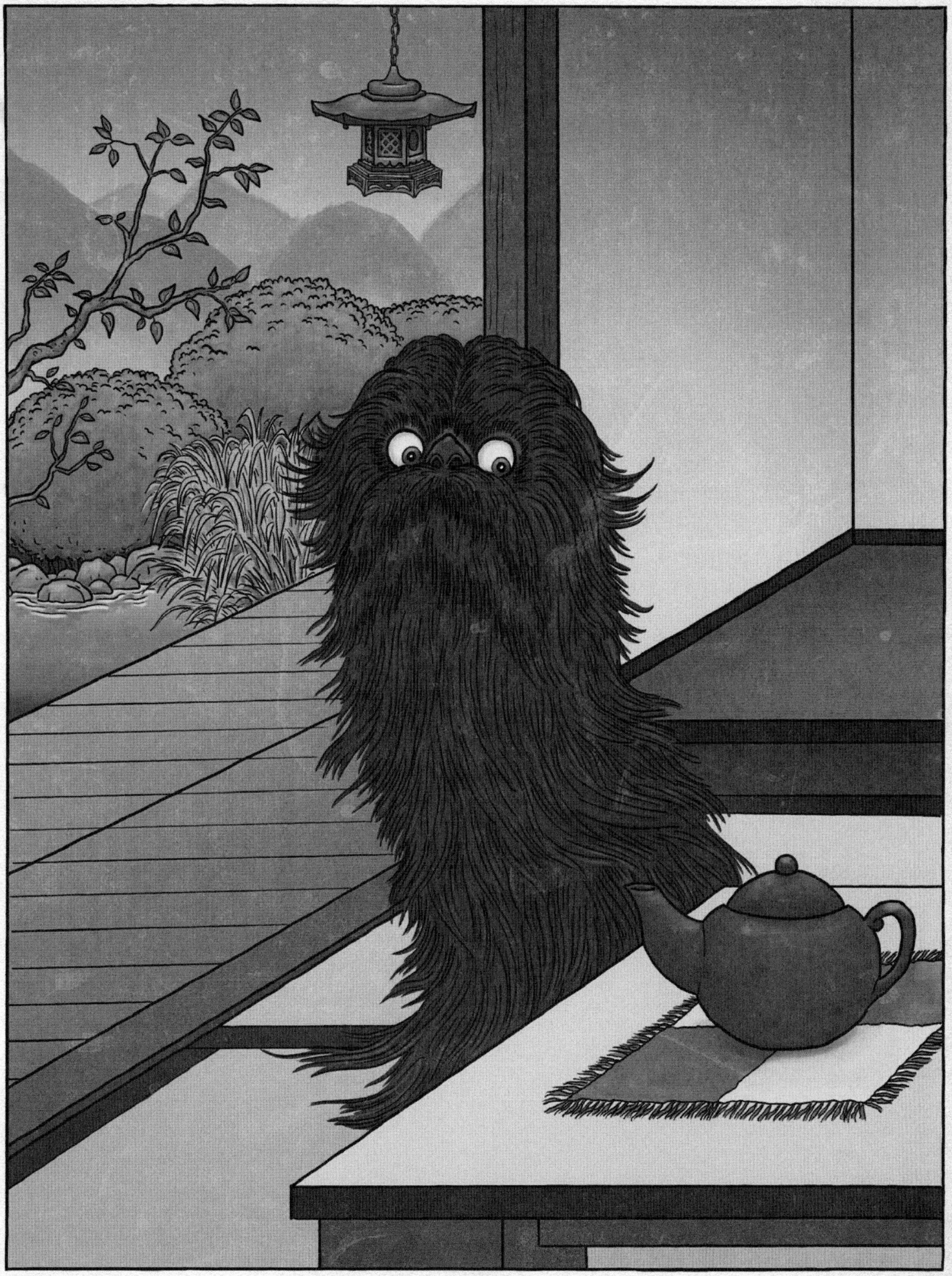

KAMIKIRI 髪切り

TRANSLATION: hair cutter
HABITAT: urban areas, dark alleys, toilets, bedrooms
DIET: human hair

APPEARANCE: Kamikiri are a kind of magical arthropod, with a scissor-like beak and hands like razors. They are small, and capable of sneaking quietly through open windows and doors without alerting their victims.

BEHAVIOR: A kamikiri's modus operandi is simple: sneaking about at night and cutting a person's hair off—suddenly and unexpectedly. They hide under roof tiles and wait for unsuspecting prey to pass by. Kamikiri's are indiscriminate in their attacks. They go after anyone with hair—men and women, servants and aristocrats. Kamikiri strike in urban areas. They stalk alleys, bathrooms, or other out of the way places. In many cases, the strike goes completely unnoticed until later, when a mop of cut hair is found lying in the street or friends and family point out the victim's striking new hairstyle. Often, the victim is asleep in bed when the kamikiri attacks. In the days when long hair was the only fashion in Japan, the kamikiri was a terrifying apparition indeed—particularly in high class, urban areas. These days, with the wide variety of hair styles including short hair, kamikiri are no longer feared as they once were.

Aside from random, malicious attacks, it is said that kamikiri strikes are sometimes a sign that the victim is about to unknowingly marry a yōkai. While these couplings are uncommon, there are a number of stories of kitsune and other shape-changers tricking unsuspecting men into marrying them. Because these improper marriages often end in catastrophe, helpful kamikiri interfere in hopes that the wedding will be called off.

LEGENDS: One account of a kamikiri attack was printed in a newspaper as follows: May 20th, 1874, about 9 p.m. in a neighborhood of Tōkyō. A servant girl named Gin left her master's mansion to use the outhouse. She suddenly felt a ghostly chill, and a moment later her hair fell disheveled about her face as her long ponytail was lopped off at the base. Gin panicked, and rushed to a neighbor's house where she promptly fainted. The neighbors investigated the outhouse, and discovered Gin's severed hair strewn about the floor. Afterwards, Gin became sick from stress and returned to live with her family in the countryside. Nobody ever used that outhouse again.

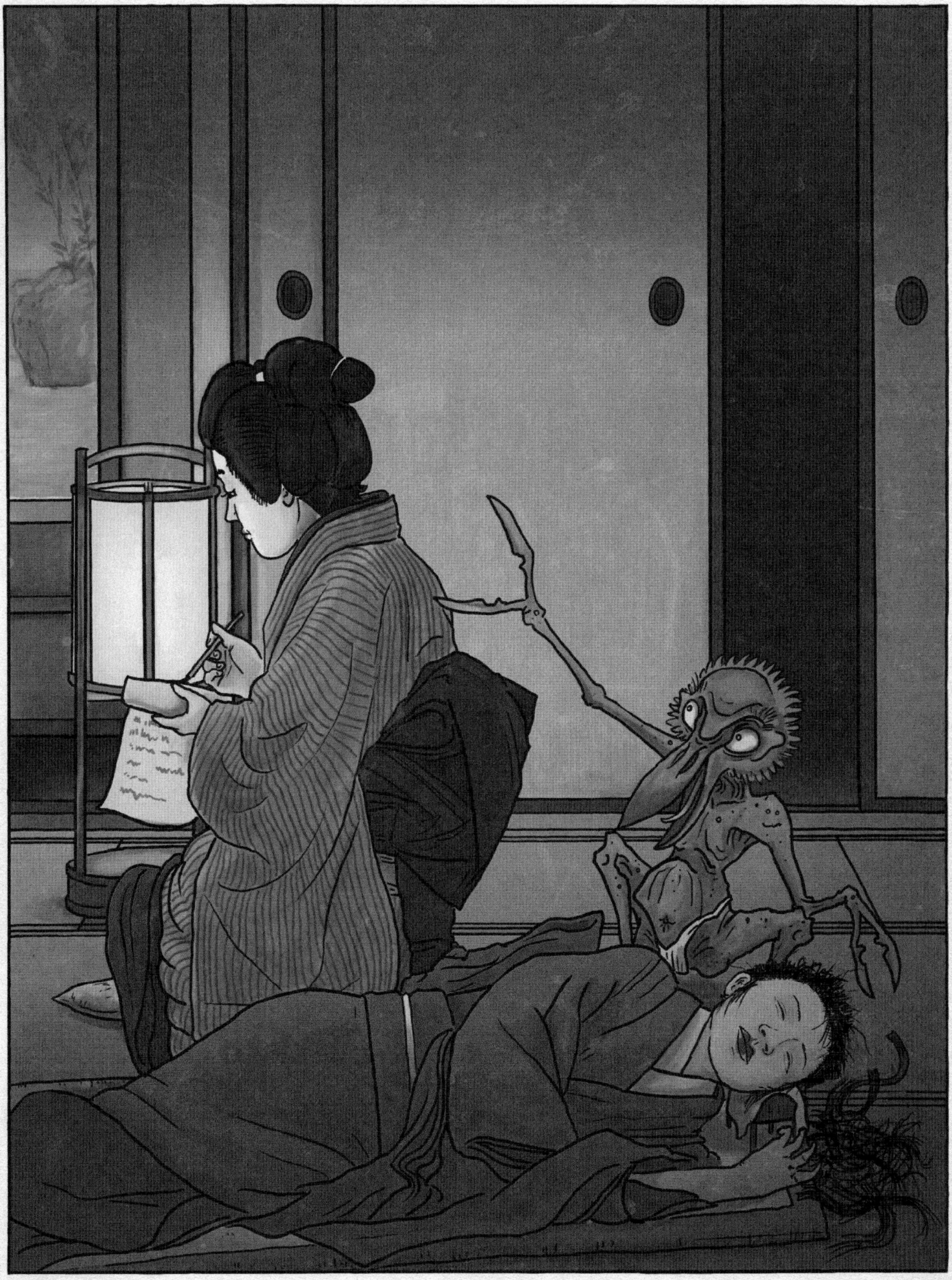

Seto taishō 瀬戸大将

Translation: General Seto, the crockery general

Appearance: Seto taishō is a tiny little soldier pieced together out of chipped teacups, cracked dishes, and other miscellaneous utensils that have fallen out of household use. Its face is a sake bottle and its armor is made of porcelain-ware. Seto taishō runs about the kitchen on tiny spoons, wielding knives or chopsticks as swords or spears.

Behavior: Seto taishō is highly aggressive. It loves to chase the cooking staff around the kitchen, causing chaos with every attack. The tiny crockery general occasionally crashes into walls or cabinets, shattering to hundreds of pieces. But it then slowly puts itself back together, and resumes its miniature kitchen war.

Origin: The word seto refers to the Seto Inland Sea, an area famous for earthenware. Just as we say "china" in English to refer to a specific kind of crockery, the Japanese use *"seto mono"* as a colloquialism for this tableware.

Shiro uneri 白溶裔

Translation: white undulation

Appearance: Born out of a dish towel or kitchen rag which has seen too many years of usage, the shiro uneri looks like a ferocious, yet tiny cloth dragon.

Behavior: Shiro uneri flies through the air, chasing cleaning staff and servants. It attacks them by wrapping its slimy, mildewy body around their necks and heads, causing them to pass out from the stench. Though they seem more interested in mischief than murder, shiro uneri have occasionally killed servants by strangulation.

Tsukumogami 付喪神

When household items, tools, clothing, and such reach an advanced age—traditionally one hundred years—it was believed they would develop a soul and transform into kami. Tsukumogami means "ninety-nine year gods"—just one year shy of one hundred. These objects were thrown out one year too soon. Instead of transforming into kami, they became degenerate, lowly spirits. Tsukumogami is written with characters that imply attachment and misery. Having worked hard for nintey-nine years before thanklessly being tossed out, these emotions cause tsukumogami to animate. There are as many kinds of tsukumogami as there are kinds of household items. Each one is as different from the next as the individual objects are. Often, tsukumogami enjoy playing pranks or terrorizing humans as revenge for their neglect or mistreatment.

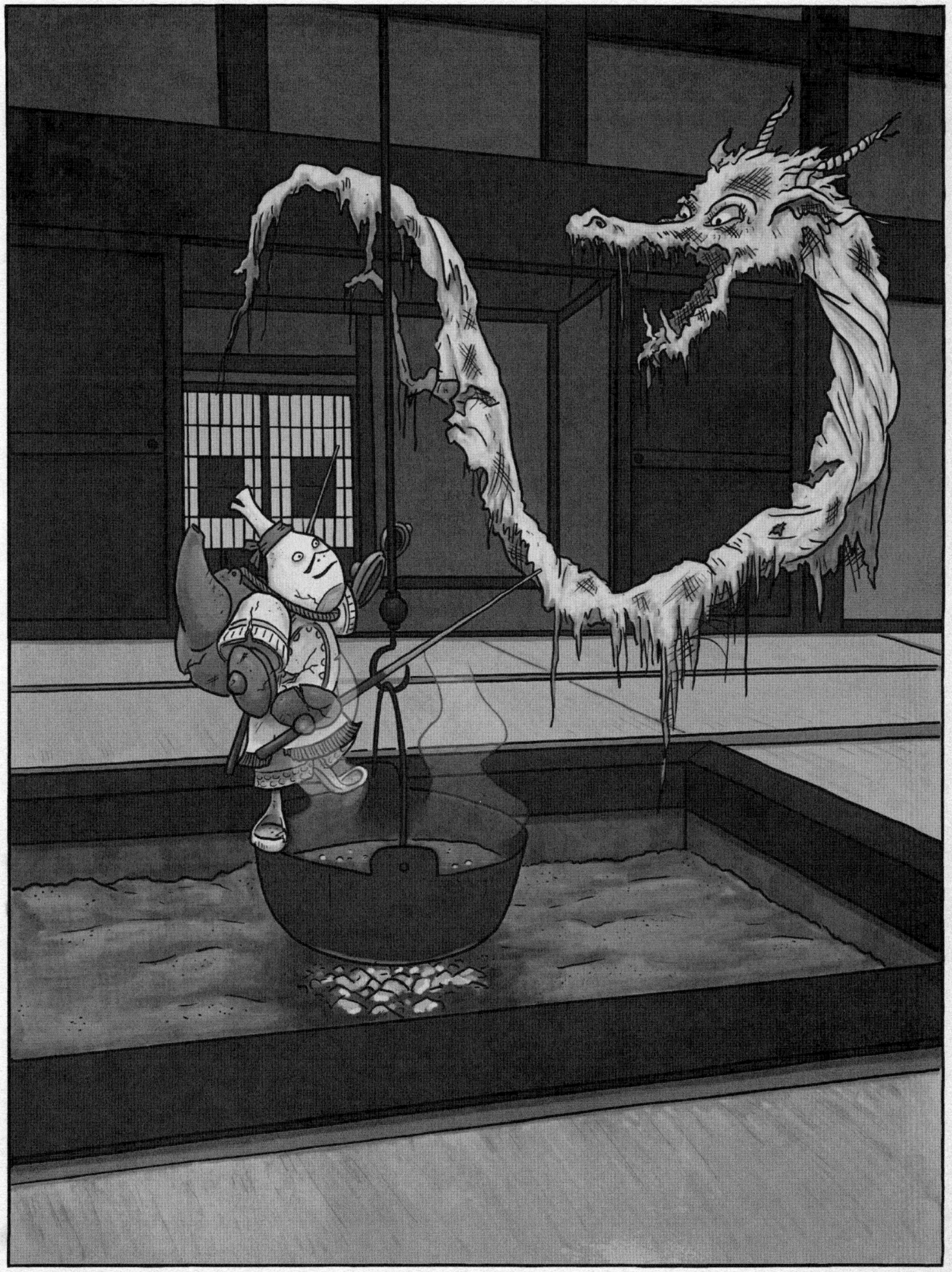

Bakezōri 化け草履

TRANSLATION: ghost zōri (zōri are traditional straw sandals)

APPEARANCE: When the straw sandals known as zōri have been mistreated and forgotten by their owners, they can transform into sandal-yōkai called Bakezōri.

BEHAVIOR: These sandal-shaped yōkai sprout arms and legs from their bodies and a single, large eye in their centers. They run about the house at night, causing mischief and making noise. Bakezōri have a favorite chant, which they sing as they run about the house on their tiny feet:

Kararin! Kororin! Kankororin! Managu mittsu ni ha ninmai!
Kararin! Kororin! Kankororin! Eyes three and teeth two!

"Eyes three" refers to the three holes where the sandal straps are attached and "teeth two" refers to the two wooden clogs on the underside of Japanese sandals. The other words are onomatopoeia representations of a zōri clacking along a hard surface.

Karakasa kozō 唐傘小僧

TRANSLATION: paper umbrella priest boy
ALTERNATE NAMES: kasa obake, karakasa obake

APPEARANCE: These silly looking yōkai are transformations of Chinese-style oiled-paper umbrellas. They have a single large eye, a long, protruding tongue, and either one or two legs upon which they hop around wildly.

BEHAVIOR: Karakasa kozō are not particularly fearsome as far as yōkai go. Their favorite method of surprising humans is to sneak up on them and deliver a large, oily lick with their enormous tongues—which may be traumatic even though it isn't dangerous. Caution is advised, however. There are other umbrella tsukumogami which are dangerous to humans, and care should be taken not to confuse them with this more playful spirit.

Mokumokuren 目目連

TRANSLATION: eye eye (i.e. many eyed) muraji (a hereditary title used in ancient Japan)

APPEARANCE: If not properly taken care of, shōji—the paper sliding doors and windows found in Japanese houses—can be easily damaged and riddled with holes. When shōji have gone too long without repair, ghostly eyes begin to pop out of the holes, watching all that goes on inside of the house.

BEHAVIOR: Mokumokuren are harmless, but incredibly creepy. Their true danger lies in who their companions might be. Mokumokuren often work in concert with other tsukumogami, and are usually a sign of a greater infestation of yōkai.

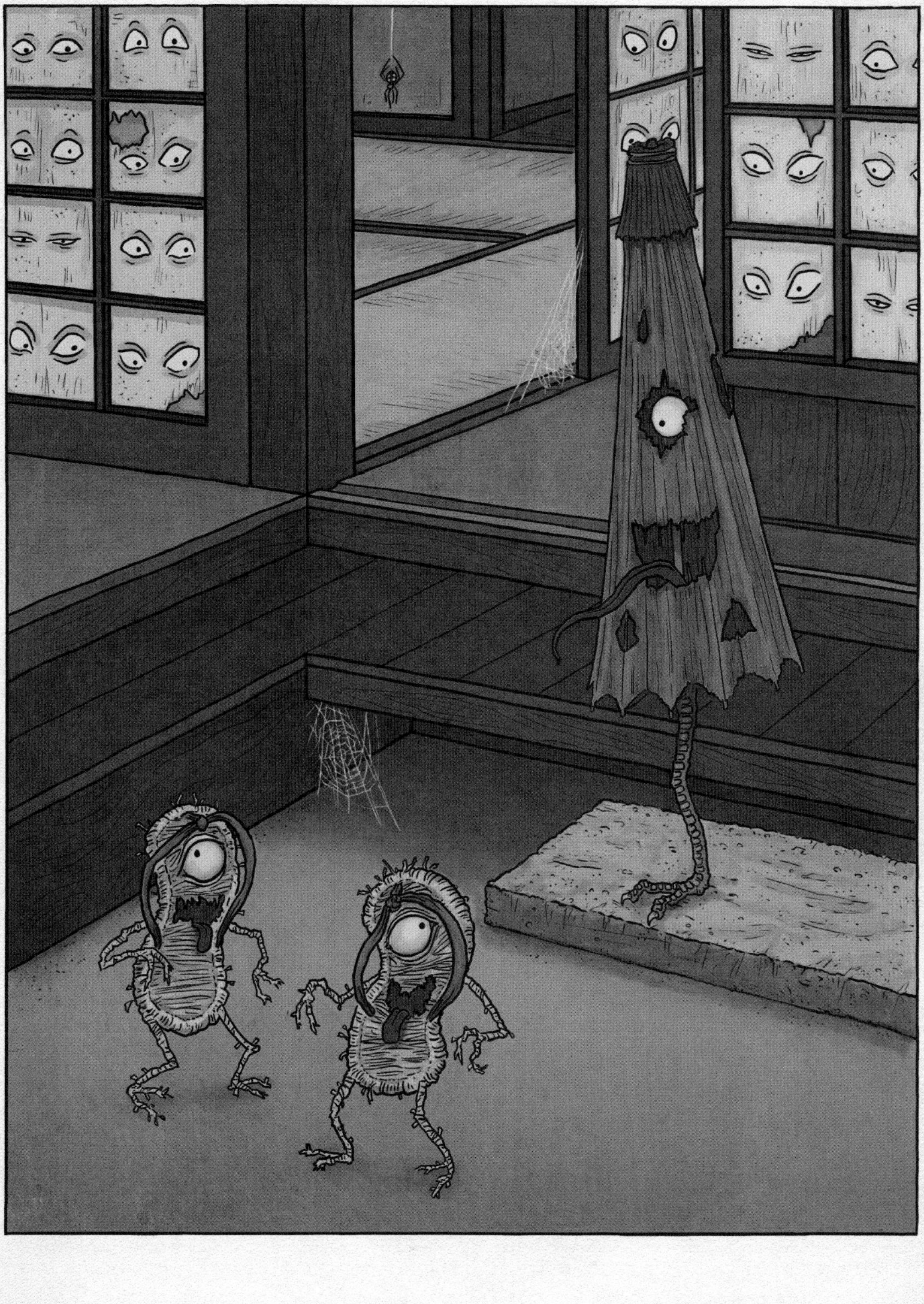

CHŌCHIN OBAKE 提灯お化け

TRANSLATION: paper lantern ghost

APPEARANCE: When a paper lantern, or a chōchin, reaches an advanced age, it may transform into a chōchin obake. The paper of the lantern splits along one of its wooden ribs, forming a gaping mouth with a wild, lolling tongue. One or two eyes pop out from the upper half of the lantern. Arms or legs may even sprout from its body as well, although this is rare.

BEHAVIOR: Like karakasa kozō, chōchin obake rarely cause physical harm, preferring simply to surprise and scare humans. They cackle and roll their huge tongues and big eyes at guests in the home. But you shouldn't be too quick to laugh them off. Occasionally, powerful onryō disguise themselves as chōchin obake—a case of one of the most dangerous supernatural entities masquerading as one of the most harmless.

KYŌRINRIN 経凛々

TRANSLATION: awe-inspiring sutra

APPEARANCE: Kyōrinrin is a spirit of knowledge formed from ancient scrolls, books, and scriptures which have been left unstudied by their owners and gathering dust. Kyōrinrin are often extravagant; they decorates themselves with the most ornate volumes and scrolls, wearing them like a kimono. A scroll with tassels becomes the headpiece, and they develop bird-like beaks and long, extendible arms.

BEHAVIOR: Compelled by the wisdom of the ages, the volumes that make up a kyōrinrin rise up as a dragon-like spirit. The kyōrinrin use their elongating arms to assault the ignorant owners who let such priceless treasures and knowledge fall into disuse.

SUZURI NO TAMASHII 硯の魂

TRANSLATION: ink stone spirit

APPEARANCE: An ink stone which has been used to copy the same manuscript over and over again for many generations begins to take on aspects of the story itself. Suzuri no tamashii can manifest phantom sounds and illusory characters from the story, which arise from the ink and wreak havoc on the writing desk.

ORIGIN: One of the most bloody tales of old Japan deals with the civil war between the Taira and Minamoto clans, known as the Genpei War. In the final naval battle of the war, the entire Taira clan was brutally wiped out. Many of the slaughtered Taira soldiers transformed into onryō, and their grudge-curse infects the ink stones which have been used to repeatedly copy their story.

BEHAVIOR: Suzuri no tamashii echo the brutal slaughter from when the Taira clan was wiped out in the final battle of the Genpei War. When used, they produce sounds like the echo of the sea, the din of battle, and the screams of warriors. The ink inside begins to ripple and billow like the sea's waves, and tiny boats and soldiers materialize out of the ink.

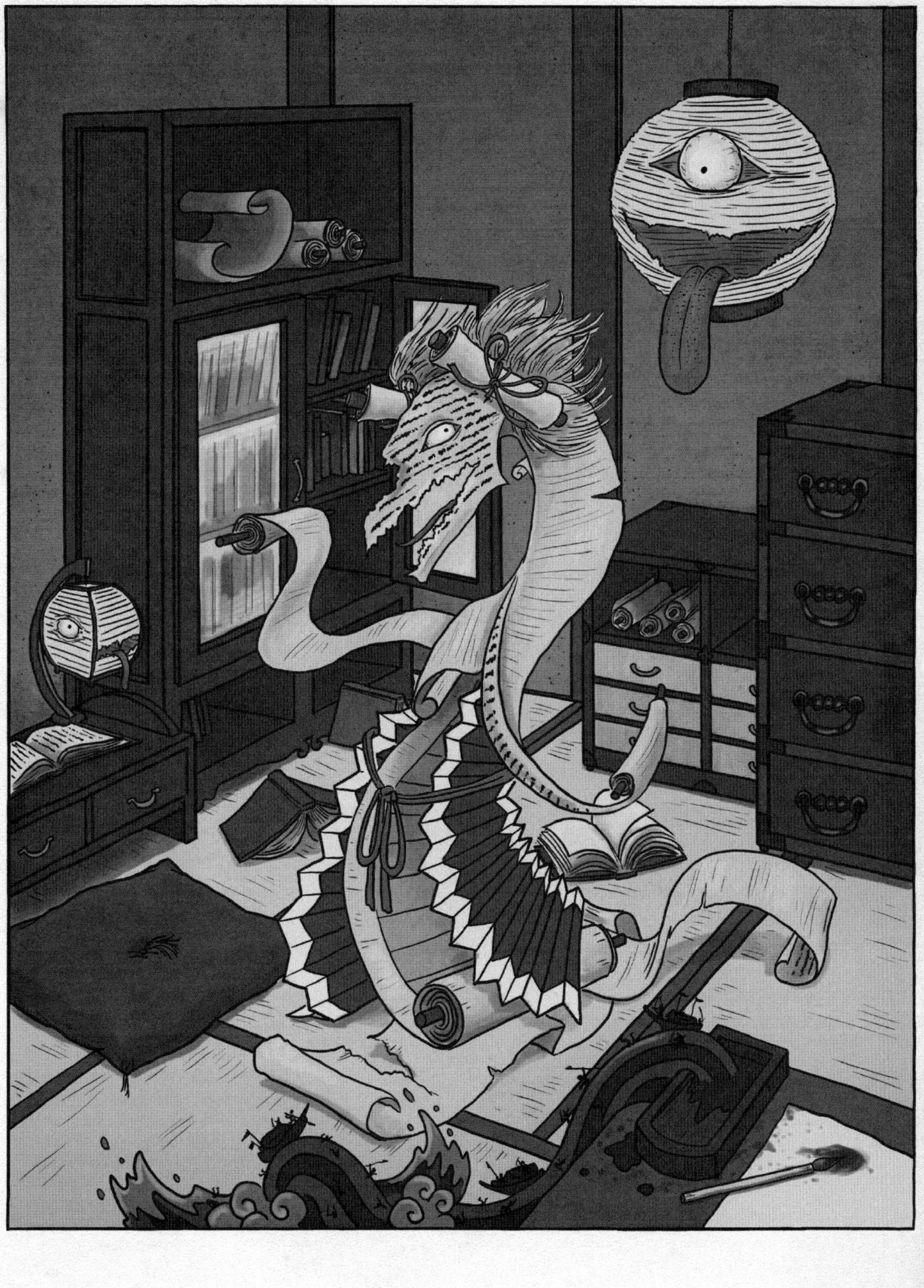

Shami chōrō 三味長老

Translation: elder shamisen

Appearance: A shami chōrō looks exactly like the shamisen it transformed from, a three-stringed guitar-like instrument.

Origin: Musical instruments, because of their high value, are often kept around long enough to turn into tsukumogami. Instruments which were once played by masters are the most likely to develop into yōkai. These instruments no longer receive any use—either because their master died or because they started using other instruments—and transform into yōkai, longing to be played again.

Shami chōrō's name is a play on words, written with characters meaning shamisen master. The name also invokes the old Japanese proverb, "*Shami kara chōrō ni wa nararezu*," meaning, "One cannot skip from novice to senior." In other words, only through many years of practice can one become a master.

Koto furunushi 琴古主

Translation: old koto master

Appearance: The Koto furunushi looks like a koto—a long, harp-like instrument that is the national instrument of Japan—transformed into a wild beast.

Behavior: A koto which was once played frequently but later forgotten about and stored away can transform into the koto furunushi. These yōkai may look like wild beasts, but they remember every song that was ever played on them. Koto furunushi play when no one is around, causing everyone to wonder where the music is coming from. They prefer to play old, forgotten tunes that have fallen out of style and vanished from people's memory.

Biwa bokuboku 琵琶牧々

Translation: takes its name from a particular legendary biwa

Appearance: A biwa is a kind of lute, frequently used to sing stories and poems. The biwa bokuboku is a biwa that has grown a human body and is dressed like a blind priest, wielding a cane,

Behavior: A biwa of extremely fine construction, upon reaching an advanced age, transforms into the self-playing biwa instrument known as a biwa bokuboku. This musical tsukumogami wanders playing music in the street for money.

Origin: These tsukumogami get their name from a legendary biwa named Bokuba. This magnificent instrument was said to magically play on its own when nobody was looking. And not just any music—Bokuba played music beautiful enough to charm even an oni.

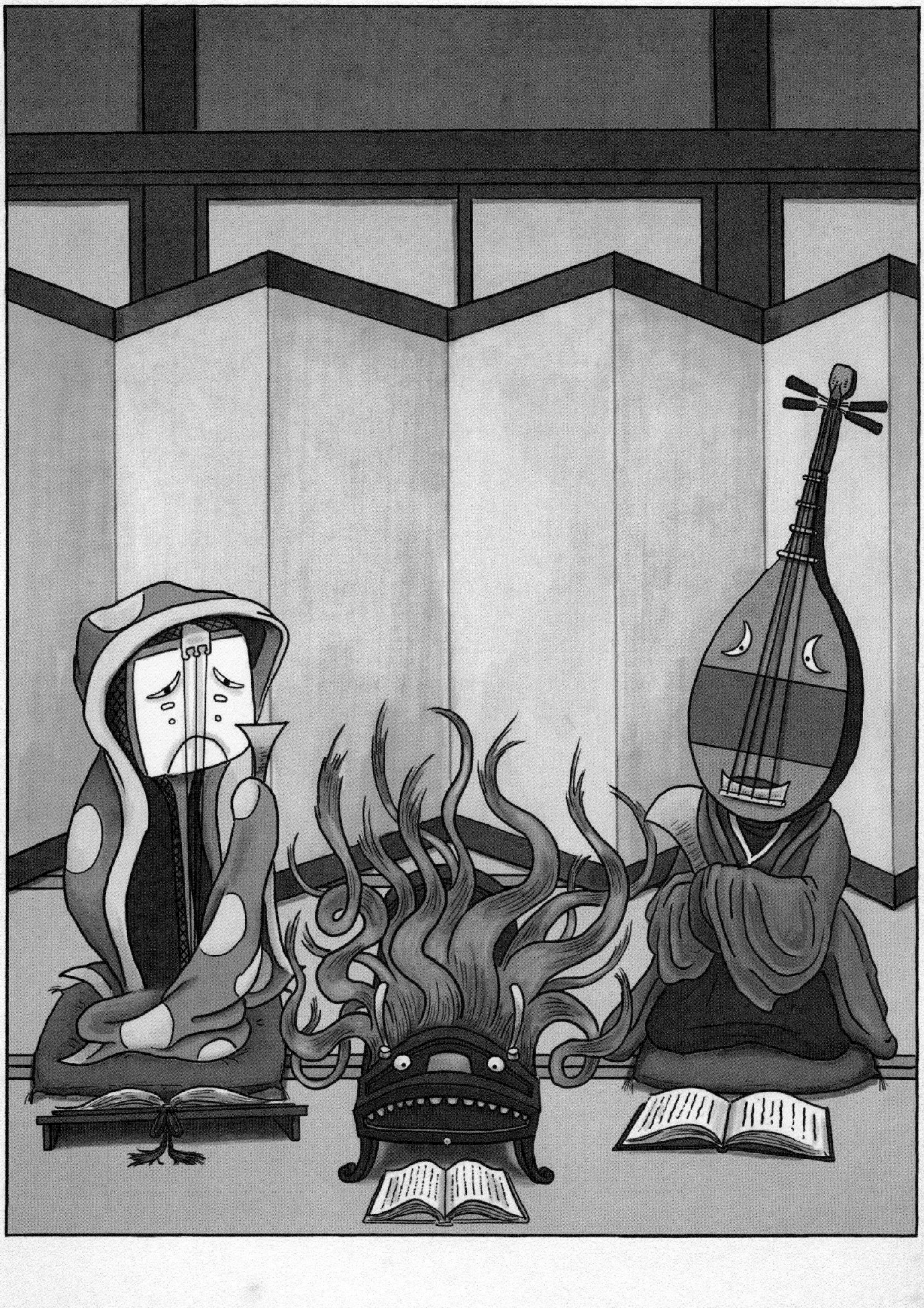

Ittan momen 一反木綿

TRANSLATION: one *tan* (about 28.8 cm by 10 m) of cotton

APPEARANCE: Ittan momen are long, narrow sheets of cloth normally used to make clothes, but reanimated as tsukumogami. They are native to Kagoshima, and can be seen flying through the sky at night.

BEHAVIOR: Ittan momen attack by wrapping their bodies around a person's face and neck, strangling or smothering them to death. As far as tsukumogami go, they are fairly malicious and even deadly.

Kosode no te 小袖の手

TRANSLATION: kosode (a short sleeved kimono) hands

APPEARANCE: Kosode no te appear in short sleeved kimonos formerly owned by prostitutes. This yōkai manifests as a pair of ghostly hands that emerge from the sleeves and assault welching clients—or whoever happens to be nearby.

ORIGIN: Kosode no te can occur for a number of reasons. One common origin is when a prostitute dies in vain, after working for many years to save up the money to buy her freedom. Upon death, such women usually had their clothes donated to a temple in exchange for a funeral and prayers. However, if the woman died still owed money from some of her clients, her spirit might reanimate her old clothing and head off in revenge. The newly formed kosode no te leaves the temple to find the prostitute's customers and scare them into to paying the money owed.

Another origin is when a dead person's kimono is sold for cash instead of being donated to a temple, as is customary. If the deceased was unable to properly pass on to nirvana upon death, that person's spirit may come back and haunt their former kimono.

Jatai 蛇帯

TRANSLATION: snake obi (a kimono sash)

APPEARANCE: The jatai is an animated kimono sash that slithers around like a giant snake during the night.

ORIGIN: An old folk belief from Ehime Prefecture and other parts of Japan says that if you lay your obi out near your pillow while you sleep, you will dream of snakes. Because the word for a snake's body (*jashin*) is the same as the word for a wicked heart, it is said that the obi itself turns into a murderous tsukumogami called a jatai. The jatai hunts after men, strangling them in their sleep.

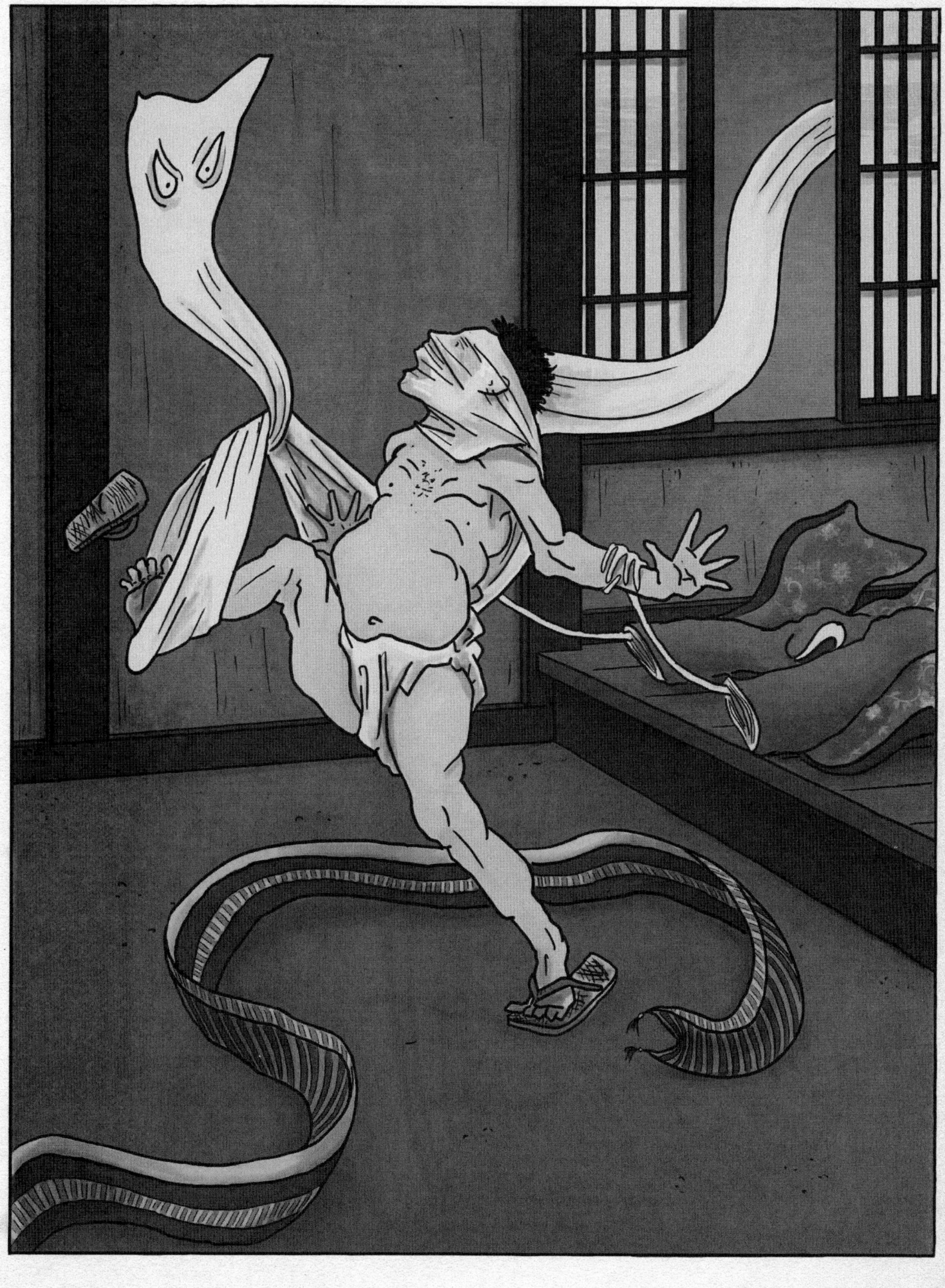

Ao andon 青行燈

TRANSLATION: blue lantern
ALTERNATE NAMES: ao andō
HABITAT: parlors and living rooms; appears during ghost story telling parties
DIET: fear

APPEARANCE: The ao andon is the incarnation of mass human terror, formed out of the built up fears of large groups of people. This fear takes the appearance of a demonic woman with long black hair, blue skin, blackened teeth, sharp claws, and horns. It wears a white or blue kimono, and glows with an eerie blue light.

During the Edo period, a popular summertime activity among the aristocratic classes was to gather and swap ghost stories, hoping the chill of fear would stave off the intense midsummer heat. These parties were called hyakumonogatari kaidankai—a gathering of one hundred ghost stories. During a game of hyakumonogatari kaidankai, one hundred candles would be lit and placed inside of blue paper lanterns, called andon. The andon created an eerie atmosphere suitable for storytelling. Throughout the night, guests would take turns telling progressively scarier stories about yōkai, demons, ghosts, and other strange things. After each story, one candle would be snuffed out. The room grew gradually darker, until only the hundredth candle remained. Its dim blue light would struggle to fill the room, and cast long, creepy shadows.

BEHAVIOR: According to superstition, after the final candle was snuffed an actual spirit would appear out of the darkness to attack the participants. Summoned by the heightened emotional state and fears of guests, this spirit was called the ao andon. The ao andon would emerge from the smoke of the final candle and attacks the guests. What exactly this attack consists of is a mystery; whether the ao andon slaughters all of the participants in a brutal finale inspired by the preceding tales, or simply jumps out to give one last shock before the guests return home has never been recorded. The reason for this is that by the time the ninety-ninth ghost story had been told, the guests were too frightened to tell the final story. Hyakumonogatari kaidankai parties traditionally concluded before the final candle could be snuffed and the ao andon could appear.

ORIGIN: As the old proverb says (in both English and Japanese): speak of the devil, and the devil appears. It was believed that merely talking about ghosts and spirits would cause them to materialize for real.

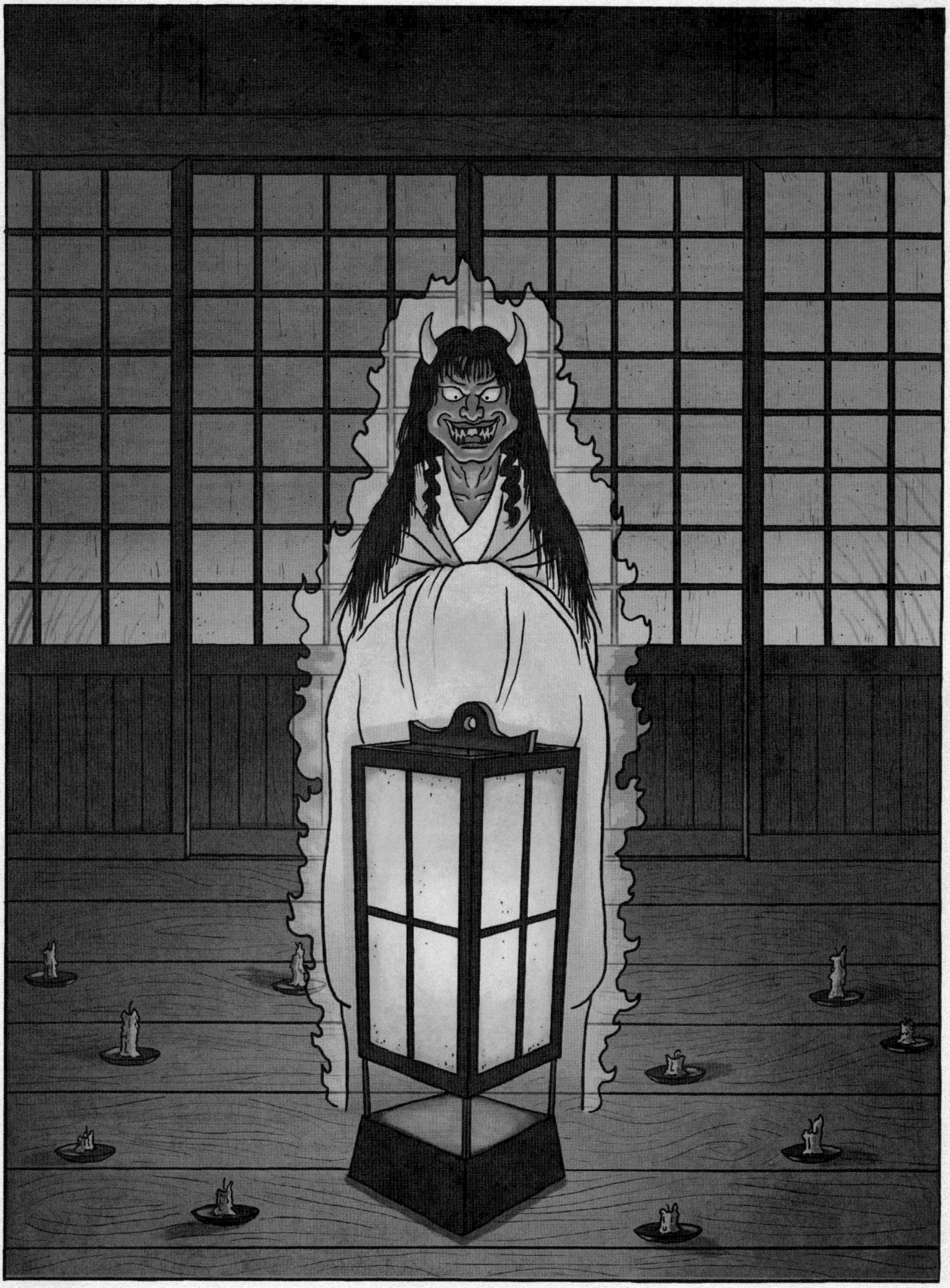

HYAKKI YAGYŌ 百鬼夜行

TRANSLATION: the night parade of one hundred demons
ALTERNATE NAMES: hyakki yakō

HABITAT: travels throughout Japan, appearing on auspicious nights each month

APPEARANCE: The hyakki yagyō is the dreaded night parade of one hundred demons—an event when all of the yōkai, oni, ghosts, tsukumogami, and other supernatural creatures leave their homes and parade through the streets of Japan in one massive spectacle of utter pandemonium. In many ways, it resembles a traditional Japanese festival, filled with songs and chants, dancing, and merriment. The parade is said to be led by nurarihyon, nozuchi, and otoroshi.

INTERACTIONS: Humans foolish enough to go outside on these nights, or curious enough to peek out of their windows in hopes of catching a glimpse of the supernatural, are either killed or spirited away by the monsters. This is attributed sometimes to divine punishment for looking upon that which must not be seen, and sometimes to sheer shock from witnessing this horrible spectable.

LEGENDS: According to the *Shūgaishō*—a medieval Japanese encyclopedia—the only way to keep safe from the night parade should it come by your home is to stay inside on the specific nights associated with the Chinese zodiac on which the night parade is said to be held. Those who hear the pandemonium parade pass by their homes should chant this magic spell:

カタシハヤ、エカセニクリ二、タメルサケ、テエヒ、アシエヒ、ワレシコ二ケリ
KA-TA-SHI-HA-YA, E-KA-SE-NI-KU-RI-NI, TA-ME-RU-SA-KE,
TE-E-HI, A-SHI-E-HI, WA-RE-SHI-KO-NI-KE-RI

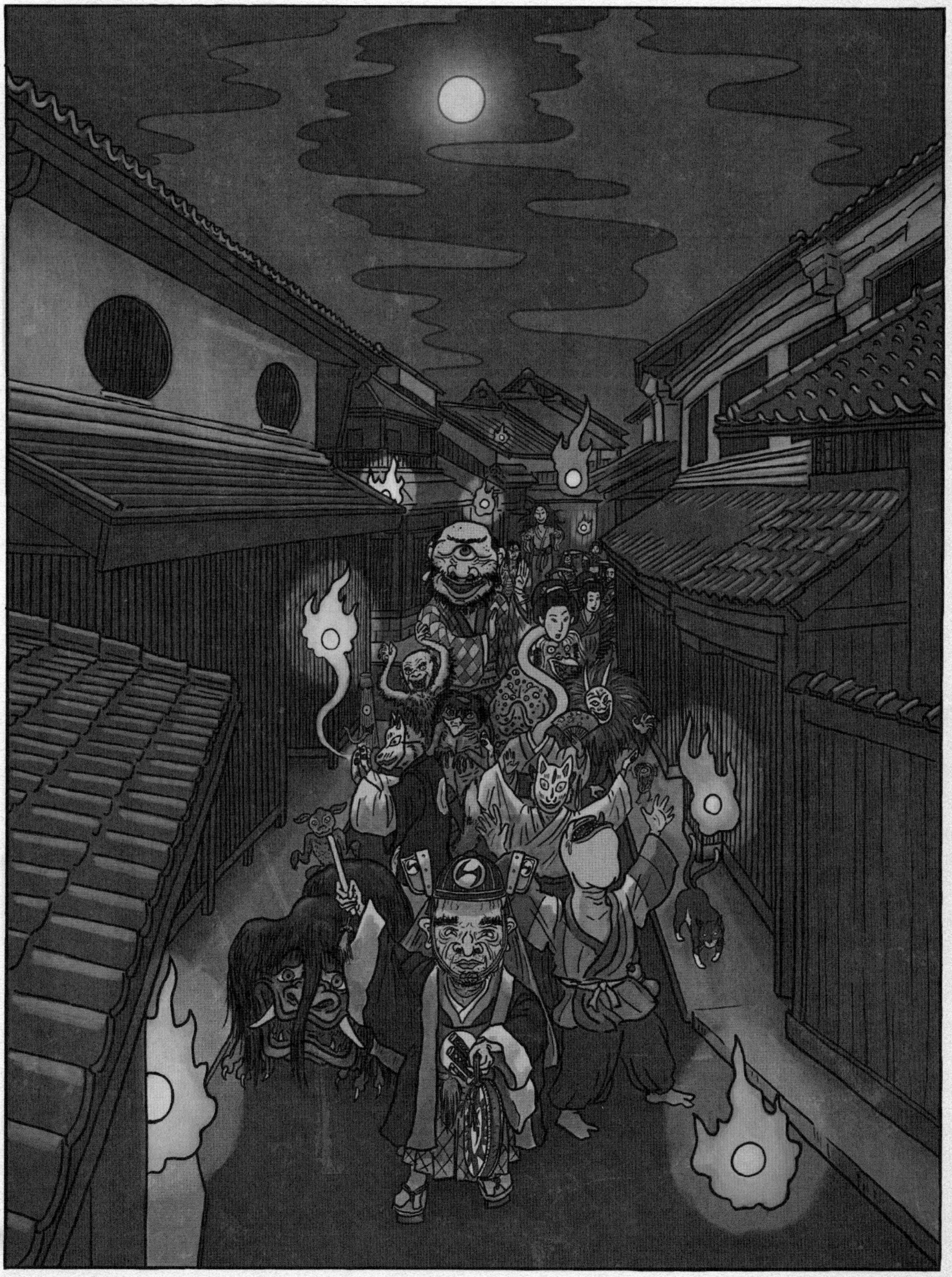

ACKNOWLEDGMENTS

Creating this book has been such a wonderful experience and a testament to the Information Age which we live in. Not even five years ago, it would have been impossible to put this together.

The Night Parade of One Hundred Demons began as a Halloween project called A-Yōkai-A-Day, in which I did a complete painting of a yōkai every day during the month of October. I posted these paintings on my website, along with a description of the yōkai. This project gained enough of a following that I repeated it again the following year, and after another great response and countless requests, I decided to create an illustrated yōkai manual.

All of the funds for the creation and publication of this book were raised online through Kickstarter. To my fans who generously pledged money in advance to support my book, I am grateful beyond words. Communicating with you daily, and sharing the progress of this project, has been a wonderful, collaborative experience. Your questions, comments, and assistance in editing and proofreading have made you all an integral part of this book. I hope it lives up your expectations. It is no exaggeration to say that without your support, *The Night Parade of One Hundred Demons* would not exist.

Everything in this book was created using free and open source software. The illustrations were created using GIMP, the text was written on LibreOffice Writer, the book layout and design were done in Scribus, and all of this was done on Ubuntu Linux. The free typefaces used in this book are The Fell Types and Iwata Gyōsho (イワタ行書) for Japanese. Many thanks are owed to the people who create free software, whose hard work and generosity make it possible for anyone to self-publish. Thanks are also owed to the people of the CreateSpace team and forums, whose advice greatly aided in the self-publishing of this book.

The information on yōkai found in this book was collected from a number of difference sources. Many works of Toriyama Sekien and other Edo period yōkai artists—which served as a primary source for most of this book—can be found in Wikimedia Commons. They can also be found in the online databases maintained by The International Research Center for Japanese Studies, which is another invaluable source of images and legends about yōkai. Additionally, a good deal of information came from the people of Fukui Prefecture, who graciously shared their yōkai stories that had been passed down to them from their grandparents.

Finally, special thanks go to my wife, whose unwavering support for this project has meant so much to me. I cannot understate how important her help with translating old Japanese documents, deciphering barely intelligible brush scripts, researching correct period hair and clothing styles, and other fact-checking—as well as critiquing my paintings—has been to this project.

Yōkai References and Further Reading

Books

Hearn, Lafcadio. *In Ghostly Japan*. Boston: Little, Brown, and Co., 1899.

Hearn, Lafcadio. *Kwaidan: Stories and Studies of Strange Things*. Boston: Houghton, Mifflin and Co., 1904.

Foster, Michael Dylan. *Pandemonium and Parade: Japanese Monsters and the Culture of Yōkai*. Los Angeles: University of California Press, 2009.

Griffis, William Elliot. *Japanese Fairy World. Stories from the Wonder-lore of Japan*. London: Trübner & Co., 1887.

Mitford, A.B. *Tales of Old Japan*. London, 1871

Mizuki, Shigeru. *Mujara*. Tōkyō: Softgarage Inc., 2008.

Ozaki, Yei Theodora. Japanese Fairy Tales. New York: A.L. Burt Company, 1908.

Sawaki, Sūshi. *Hyakkai zukan*. 1737.

Toriyama, Sekien. *Gazu hyakki yagyō*. 1776.

Toriyama, Sekien. *Konjaku gazu zoku hyakki*. 1779.

Toriyama, Sekien. *Konjaku hyakki shūi*. 1780.

Toriyama, Sekien. *Gazu hyakki tsurezure bukuro*. 1784.

Yodo, Hiroko and Matt Alt. *Yokai Attack! The Japanese Monster Survival Guide*. Tōkyō: Kodansha International Ltd., 2008.

Online

atelier CROMAGNON. <http://www.cromagnon.jp>

Database of Images of Strange Phenomena and Yōkai. International Research Center for Japanese Studies. <http://www.nichibun.ac.jp/YoukaiGazouMenu/>.

Folktale Data of Strange Phenomena and Yōkai. International Research Center for Japanese Studies. <http://www.nichibun.ac.jp/YoukaiDB/>.

INDEX OF YŌKAI

Made in the USA
Middletown, DE
22 July 2021

44603876R00126